W9-BID-365

# NETWORKS OF OUTRAGE
# AND HOPE

Pour Alain Touraine
My intellectual father,
theorist of social movements

# NETWORKS OF
# OUTRAGE AND HOPE
## SOCIAL MOVEMENTS IN
## THE INTERNET AGE
### SECOND EDITION

## MANUEL CASTELLS

polity

Copyright © Manuel Castells 2012, 2015

The right of Manuel Castells to be identified as Author of this Work has been asserted in accordance with the UK Copyright, Designs and Patents Act 1988.

First published in 2012 by Polity Press
This edition first published in 2015 by Polity Press
Reprinted 2016, 2017

Polity Press
65 Bridge Street
Cambridge CB2 1UR, UK

Polity Press
350 Main Street
Malden, MA 02148, USA

All rights reserved. Except for the quotation of short passages for the purpose of criticism and review, no part of this publication may be reproduced, stored in a retrieval system, or transmitted, in any form or by any means, electronic, mechanical, photocopying, recording or otherwise, without the prior permission of the publisher.

ISBN-13: 978-0-7456-9575-4
ISBN-13: 978-0-7456-9576-1(pb)

A catalogue record for this book is available from the British Library.

Library of Congress Cataloging-in-Publication Data

Castells, Manuel, 1942–
Networks of outrage and hope : social movements in the Internet age / Manuel Castells.
    pages cm
Revised edition of the author's Networks of outrage and hope published in 2012.
    ISBN 978-0-7456-9575-4 (hardback) -- ISBN 978-0-7456-9576-1 (pbk.)
1. Information technology--Social aspects. 2. Internet--Social aspects. 3. Information society. 4. Information networks. 5. Social movements. 6. Technology and civilization.
    I. Title.
    HM851.C369 2015
    302.23'1--dc23
    2014043395

Typeset in 10.75 on 14 pt Janson Text by
Servis Filmsetting Ltd, Stockport, Cheshire SK2 5AJ
Printed and bound in the United States by LSC Communication

The publisher has used its best endeavours to ensure that the URLs for external websites referred to in this book are correct and active at the time of going to press. However, the publisher has no responsibility for the websites and can make no guarantee that a site will remain live or that the content is or will remain appropriate.

Every effort has been made to trace all copyright holders, but if any have been inadvertently overlooked the publisher will be pleased to include any necessary credits in any subsequent reprint or edition.

For further information on Polity, visit our website:
politybooks.com

# CONTENTS

# PREFACE 2015

São Paulo, June 14, 2013. I had just finished my lecture presenting the first edition of the book you have in your hands before an audience of several hundred people. The first question that opened the subsequent discussion came from one of the many journalists present in the auditorium, "Why do you think these kinds of movements do not happen in Brazil?" Before I could improvise a sophisticated theory about Brazilian exceptionalism, someone in the room shouted "We cannot get out! The Avenida Paulista is blocked!" Indeed, the Movimiento do Passe Livre had taken its protest to the streets. The movement would go on for weeks, then for months in a very similar form to the networked social movements that had taken place in 2010–11 elsewhere, as analyzed in this volume. Indeed, Brazil was not an exception, but an addition to an expanding galaxy of new forms of social movements. Then came Gezi Park in Istanbul, the occupation of Maidan Square in Kiev, Hong Kong's Umbrella Revolution, Mexicans' mobilization against the assassinations of the narco-state, and a multiplicity of less known protests that seem to give credibility to the main proposition of this book: that networked social movements, as identified and analyzed in the research presented here, may well be the social movements characteristic of the network society, the social structure of the Information Age.

However, the recurrence of these movements around the world at an accelerated pace is not a good enough reason to revise substantially in December 2014 a book that was finished in June 2012; because I am not in the trade of updating information – a book at a time – in the age of the Internet and instant communication of any relevant information. Yes, the reader will find in this expanded second edition a number of accounts of networked social movements that were not included in the first edition for the simple reason that they had not yet happened at the time of my research. But rather than compiling new information, the purpose of these empirical reports is to enrich the analytical interpretation of the form and meaning of networked social movements beyond the specific contexts where they originated in 2010–11. Thus, the verification of the persistence of certain key features as common to most movements in spite of the differences of contexts, goals, and demands appears to lend some explanatory value to the synthetic characterization presented in this volume; a characterization that reproduces most of the grounded theory I proposed in the first edition of this book.

Furthermore, with the hindsight of time, I have been able to examine the fundamental question that most observers addressed to these movements: "So what?!" What are the specific outcomes of the movements in tangible social terms? And particularly, what is their impact on the political system and on policy making, if any? By broadening the scope of the observation and by analyzing the evolution of the movements over a longer time span, I am now able to venture a number of hypotheses on the relationship between networked social movements and political change. Moreover, I have been able to introduce a fundamental distinction between networked social movements and populist reactions, of diverse ideological nature, prompted by the ubiquitous crisis of political legitimacy in a time of crisis and change at the global level. Thus, there are two entirely new chapters in this volume. One chapter focuses on an analytical commentary on a number of important social movements not present in the first edition: in Brazil, Turkey, Mexico, Chile, as well as on the anti-establishment political reactions in Europe and the United States. Another new chapter considers the relationship between different social movements and political change, including the attempt by some of the movements, for instance in Spain, to be involved in institutional politics while pursuing a transformative strategy. Yet, I decided not to change the text of the case studies that formed the basis of the first edition since the social movements I analyzed will stand in history by the practices they enacted, not by a reconstructed logic that I would add *ex post*. I simply have included a few comments to explain the relative fading of the Icelandic revolution, and a few others to put into perspective the dramatic turn of events in the Arab world as the result of geopolitical interventions in the space opened by the overthrowing of dictatorships by social movements. To limit the size of the book in its second incarnation, I have deleted most of the appendices to the chapter case studies, including chronologies of the movements and relevant statistical material. The interested reader can find this information in the first edition of the book.

Ultimately, what this new edition tries to achieve is to further the debate on the meaning and prospects of networked social movements; broadening and deepening the observation as much as possible in the hope that researchers, activists, and action researchers will investigate, in real time, the practices that are shaping the twenty-first-century societies around the world.

In pursuing this effort of observation and analysis of networked social movements, I have continued to rely on friends and colleagues, many of them social activists and participants in the movements. I want to personalize my gratitude and acknowledge their essential contribution to Arnau Monterde and Javier Toret in Barcelona, Joan Donovan in Los Angeles, Marcelo Branco in Porto Alegre, Gustavo Cardoso in Lisbon, Sasha Costanza-Chock in Boston, Birgan Gokmenoglu in Istanbul, Fernando Calderon in Buenos Aires/Santiago de Chile, and Andrea Apolaro in Montevideo. I am particularly grateful to the Redes Frente Amplistas of Uruguay for their invitation to participate in the First Latin American meeting of networked social movements in Montevideo in June 2013. The discussions in that meeting have been a source of ideas that have informed my reflection on social movements as presented in this volume. I have also benefited from my participation in several international meetings organized in Barcelona by the Research Group on Communication and Civil Society, Internet Interdisciplinary Institute, Open University of Catalonia. I want to acknowledge the Foundation Frontiers of the Mind, of Porto Alegre, for its invitation to Brazil in 2013, and for organizing a series of most interesting debates that informed my understanding of the Brazilian movement.

To all these institutions and the persons involved in organizing the events around the presentation of my work, I want to express my heartfelt gratitude in the acknowledgment that the elaboration, or re-elaboration, of a book is always a collective endeavor of many wills and intellectual contributions.

I also thank my colleague Gustavo Cardoso, from ICST/

University of Lisbon, for graciously providing me with the most complete chart of users of social networks, obtained from the Global Survey he directed in 2013, as well as Alex Rodriguez, the director of Vanguardia Dossiers, the original publication of the chart, for his generous permission to reprint it in this book.

Last but not least, this book reaches you in this new version only because of the intellectual advice of my publisher and friend, Professor John Thompson, of Cambridge University, and because of the excellent editing of my personal assistant, Ms Reanna Martinez, at the Annenberg School of Communication, University of Southern California, Los Angeles. I want also to acknowledge the careful editorial and production work of my publishers at Polity Press. I hope all this work will be worthy of your attention.

*Barcelona and Santa Monica, June–December 2014*

# ACKNOWLEDGMENTS 2012

November 2011 was a good month for me. I had been invited to Cambridge by my friend John Thompson, one of the most distinguished sociologists in media politics, to give a series of lectures in the University of Cambridge's CRASSH program. I was housed in the magnificent medieval quarters of St John's College, where the monastic atmosphere and collegial interaction provided a serene space/time to reflect on my ideas, after an intense year of being immersed in the theory and practice of social movements. Like many people around the world, I had been struck first, and then mobilized, by the uprisings that started in Tunisia in December 2010 and diffused virally throughout the Arab world. During the previous years, I had followed the emergence of social movements that were powered by the use of the Internet and wireless communication networks, in Madrid in 2004, in Iran in 2009, in Iceland in 2009, and in a number of countries around the world. I had spent most of the last decade studying the transformation of power relationships in interaction with the transformation of communication, and I detected the development of a new pattern of social movements, perhaps the new forms of social change in the twenty-first century. This phenomenon resonated with my personal experience, as a veteran of the May 1968 movement in Paris. I felt the same kind of exhilaration I felt at that time: suddenly, everything appeared to be possible; the world was not necessarily doomed to political cynicism and bureaucratic enforcement of absurd ways of life. The symptoms of a new revolutionary era, an age of revolutions aimed at exploring the meaning of life rather than seizing the state, were apparent everywhere, from Iceland to Tunisia, from WikiLeaks to Anonymous, and, soon, from Athens to Madrid to New York. The crisis of global financial capitalism was not necessarily a dead end – it could even signal a new beginning in unexpected ways.

Throughout 2011 I began to collect information on these new social movements, discussed my findings with my students at the University of Southern California, and then gave some lectures to communicate my preliminary thoughts at Northwestern University, at the College d'Etudes Mondiales in Paris, at the Oxford Internet Institute, at Barcelona's Seminar on Communication and Civil Society in the Internet Interdisciplinary Institute of the Universitat Oberta de Catalunya, and at the London School of Economics. I became increasingly convinced that something truly meaningful was taking place around the world. Then two days before returning to Barcelona from Los Angeles, on 19 May, I received an email from a young woman from Madrid whom I had never met before, letting me know that they were occupying the squares of Spanish cities, and wouldn't it be nice if I joined in some way, given my writings on the subject? My heart accelerated. Could it be possible? Hope again? As soon as I landed in Barcelona I headed to Plaza Catalunya. There they were, by the hundreds, peacefully and seriously

debating under the sun. I met the *indignadas*. It turned out
that my two main research collaborators in Barcelona, Joana
and Amalia, were already a part of the movement. But not
with the intention of conducting research. They were just
*indignadas* like all the others, and had decided to act. I did not
camp myself; my old bones would not take easily to sleeping
on the pavement. But since then I have followed daily the
activities of the movement, visiting the camps at times, in
Barcelona and Madrid; occasionally talking, at the request of
someone, in Acampada Barcelona or Occupy London; and
helping to elaborate some of the proposals that emerged
from the movement. I connected spontaneously with the
values and style of the movement, largely free of obsolete
ideologies and manipulative politics. There began a journey
of trying to support these movements while exploring their
meaning. With no specific purpose, and certainly no intention of writing a book – not in the short term anyway. Living
it was much more fascinating than writing about it, particularly after having already written 25 books.

So, there I was in Cambridge, with the opportunity to
lecture/debate with a fantastic group of smart students who
were also committed citizens. I decided to focus my lecture
series on "Social Movements in the Internet Age," to put
my ideas in order for myself, with the hope of better understanding the meaning of these variegated movements in my
interaction with students and colleagues. It went very well. It
was intense, rigorous, truthful and absent of academic pomp.
At the end of the month, while saying farewell, my colleague
John Thompson insisted that I should write a book on the
basis of these lectures. A short, quick book, and less academic
than usual. Short? Quick? I have never done that. My books
are usually over five years in the making and over 400 pages
when published. Yes, he said, you may do another one in five
years, but what is needed now is a simple book that organizes

the debate and contributes to the reflection of the movement and to the broader understanding of these new movements by people at large. He succeeded in making me feel guilty for not doing it, since my only potential useful contribution to a better world comes from my lifelong experience as a social researcher, writer and lecturer, not from my often confused activism. I yielded to his request, and here I am, four months later. It was quick, and exhausting. It is short by my standards. As for its relevance, that is for you to judge. So, my first acknowledgment goes to John, the initiator of this enterprise. He backed up his interest by following and commenting on my draft chapters during the elaboration of this project. Thus, I am deeply indebted to him for his generosity and intellectual contribution.

Yet, for all the impulse I received in and from Cambridge, I would not have been able to keep my promise without the help of an extraordinary group of young researchers with whom I worked regularly in Barcelona and in Los Angeles. As soon as I returned from England, I realized that I was in big trouble, and called my friends and co-investigators to the rescue. Joana Conill, Amalia Cardenas, and I had created a small research team at the Open University of Barcelona (UOC) to study the rise of alternative economic cultures in Barcelona. Many of the groups and individuals we observed became in fact participants in the *indignadas* movement. Since Joana and Amalia were already within the movement, they agreed to help with information and analysis, on the condition of not being involved in the final writing of the research, for their own personal reasons. Amalia also collected and analyzed information on Iceland and on Occupy Wall Street, while I used my networks of colleagues and former students around the world to retrieve information, check facts, and listen to ideas, particularly about the Arab countries. Other persons in the movement also agreed to discuss with me

XVIIIACKNOWLEDGMENTS 2012

or with my collaborators some of the issues and history of the movement. I want to thank particularly Javier Toret and Arnau Monterde, both in Barcelona.

Then, in Los Angeles, my research collaborator Lana Swartz, an outstanding doctoral student at the Annenberg School of Communication at USC, was also involved in Occupy Los Angeles, and also accepted with incredible generosity, intelligence, and rigor to help me in the data collection and analysis of the Occupy movement in the United States. Joan Donovan, an active participant in Occupy Los Angeles and Inter-Occupy, a veteran of many battles for social justice, and a doctoral student at UC San Diego, gave me some key ideas that helped my understanding. Dorian Bon, a student at Columbia University, conveyed to me his experience in the student movement connected to Occupy Wall Street. My friend and colleague Sasha Costanza-Chock, a professor at MIT, shared with me his unpublished survey data on the Occupy movement in the US. Maytha Alhassen, an Arab-American journalist and doctoral student in American Studies and Ethnicity at the University of Southern California in Los Angeles, who had traveled in the Arab countries during the time of the uprisings, worked closely with me, reporting on key events that she witnessed first-hand, allowing me access to Arabic sources, and most importantly educating me about what had really happened everywhere. Of course, I am the only one responsible for the many mistakes I have probably made in my interpretation. But without her invaluable help there would have been many more mistakes. It is because of the quality of her contribution that I dared to go into the analysis of specific processes in the Arab uprisings.

Thus my gratitude and recognition goes to this very diverse group of exceptional individuals who agreed to collaborate in the project of this book, which became a truly collective endeavor, although the end result was elaborated in the solitude of authorship.

As for my previous books, Melody Lutz, a professional writer and my personal editor, was the key link between me, the author, and you, the reader, making our communication possible. My heartfelt recognition goes to Melody.

The complexity of the process of work that I just outlined, which led to this book, required exceptional management and organizational skills, and a great deal of patience. Thus, my deepest thanks go to Clelia Azucena Garciasalas, my personal assistant at the Annenberg School of Communication, who directed the entire project, coordinated research and editing, filled in the gaps, collected information, corrected mistakes, and made sure that you would have in your hands this volume with full assurance of her quality control. I also want to thank the contribution of Noelia Diaz Lopez, my personal assistant at the Open University of Catalonia, for her ongoing outstanding support of all my research activities.

Finally, as with my previous research and writing, none of this would have been possible without the supportive family environment that this author enjoys. For this, my love and my gratitude go to my wife Emma Kiselyova, my daughter Nuria, my stepdaughter Lena, my grandchildren Clara, Gabriel, and Sasha, my sister Irene, and my brother-in-law Jose.

Thus, it is in the crossroads between emotion and cognition, work and experience, personal history and hope for the future that this book was born. For you.

*Barcelona and Santa Monica, December 2011–April 2012*

# OPENING:

## NETWORKING MINDS, CREATING

## MEANING, CONTESTING POWER

No one expected it. In a world darkened by economic distress, political cynicism, cultural emptiness and personal hopelessness, it just happened. Suddenly dictatorships could be overthrown with the bare hands of the people, even if their hands had been bloodied by the sacrifice of the fallen. Financial magicians went from being the objects of public envy to the targets of universal contempt. Politicians became exposed as corrupt and as liars. Governments were denounced. Media were suspected. Trust vanished. And trust is what glues together society, the market, the institutions. Without trust, nothing works. Without trust, the social contract dissolves and people disappear as they transform into defensive individuals fighting for survival. Yet, at the fringe of a world that had come to the brink of its capacity for humans to live together and to share life with nature, individuals did come together again to find new forms of being us, the people. There were first a few, who were joined by hundreds, then networked by thousands, then supported by millions with their voices and their internal quest for hope, as muddled as it was, that cut across ideology and hype, to connect with the real concerns of real people in the real human experience that had been reclaimed. It began on the Internet social networks, as these are spaces of autonomy, largely beyond the control of governments and corporations that had monopolized the channels of communication as the foundation of their power, throughout history. By sharing sorrow and hope in the free public space of the Internet, by connecting to each other, and by envisioning projects from multiple sources of being, individuals formed networks, regardless of their personal views or organizational attachments. They came together. And their togetherness helped them to overcome fear, this paralyzing emotion on which the powers that be rely in order to prosper and reproduce, by intimidation or discouragement, and when necessary by sheer violence, be it naked or institutionally enforced. From the safety of cyberspace, people from all ages and conditions moved toward occupying urban space, on a blind date with each other and with the destiny they wanted to forge, as they claimed their right to make history – their history – in a display of the self-awareness that has always characterized major social movements.[1]

The movements spread by contagion in a world networked by the wireless Internet and marked by fast, viral diffusion of images and ideas. They started in the South and in the North, in Tunisia and in Iceland, and from there the spark lit fire in a diverse social landscape devastated by greed and manipulation in all quarters of the blue planet. It was not just poverty, or the economic crisis, or the lack of democracy that caused the multifaceted rebellion. Of course, all these poignant manifestations of an unjust society and of an undemocratic polity were present in the protests. But it was primarily the humiliation provoked by the cynicism and arrogance of those in power, be it financial, political or cultural, that brought together those who turned fear into outrage, and outrage into hope for a better humanity. A humanity that had to be reconstructed from scratch, escaping the multiple ideological and institutional traps that had led to dead ends again and again, forging a new path by treading it. It was the search for dignity amid the suffering of humiliation – recurrent themes in most of the movements.

Networked social movements first spread in the Arab world and were confronted with murderous violence by Arab dictatorships. They experienced diverse fates, from victory to concessions to repeated massacres to civil wars. Other movements arose against the mishandled management of the economic crisis in Europe and in the United States by governments who sided with the financial elites responsible for the crisis at the expense of their citizens: in Spain, in Greece, in Portugal, in Italy (where women's mobilizations contributed to finishing off the buffoon-esque *commedia dell'arte* of Berlusconi), in Britain (where occupations of squares and the defense of the public sector by trade unions and students joined hands) and with less intensity but similar symbolism in most other European countries. In Israel, a spontaneous movement with multiple demands became the largest grassroots mobilization in Israeli history, obtaining the satisfaction of many of its requests. In the United States, the Occupy Wall Street movement, as spontaneous as all the others, and as networked in cyberspace and urban space as the others, became the event of the year, and affected most of the country, so much so that *Time* magazine named "The Protester" the person of the year. And the motto of the 99 percent, whose well-being had been sacrificed to the interests of the 1 percent, who control 23 percent of the country's wealth, became a mainstream topic in American political life. On October 15, 2011, a global network of occupying movements under the banner of "United for Global Change" mobilized hundreds of thousands in 951 cities in 82 countries around the world, claiming social justice and true democracy. In all cases the movements ignored political parties, distrusted the media, did not recognize any leadership and rejected all formal organization, relying on the Internet and local assemblies for collective debate and decision-making.

This book attempts to shed light on these movements: on their formation, their dynamics, their values and their prospects for social transformation. This is an inquiry into the social movements of the network society, the movements that will ultimately make societies in the twenty-first century by engaging in conflictive practices rooted in the fundamental contradictions of our world. The analysis presented here is based on observation of the movements, but it will not try to describe them, nor will it be able to provide definitive proof for the arguments conveyed in this text. There is already available a wealth of information, articles, books, media reports, and blog archives that can be easily consulted by browsing the Internet. And it is too early to construct a systematic, scholarly interpretation of the movements. Thus, my purpose is more limited: to suggest some hypotheses, grounded on observation, on the nature and perspectives of networked social movements, with the hope of identifying the new paths of social change in our time, and to stimulate a debate on the practical (and ultimately political) implications of these hypotheses.

This analysis is based on a grounded theory of power that I presented in my book *Communication Power* (2009), a theory that provides the background for the understanding of the movements studied here.

I start from the premise that power relationships are constitutive of society because those who have power construct the institutions of society according to their values and interests. Power is exercised by means of coercion (the monopoly of violence, legitimate or not, by the control of the state) and/or by the construction of meaning in people's minds, through mechanisms of symbolic manipulation. Power relations are embedded in the institutions of society, and particularly in the state. However, since societies are contradictory and conflictive, wherever there is power there is also counterpower, which I understand to be the capacity of social actors to challenge the power embedded in the institutions of society for the purpose of claiming representation for their own values and interests. All institutional systems reflect power relations, as well as the limits to these power relations as negotiated by an endless historical process of conflict and bargaining. The actual configuration of the state and other institutions that regulate people's lives depends on this constant interaction between power and counterpower.

Coercion and intimidation, based on the state's monopoly of the capacity to exercise violence, are essential mechanisms for imposing the will of those in control of the institutions of society. However, the construction of meaning in people's minds is a more decisive and more stable source of power. The way people think determines the fate of the institutions, norms and values on which societies are organized. Few institutional systems can last long if they are based just on coercion. Torturing bodies is less effective than shaping minds. If a majority of people think in ways that are contradictory to the values and norms institutionalized in the laws and regulations enforced by the state, the system will change, although not necessarily to fulfill the hopes of the agents of social change. This is why the fundamental power struggle is the battle for the construction of meaning in the minds of the people.

Humans create meaning by interacting with their natural and social environment, by networking their neural networks with the networks of nature and with social networks. This networking is operated by the act of communication. Communication is the process of sharing meaning through the exchange of information. For society at large, the key source of the social production of meaning is the process of socialized communication. Socialized communication exists in the public realm beyond interpersonal communication. The ongoing transformation of communication technology in the digital age extends the reach of communication media to all domains of social life in a network that is at the same time global and local, generic and customized in an ever-changing pattern. The process of constructing meaning is characterized by a great deal of diversity. There is, however, one feature common to all processes of symbolic construction: they are largely dependent on the messages and frames created, formatted and diffused in multimedia communication networks. Although each individual human mind constructs its own meaning by interpreting the communicated materials on its own terms, this mental processing is conditioned by the communication environment. Thus, the transformation of the communication environment directly affects the forms of meaning construction, and therefore the production of power relationships. In recent years, the fundamental change in the realm of communication has been the rise of what I have called mass self-communication – the use of the Internet and wireless networks as platforms of digital communication. It is mass communication because it processes messages from many to many, with the potential of reaching a multiplicity of receivers, and of connecting to endless networks that transmit digitized information around the neighborhood or around the world. It is self-communication because the production of the message is autonomously decided by the sender, the designation of the receiver is self-directed and the retrieval of messages from the networks of communication is self-selected. Mass self-communication is based on horizontal networks of interactive communication that, by and large, are difficult to control by governments or corporations. Furthermore, digital communication is multimodal and allows constant reference to a global hypertext of information whose components can be remixed by the communicative actor according to specific projects of communication. Mass self-communication provides the technological platform for the construction of the autonomy of the social actor, be it individual or collective, vis-à-vis the institutions of society. This is why governments are afraid of the Internet, and this is why corporations have a love–hate relationship with it and are trying to extract profits while limiting its potential for freedom (for instance, by controlling file sharing or open source networks).

In our society, which I have conceptualized as a network society, power is multidimensional and is organized around networks programmed in each domain of human activity according to the interests and values of empowered actors.[2] Networks of power exercise their power by influencing the human mind predominantly (but not solely) through multimedia networks of mass communication. Thus, communication networks are decisive sources of power-making.

Networks of power in various domains of human activity are networked among themselves. Global financial networks and global multimedia networks are intimately linked, and this particular meta-network holds extraordinary power. But not all power, because this meta-network of finance and media is itself dependent on other major networks, such as the political network, the cultural production network (which encompasses all kinds of cultural artefacts, not just communication products), the military/security network, the global criminal network and the decisive global network of production and application of science, technology and knowledge management. These networks do not merge. Instead, they engage in strategies of partnership and competition by forming ad hoc networks around specific projects. But they all share a common interest: to control the capacity of defining the rules and norms of society through a political system that primarily responds to their interests and values. This is why the network of power constructed around the state and the political system does play a fundamental role in the overall networking of power. This is, first, because the stable operation of the system, and the reproduction of power relationships in every network, ultimately depend on the coordinating and regulatory functions of the state, as was witnessed in the collapse of financial markets in 2008 when governments were called to the rescue around the world. Furthermore, it is via the state that different forms of exercising power in distinct social spheres relate to the monopoly of violence as the capacity to enforce power in the last resort. So, while communication networks process the construction of meaning on which power relies, the state constitutes the default network for the proper functioning of all other power networks.

And so, how do power networks connect with one another while preserving their sphere of action? I propose that they do so through a fundamental mechanism of power-making in the network society: switching power. This is the capacity to connect two or more different networks in the process of making power for each one of them in their respective fields.

Thus, who holds power in the network society? The *programmers* with the capacity to program each one of the main networks on which people's lives depend (government, parliament, the military and security establishment, finance, media, science and technology institutions, etc.). And the *switchers* who operate the connections between different networks (media moguls introduced in the political class, financial elites bankrolling political elites, political elites bailing out financial institutions, media corporations intertwined with financial corporations, academic institutions financed by big business, etc.).

If power is exercised by programming and switching networks, then counterpower, the deliberate attempt to change power relationships, is enacted by reprogramming networks around alternative interests and values, and/or disrupting the dominant switches while switching networks of resistance and social change. Actors of social change are able to exert decisive influence by using mechanisms of power-making that correspond to the forms and processes of power in the network society. By engaging in the production of mass media messages, and by developing autonomous networks of horizontal communication, citizens of the Information Age become able to invent new programs for their lives with the materials of their suffering, fears, dreams and hopes. They build their projects by sharing their experience. They subvert the practice of communication as usual by occupying the medium and creating the message. They overcome the powerlessness of their solitary despair by networking their desire. They fight the powers that be by identifying the networks that are.

Social movements, throughout history, are the producers of new values and goals around which the institutions of society are transformed to represent these values by creating new norms to organize social life. Social movements exercise counterpower by constructing themselves in the first place through a process of autonomous communication, free from the control of those holding institutional power. Because mass media are largely controlled by governments and media corporations, in the network society communicative autonomy is primarily constructed in the Internet networks and in the platforms of wireless communication. Digital social

networks offer the possibility for largely unfettered deliberation and coordination of action. However, this is only one
component of the communicative processes through which
social movements relate to society at large. They also need
to build public space by creating free communities in the
urban space. Since the institutional public space, the consti-
tutionally designated space for deliberation, is occupied by
the interests of the dominant elites and their networks, social
movements need to carve out a new public space that is not
limited to the Internet, but makes itself visible in the places
of social life. This is why they occupy urban space and symbolic buildings. Occupied spaces have played a major role in
the history of social change, as well as in contemporary practice, for three basic reasons:

1. They create community, and community is based on
   togetherness. Togetherness is a fundamental psychological mechanism to overcome fear. And overcoming fear
   is the fundamental threshold for individuals to cross in
   order to engage in a social movement, since they are well
   aware that in the last resort, they will have to confront
   violence if they trespass the boundaries set up by the
   dominant elites to preserve their domination. In the history of social movements, the barricades erected in the
   streets had very little defensive value; in fact, they became
   easy targets either for the artillery or for the riot squads,
   depending on the context. But they always defined an "in
   and out," an "us versus them," so that by joining an occupied site, and defying the bureaucratic norms of the use
   of space, other citizens could be part of the movement
   without adhering to any ideology or organization, just by
   being there for their own reasons.
2. Occupied spaces are not meaningless: they are usually
   charged with the symbolic power of invading sites of state

power, or financial institutions. Or else, by relating to history, they evoke memories of popular uprisings that had expressed the will of citizens when other avenues of representation were closed. Often, buildings are occupied either for their symbolism or to affirm the right of public use of idle, speculative property. By taking and holding urban space, citizens reclaim their own city, a city from where they were evicted by real estate speculation and municipal bureaucracy. Some major social movements in history, such as the 1871 Paris Commune or the Glasgow strikes of 1915 (at the origin of public housing in Britain), started as rent strikes against housing speculation.[3] The control of space symbolizes the control over people's lives.

3. By constructing a free community in a symbolic place, social movements create a public space, a space for deliberation, which ultimately becomes a political space, a space for sovereign assemblies to meet and to recover their rights of representation, which have been captured in political institutions predominantly tailored for the convenience of the dominant interests and values. In our society, the public space of the social movements is constructed as a hybrid space between the Internet social networks and the occupied urban space: connecting cyberspace and urban space in relentless interaction, constituting, technologically and culturally, instant communities of transformative practice.

The critical matter is that this new public space, the networked space between the digital space and the urban space, is a space of autonomous communication. The autonomy of communication is the essence of social movements because it is what allows the movement to be formed, and what enables the movement to relate to society at large beyond the control of the power holders over communication power.

Where do social movements come from? And how are
they formed? Their roots are in the fundamental injustice of
all societies, relentlessly confronted by human aspirations of
justice. In each specific context, the usual horses of humanity's apocalypses ride together under a variety of their hideous
shapes: economic exploitation, hopeless poverty, unfair
inequality, undemocratic polity, repressive states, unjust
judiciary, racism, xenophobia, cultural negation, censorship,
police brutality, warmongering, religious fanaticism (often
against others' religious beliefs), carelessness toward the blue
planet (our only home), disregard of personal liberty, violation of privacy, gerontocracy, bigotry, sexism, homophobia,
and other atrocities in the long gallery of portraits featuring
the monsters we are. And of course, always, in every instance
and in every context, sheer domination of males over females
and their children, as the primary foundation of a/n (unjust)
social order. Thus, social movements always have an array
of structural causes and individual reasons to rise up against
one or many of the dimensions of social domination. Yet, to
know their roots does not answer the question of their birth.
And since, in my view, social movements are the sources of
social change, and therefore of the constitution of society, the
question is a fundamental one. So fundamental that entire
libraries are dedicated to a tentative approach to the answer,
and so, consequently, I will not deal with it here, since this
book is not intended to be another treatise on social movements but a small window on a nascent world. But I will say
this: social movements, certainly now, and probably in history
(beyond the realm of my competence), are made of individuals. I say it in plural, because in most of what I have read of
analyses of social movements in any time and society, I find
few individuals, sometimes only the one hero, accompanied
by an undifferentiated crowd, called social class, or ethnia, or
gender, or nation, or believers, or any of the other collective

denominations of the subsets of human diversity. Yet, while grouping people's living experience in convenient analytical categories of social structure is a useful method, the actual practices that allow social movements to rise and change institutions and, ultimately, social structure, are enacted by individuals: persons in their material flesh and minds. And so the key question to understand is when and how and why one person or one thousand persons decide, individually, to do something that they are repeatedly warned not to do because they will be punished. There are usually a handful of persons, sometimes just one, at the start of a movement. Social theorists usually call these people agency. I call them individuals. And then we have to understand the motivation of each individual: how these individuals network by connecting mentally to other individuals, and why they are able to do so, in a process of communication that ultimately leads to collective action; how these networks negotiate the diversity of interests and values present in the network to focus on a common set of goals; how these networks relate to the society at large, and to many other individuals; and how and why this connection works in a large number of cases, activating individuals to broaden the networks formed in the resistance to domination, and to engage in a multimodal assault against an unjust order.

At the individual level, social movements are emotional movements. Insurgency does not start with a program or political strategy. This may come later, as leadership emerges, from inside or from outside the movement, to foster political, ideological and personal agendas that may or may not relate to the origins and motivations of participants in the movement. But the big bang of a social movement starts with the transformation of emotion into action. According to the theory of affective intelligence,[4] the emotions that are most relevant to social mobilization and political behavior are fear

(a negative affect) and enthusiasm (a positive affect).[5] Positive
and negative affects are linked to two basic motivational
systems that result from human evolution: approach and
avoidance. The approach system is linked to goal-seeking
behavior that directs the individual to rewarding experiences.
Individuals are enthusiastic when they are mobilized toward
a goal that they cherish. This is why enthusiasm is directly
related to another positive emotion: hope. Hope projects
behavior into the future. Since a distinctive feature of the
human mind is the ability to imagine the future, hope is a
fundamental ingredient in supporting goal-seeking action.
However, for enthusiasm to emerge and for hope to rise,
individuals have to overcome the negative emotion resulting
from the avoidance motivational system: anxiety. Anxiety is
a response to an external threat over which the threatened
person has no control. Thus, anxiety leads to fear, and has
a paralyzing effect on action. The overcoming of anxiety in
socio-political behavior often results from another negative
emotion: anger. Anger increases with the perception of an
unjust action and with the identification of the agent responsible for the action. Neurological research shows that anger
is associated with risk-taking behavior. Once the individual
overcomes fear, positive emotions take over, as enthusiasm
activates action and hope anticipates the rewards for the
risky action. However, for a social movement to form, the
emotional activation of individuals must connect to other
individuals. This requires a communication process from
one individual experience to others. For the communication
process to operate, there are two requirements: cognitive
consonance between senders and receivers of the message,
and an effective communication channel. The empathy in
the communication process is determined by experiences
similar to those that motivated the original emotional
outburst. Concretely speaking: if many individuals feel

humiliated, exploited, ignored or misrepresented, they are ready to transform their anger into action, as soon as they overcome their fear. And they overcome their fear by the extreme expression of anger, in the form of outrage, when learning of an unbearable event suffered by someone with whom they identify. This identification is better achieved by sharing feelings in some form of togetherness created in the process of communication. Thus, the second condition for individual experiences to link up and form a movement is the existence of a communication process that propagates the events and the emotions attached to it. The faster and more interactive the process of communication is, the more likely the formation of a process of collective action becomes, rooted in outrage, propelled by enthusiasm and motivated by hope.

Historically, social movements have been dependent on the existence of specific communication mechanisms: rumors, sermons, pamphlets, and manifestos, spread from person to person, from the pulpit, from the press, or by whatever means of communication were available. In our time, mul-timodal, digital networks of horizontal communication are the fastest and most autonomous, interactive, reprogramma-ble and self-expanding means of communication in history. The characteristics of communication processes between individuals engaged in the social movement determine the organizational characteristics of the social movement itself: the more interactive and self-configurable communication is, the less hierarchical is the organization and the more participatory is the movement. This is why the networked social movements of the digital age represent a new species of social movement.[6]

If the origins of social movements are to be found in the emotions of individuals and in their networking on the basis of cognitive empathy, what is the role of the ideas, ideologies, and programmatic proposals traditionally considered to be the stuff of which social change is made? They are in fact the indispensable materials for the passage from emotion-driven action to deliberation and project construction. Their embedding in the practice of the movement is also a communication process, and how this process is constructed determines the role of these ideational materials in the meaning, evolution, and impact of the social movement. The more the ideas are generated from within the movement, on the basis of the experience of their participants, the more representative, enthusiastic and hopeful the movement will be, and vice versa. It is too often the case that movements become raw materials for ideological experimentation or political instrumentation by defining goals and representations of the movement that have little to do with their reality. Sometimes even in its historical legacy, the human experience of the movement tends to be replaced by a reconstructed image for the legitimization of political leaders or for the vindication of the theories of organic intellectuals. A case in point is how the Commune of Paris came to be in its ideological reconstruction, in spite of the historians' efforts to restore its reality, a proto-proletarian revolution in a city that at the time counted few industrial workers among its dwellers. Why a municipal revolution, sparked by a rent strike and partly led by women, came to be misrepresented has to do with the inaccuracy of Karl Marx's sources in his writings about the Commune, mainly based on his correspondence with Elizabeth Dmitrieva, president of the Women's Union, a committed socialist Communard who saw just what she and her mentor wanted to see.[7] The misrepresentation of the movements by their leaders, ideologues, or chroniclers does have considerable consequences, as it introduces an irreversible cleavage between the actors of the movement and the projects constructed on their behalf, often without their knowledge and consent.

The next question for the understanding of social movements has to do with the evaluation of the actual impact of the joint action of these networks of individuals on the institutions of society, as well as on themselves. This will require a different set of data and analytical instruments, as the characteristics of institutions and of the networks of domination will have to be brought into confrontation with the characteristics of the networks of social change. In a nutshell, for the networks of counterpower to prevail over the networks of power embedded in the organization of society, they will have to reprogram the polity, the economy, the culture or whatever dimension they aim to change by introducing in the institutions' programs, as well as in their own lives, other instructions, including, in some utopian versions, the rule of not ruling anything. Furthermore, they will have to switch on the connection between different networks of social change, e.g. between pro-democracy networks and economic justice networks, women's rights networks, environmental conservation networks, peace networks, freedom networks, and so on. To understand under which conditions these processes take place and which are the social outcomes that result from each specific process cannot be a matter of formal theory. It requires one to ground the analysis on observation.

The theoretical tools I have proposed here are simply so, tools, whose usefulness or futility can only be evaluated by using them to examine the practices of networked social movements this book intends to analyze. However, I will not code the observation of these movements in abstract terms to fit into the conceptual approach presented here. Rather, my theory will be embedded in a selective observation of the movements, to bring together at the end of my intellectual journey the most salient findings of this study in an analytical framework. This is what I intend to be my contribution to the understanding of networked social movements as harbingers of social change in the twenty-first century.

One last word about the origins and conditions of the reflections I am presenting here. I have been a marginal participant in the Barcelona *indignadas* movement, and a supporter and sympathizer of movements in other countries. But I have kept, as is usual in my case, as much distance as I could between my personal beliefs and my analysis. Without pretending to achieve objectivity, I have tried to present the movements in their own words and by their own actions, using some direct observation and a considerable amount of information: some from individual interviews and some from secondary sources that are detailed in the references to each chapter and in the appendices to this book. In fact, I am in full accordance with the basic principle of this leaderless movement of multiple faces: I only represent myself, and this is simply my reflection on what I have seen, heard, or read. I am an individual, doing what I learned to do throughout my life: investigate processes of social transformation, with the hope that this investigation could be helpful to the endeavors of those fighting, at great risk, for a world we would like to live in.

## NOTES

1  For an excellent, analytical, and informed overview of the social movements that sprung up everywhere in 2011, see Paul Mason, *Why It's Kicking Off Everywhere: The New Global Revolutions* (2012, Verso, London).

2  For my characterization of the network society, see my book, *The Rise of the Network Society* (1996; 2010, 2nd edn. Blackwell, Oxford). For a succinct presentation of my network theory of power, see my 2011 article, "A Network Theory of Power," *International Journal of Communication*, 5, 773–87.

3 For a presentation of a historical analysis of urban social movements, see my book, *The City and the Grassroots* (1983, University of California Press, Berkeley, CA), pp. 15–48.

4 W. Russell Neuman, G.E. Marcus, A.N. Crigler, and M. MacKuen (eds.), *The Affect Effect: Dynamics of emotions in political thinking and behavior* (2007, University of Chicago Press, Chicago, IL).

5 I have discussed the contributions of the theory of affective intelligence to the study of socio-political mobilization in my book, *Communication Power* (2009, Oxford University Press, Oxford), pp. 146–55.

6 A pioneer analysis of the rise of contemporary networked social movements is Jeff Juris's *Networked Futures* (2008, Duke University Press, Durham, NC).

7 I discuss the historical record of the Commune of Paris in my book, *The City and the Grassroots* (1983), pp. 15–26.

# PRELUDE TO REVOLUTION:

## WHERE IT ALL STARTED

What do Tunisia and Iceland have in common? Nothing at all. And yet, the political insurgencies that transformed the institutions of governance in both countries in 2009–11 have become the point of reference for the social movements that shook up the political order in the Arab world and challenged the political institutions in Europe, and in the United States. In the first mass demonstration in Cairo's Tahrir Square on January 25, 2011, thousands shouted "Tunisia is the solution," purposely modifying the slogan "Islam is the solution" that had dominated social mobilizations in the Arab world in recent years. They were referring to the toppling of the dictatorship of Ben Ali, who fled his country on January 14 after weeks of grassroots protests that overcame the bloody repression of the regime. When Spain's *indignadas* started camping in the main squares of cities around the country in May 2011, they proclaimed that "Iceland is the solution." And when New Yorkers occupied public spaces around Wall Street on September 17, 2011,

*THIS IS CURRENT REVOLUTIONS*

they named their first encampment Tahrir Square, as did
the occupiers of Catalunya Square in Barcelona. What could
be the common thread that united in people's minds their
experiences of revolt in spite of the vastly diverse cultural,
economic and institutional contexts? In a nutshell: their
feeling of empowerment. It was born from their disgust
with their governments and the political class, be it dictatorial or, in their view, pseudo-democratic. It was prompted
by their outrage toward the perceived complicity between
the financial elite and the political elite. It was triggered by
the emotional upheaval that resulted from some unbearable
event. And it was made possible by overcoming fear through
togetherness built in the networks of cyberspace and in the
communities of urban space. Moreover, both in Tunisia and
in Iceland, there were tangible political transformations, as
well as new civic cultures emerging from the movements in
a very short span of time. They materialized the possibility of fulfilling some of the key demands of the protesters.
Thus, it is analytically meaningful to focus briefly on these
two processes to identify the seeds of social change that
were spread by the wind of hope to other contexts; at times
to germinate in new social forms and values, and in other
instances to be suffocated by machines of repression put on
alert by the powers that be who were at first surprised, then
afraid, and ultimately called into preventive action all over
the world. New avenues of political change, through autonomous capacity to communicate and organize, have been
discovered by a young generation of activists, beyond the
reach of the usual methods of corporate and political control. And, while there were already a number of precedents
of such new social movements in the last decade (particularly
in Spain in 2004 and in Iran in 2009), we may say that in
its full-fledged manifestation it all started in Tunisia and in
Iceland.

## TUNISIA: "THE REVOLUTION OF
## LIBERTY AND DIGNITY"[1]

It began in a most unlikely site: Sidi Bouzid, a small town
of 40,000 residents in an impoverished central region of
Tunisia, south of Tunis. The name of Mohamed Bouazizi, a
26-year-old street vendor, has now been engraved in history
as the one who changed the destiny of the Arab world. His
self-immolation by fire at half past eleven on the morning of
December 17, 2010 in front of a government building was
his ultimate cry of protest against the humiliation of repeated
confiscation of his fruit and vegetable stand by the local police
after he refused to pay a bribe. The last confiscation took
place one hour earlier that day. He died on January 3, 2011
in the Tunis hospital where the dictator had transported him
to placate the wrath of the population. Indeed, only a few
hours after he set himself on fire, hundreds of youth, sharing
similar experiences of humiliation by the authorities, staged
a protest in front of the same building. Mohamed's cousin,
Ali, recorded the protest and distributed the video over the
Internet. There were other symbolic suicides and attempted
suicides that fed the anger and stimulated the courage of
youth. In a few days, demonstrations started spontaneously
around the country, beginning in the provinces and then
spreading to the capital in early January, in spite of savage
repression by the police, who killed at least 147 persons and
injured hundreds. But on January 12, 2011, General Rachid
Ammar, the Chief of Staff of the Tunisian Armed Forces,
refused to open fire on the protesters. He was immediately
dismissed, but on January 14, 2011, the dictator Ben Ali and
his family left Tunisia to find refuge in Saudi Arabia when
confronted with the withdrawal of support from the French
government, Ben Ali's closest ally since his coming to power
in 1987. He had become an embarrassment to his interna-

tional sponsors, and a replacement had to be found within the political elite of the regime itself. Yet, the demonstrators were not appeased by this victory. In fact they were encouraged to pressure for the removal of all commanding personnel of the regime, demanding political freedom and freedom of the press, and calling for truly democratic elections under a new electoral law. They kept shouting *"Degage! Degage!* (Get out of here!)" vis-à-vis all powers that be: corrupt politicians, financial speculators, brutal police and subservient media. The diffusion of videos of protests and police violence over the Internet was accompanied by calls to action in the streets and squares of cities around the country, starting in the Central Western provinces and then moving to Tunis itself. The connection between free communication on Facebook, YouTube and Twitter and the occupation of urban space created a hybrid public space of freedom that became a major feature of the Tunisian rebellion, foreshadowing the movements to come in other countries. Convoys of solidarity were formed by hundreds of cars converging in the capital. On January 22, 2011, the Convoy of Liberty (*Qâfilat al-hurriyya*), beginning in Sidi Bouzid and Menzel Bouzaiane, reached the Kasbah in the Tunis Medina, calling for the resignation of the provisional government of Mohamed Ghannouchi, an obvious continuation of the regime in personnel and policies. Asserting symbolically the people's power, that day the protesters occupied the Place du Gouvernement, at the heart of the Kasbah, the site of most government ministries. They set up tents and organized a permanent forum that engaged in animated debates lasting well into the night. Discussions would go on in some cases for two weeks in a row. They filmed themselves and diffused the video of the debates on the Internet. But their language was not only digital. The walls of the square were covered with slogans in Arabic, French and English, since the movement wanted to relate

to the outside world to claim their rights and aspirations.
They sang rhythmic slogans and protest songs. Most frequently they chanted the most popular line of the national
anthem: "If the people one day wish to live, destiny will have
to respond" (*Idhâ I-sha 'bu yawman arâda I-hayât, fa-lâ budda
an yastadjiba al-qadar*). Although there were no leaders, some
informal organization emerged to take care of the logistics
and to enforce rules of engagement in the debates in the
square: discussions should be polite and respectful and free
from shouting, with everybody entitled to express an opinion, and devoid of endless tirades so that there would be
enough time for everyone to exercise the newly found freedom of speech. A soft surveillance network, organized by the
protesters themselves, made sure the rules were respected.
The same informal organization protected the encampment
against violence and provocation, either from the outside or
from within. There was indeed police violence, and the occupiers were evicted from the square several times, but they
came back on February 20, 2011 to re-occupy the square,
and then again on April 1, 2011. They debated everything
– rejecting a rotten government, calling for true democracy,
asking for a new electoral regime, defending the rights of
the regions against centralism – but also asked for jobs, as
a large proportion of the young demonstrators were unemployed and requesting better education. They were outraged
by the control of both politics and the economy by the clan
of the Trabelsi, the family of the second wife of Ben Ali,
whose crooked deals had been exposed in the diplomatic
cables revealed by WikiLeaks. They also discussed the role
of Islam in providing a moral guide against corruption and
abuse. Yet, this was not an Islamic movement, in spite of the
presence of a strong Islamist current among the protesters,
for the simple reason that there is widespread influence of
political Islamism in the Tunisian society. But secularism and

Islamism coexisted in the movement without major tensions. Indeed, in terms of the community of reference, this was a national Tunisian movement that used the national flag and sang the national anthem as a rallying cry, claiming the legitimacy of the nation against the appropriation of the nation by an illegitimate political regime backed by the former colonial powers, particularly France and the United States. This was neither an Islamic revolution nor a Jasmine revolution (the poetic name given by the Western media for no clear reason, which in fact was the original name for the coup of Ben Ali in 1987!). In the words of the protesters themselves, this was a "Revolution for liberty and dignity" (*Thawrat al-hurriya wa-I Karâma*). The search for dignity in response to institutionally backed humiliation was an essential emotional driver of the protests.

Who were these protesters? After a few weeks of demonstrations we can say that a cross-section of the Tunisian society was in the streets, with a strong presence of the professional class. Moreover, the large majority of the population supported the demand to end the dictatorial regime. Yet, in the view of most observers, those who started the movement and those who played the most active role in the protest were mainly unemployed educated youth. Indeed, while the unemployment rate in Tunisia was 13.3 percent, it had risen to 21.1 percent among young college graduates. This mixture of education and lack of opportunities was a breeding ground for revolt in Tunisia, as in all other Arab countries. It was also significant that unionized workers were important participants once the movement had reached a critical mass. While the leadership of the Union Generale des Travailleurs Tunisiens (UGTT) was delegitimized by its deep connection with the regime (particularly its secretary general, Abdeslem Jrad), the rank and file and the middle-level cadres used the opportunity to voice their demands and launched a number

of strikes that contributed to bringing the country out of control of the authorities. Instead, the opposing political parties
were ignored by the activists and had no organized presence
in the revolt. The protesters generated spontaneously their
own ad hoc leadership in specific times and places. Most of
these self-appointed leaders were in their twenties and early
thirties. Although the movement was intergenerational, the
trust was created among the youth. A post on Facebook
expressed clearly a certain state of mind: "Most politicians
have white hair and a black heart. We want people who have
black hair and a white heart."

Why did this movement succeed so quickly in subverting
a stable dictatorship with a façade of institutional democracy,
a huge surveillance system of the entire society (as many as
one percent of Tunisians worked in one way or another for
the Minister of Interior) and strong support from the major
Western powers? After all, social struggles and gestures of
opposition have been swiftly repressed by the regime with relative ease on prior occasions. Intense working-class struggles
had taken place in Ben Guerdane (2009) and in the phosphate
mines of Gafsa (2010), but they were violently repressed with
scores of people killed, injured and arrested, and ultimately
contained. Dissidents were tortured and jailed. Street demonstrations were rare. We know that the spark of the revolt came
from the sacrifice of Mohamed Bouazizi. But how did the
spark set fire to the prairie and how and why did it spread?

New, distinctive factors made possible the success of the
Tunisian popular revolts in 2011 over a sustained period
of time. Among these factors appears prominently the role
played by the Internet and Al Jazeera in triggering, amplify-
ing and coordinating spontaneous revolts as an expression of
outrage, particularly among the youth. Granted, any social
uprising – and Tunisia was no exception – takes place as an
expression of protest against dire economic, social and politi-

cal conditions, such as unemployment, high prices, inequality, poverty, police brutality, lack of democracy, censorship, and corruption as a way of life throughout the state. But from these objective conditions emerged emotions and feelings – feelings of outrage often induced by humiliation – and these feelings prompted spontaneous protests initiated by individuals: by young people using their networks; the networks where they live and express themselves. Certainly, this includes the Internet's social networks as well as mobile phone networks. But this also means their social networks: their friends, their families and, in some cases, their soccer clubs, most of them offline. It was in the connection between social networks on the Internet and social networks in people's lives where the protest was forged. Thus, the pre-condition for the revolts was the existence of an Internet culture, made up of bloggers, social networks and cyberactivism. For instance, blogger journalist Zouhair Yahiaoui was imprisoned in 2001 and died in prison. Other critical bloggers, such as Mohamed Abbou (2005) and Slim Boukdir (2008), were jailed for their exposure of government's wrongdoings.

These growing free voices that spread on the Internet in spite of censorship and repression found a powerful ally in satellite television beyond government control, particularly Al Jazeera. There was a symbiotic relationship between mobile phone citizen journalists uploading images and information to YouTube and Al Jazeera using feeds from citizen journalism and then broadcasting them to the population at large (40 percent of Tunisians in urban centers watched Al Jazeera, since official television had been reduced to a primitive propaganda tool). This Al Jazeera–Internet link was essential during the weeks of the revolts, both in Tunisia and in relation to the Arab world. Al Jazeera went so far as to develop a communication program to allow mobile phones to connect directly to its satellite without requiring sophisticated equipment. Twitter also played a major role in discussing the events and coordinating actions. Demonstrators used the hashtag #sidibouzid on Twitter to debate and communicate, thus indexing the Tunisian revolution. According to the study on information flows in the Arab revolutions conducted by Lotan et al. (2011: 1389), "bloggers played an important role in surfacing and disseminating news from Tunisia, as they had a substantially higher likelihood to engage their audience to participate, compared with any other actor type."

Given the role of the Internet in spreading and coordinating the revolt, it is significant to point out that Tunisia has one of the highest rates of Internet and mobile phone penetration in the Arab world. In November 2010, 67 percent of the urban population had access to a mobile phone, and 37 percent were connected to the Internet. In early 2011, 20 percent of Internet users were on Facebook, a percentage that is two times higher than in Morocco, three times higher than in Egypt, five times higher than in Algeria or Libya, and twenty times higher than in Yemen. Furthermore, the proportion of Internet users among the urban population and particularly among the urban youth was much higher. Since there is a direct connection between young age, higher education and the use of the Internet, the unemployed college graduates who were the key actors in the revolution were also frequent Internet users, and some were sophisticated users who utilized the communicative potential of the Internet to build and expand their movement. The communicative autonomy provided by the Internet made possible the viral diffusion of videos, messages and songs that incited rage and gave hope. For instance, the song "Rais Lebled" by a famous rapper from Sfax, El General, denouncing the dictatorship became a hit on the social networks. Of course, El General was arrested, but this incensed the protesters even further and strengthened their determination in the struggle for "complete transition," as they put it.

Thus, it seems that in Tunisia we find a significant convergence of three distinctive features:

1. The existence of an active group of unemployed college graduates, who led the revolt, bypassing any formal, traditional leadership;
2. The presence of a strong cyberactivism culture that had engaged in the open critique of the regime for over one decade;
3. A relatively high rate of diffusion of Internet use, including household connections, schools and cybercafés.

The combination of these three elements, which fed into each other, provides a clue to understanding why Tunisia was the harbinger of a new form of networked social movement in the Arab world.

The Tunisian protesters kept up their demands for full democratization of the country throughout 2011 in spite of persistent police repression and continuing presence of politicians from the old regime in the provisional government and in the high levels of administration. The army, however, was generally supportive of the democratization process, trying to find new legitimacy from its refusal to engage in further bloody repression during the revolution. With the support of a newly independent media, particularly in the case of the print press, the democratic movement opened a new political space and reached the milestone of clean, open elections on October 23, 2011. Ennahad, a moderate Islamist coalition, became the leading political force in the country, receiving 40 percent of the votes and obtaining 89 of the 217 seats of the Constitutional Assembly. Its leader, the veteran Islamist political intellectual Rached Gannouchi, became prime minister.

He represents the brand of Islamism that would have come to power through free elections in most Arab countries, if the will of the people would have been respected. He does not represent a return to tradition or to the imposition of Sharia. In an often quoted interview given in his London exile in 1990, Rached Gannouchi put his political vision of Islamism in simple terms: "The only way to accede to modernity is by our own path, that which has been traced for us by our religion, our history and our civilization" (*Jeune Afrique*, July 1990, my translation). So, there is no rejection of modernity, but defence of a project of self-determined modernity. His most explicit contemporary reference is the Freedom and Development Party led by Erdogan in Turkey, but this has been consistent with his own position over the years. There are no indications that an Islamic fundamentalist regime will be the outcome of the Tunisian Revolution. The president, Moncef Marzuki, is a secular personality, and the draft of the new Constitution is no more reliant on God's will than is the Constitution of the United States. Indeed, the acceptance of a modern Islamist party at the forefront of the political system has marginalized, without excluding, the radical Islamic forces. However, this may change if the new democratic governments are not able to tackle the dramatic issues of mass unemployment, extreme poverty, widespread corruption and bureaucratic arrogance that have not been dissolved by the atmosphere of freedom. Tunisia will confront major challenges in the coming years. But it will do so with a reasonably democratic polity in place and, more importantly, with a conscious and active civil society, still occupying cyberspace and ready to come back into the urban space if and when necessary. Whatever the future will be, the hope for a humane and democratic Tunisian society will be the direct result of the sacrifice of Mohamed Bouazizi and of the struggle for the dignity he defended for himself, which had been taken up by his compatriots.

## ICELAND'S KITCHENWARE REVOLUTION: FROM FINANCIAL COLLAPSE TO CROWDSOURCING A NEW (FAILED) CONSTITUTION[2]

The opening scenes of what is perhaps the best documentary film on the global financial crisis of 2008, Charles Ferguson's *Inside Job*, showcase Iceland. Indeed, the rise and fall of the Icelandic economy epitomizes the flawed model of speculative wealth creation that characterized financial capitalism in the last decade. In 2007, Iceland's average income was the fifth highest in the world. Icelanders earned 160 percent more than Americans. Its economy had been historically based in the fishing industry, representing 12 percent of GDP and 40 percent of exports. Yet, even adding tourism, software, and aluminum as dynamic economic activities, and as profitable as fishing had been, the sources of the sudden Icelandic wealth were elsewhere. It resulted from the fast growth of the financial sector in the wake of the global expansion of speculative financial capitalism. The fast integration of Iceland in international finance was led by three Icelandic banks: Kaupthing, Landsbanki, and Glitnir, which grew from local service banks in the late 1980s to major financial institutions by the mid-2000s. The three banks increased the value of their assets from 100 percent of GDP in 2000 to almost 800 percent of GDP by the year 2007. The strategy they followed for their outstanding growth was similar to that of many financial entities in the United States and the UK. They used their shares as collateral to borrow extensively from each other and then used these loans to finance the purchase of additional shares from the three banks, thus increasing the price of their shares and boosting their balance sheets. Furthermore, they plotted together to broaden the scope of their speculative operations on a global scale. Their fraudulent schemes

were disguised through a web of jointly owned firms head-
quartered in offshore banking locations, such as the Isle of
Man, the Virgin Islands, Cuba, and Luxembourg. Bank customers were persuaded to increase their debt, converting it
into lower interest Swiss francs or Japanese yen. Unlimited
credit permitted people to engage in unlimited consumption,
artificially stimulating domestic demand and propelling economic growth. Furthermore, to cover their operations, the
banks made favorable loans to selected politicians, as well as
generous financial contributions to political parties for their
election campaigns.

In February of 2006, Fitch downgraded the outlook of
Iceland's economy to negative, triggering what was labeled
a "mini crisis." To stop the main banks from losing credit,
Iceland's Central Bank borrowed extensively to increase their
foreign exchange reserves. The Chamber of Commerce,
dominated by representatives of the large banks, hired as
consultants two prominent academics: Frederic Mishkin,
from the Columbia Business School, and Richards Portes,
from the London Business School, both of whom certified
the solvency of the Icelandic banks. However, by 2007, the
government could no longer ignore the suspicious balance
sheets of the banks, and realized that if one of the major
banks failed, the whole financial system would follow. A
special commission was appointed to assess the problem.
The commission did very little, and did not even contem-
plate regulating the banking sector. Soon thereafter, the
three banks, Landsbanki, Kaupthing, and Glitnir, faced the
urgency of repaying their short-term debt, as most of their
assets were fictitious and long-term. Having more imagination than scruples, they designed new schemes to solve
their insolvency. Landsbanki set up Internet-based financial
accounts under the name of Icesave, offering high returns on
short-term deposits. They offered this service through new

branches in the UK and the Netherlands. It was a success: millions of pounds were deposited in the Icesave accounts. In the UK alone, 300,000 Icesave accounts were opened. The deposits appeared to be safe as Iceland was a member of the EEA (European Economic Area), and therefore was covered by the EEA's deposit insurance system, meaning that they were guaranteed by the Icelandic government, as well as by the governments of the countries where the branches of the banks were located. A second strategy used by the three big banks to raise money in a hurry to pay their short-term debt was what became known as "love letters." The banks swapped debt securities with each other to use the others' debt as collateral to borrow more money from the Central Bank of Iceland. Furthermore, the Central Bank of Luxembourg lent the three banks €2.5 billion, with most of the collateral in the form of "love letters." Political support from the government for the big banks continued in spite of their obvious insolvency. In April 2008, the IMF sent a confidential memo to the Haarde government requesting the control of the banks and offering help, to no avail. The only reaction from the government was to instruct the Central Bank to take more loans in foreign exchange reserves. On September 29, Glitnir bank asked the Governor of the Central Bank for immediate help, as it could not cover its financial obligations. In response, the Central Bank bought 75 percent of Glitnir's shares. Yet, this action had the opposite effect: instead of reassuring the financial markets, the move prompted the free fall of Iceland's credit rating. In a few days, the stock market, bank bonds and real estate prices plummeted. The three banks collapsed, leaving US$25 billion in debt. The financial crisis caused losses, in Iceland and abroad, equivalent to seven times the GDP of Iceland. In proportion to the size of the economy, it was the largest destruction of financial value in history. The personal income of Icelanders was substantially reduced and their assets were sharply devalued. Iceland's GDP fell by 6.8 percent in 2009, and by an additional 3.4 percent in 2010. As its financial house of cards collapsed, Iceland's economic crisis became the catalyst of the Kitchenware Revolution.

Every revolution has its date of birth and its rebel hero. On October 11, 2008, singer Hordur Torfason sat in front of the building of the Althing (the Icelandic parliament) in Reykjavik with his guitar, and sang his anger against the "banksters" and their subservient politicians. A few people joined him. Then someone recorded the scene and uploaded it to the Internet. Within days, hundreds and then thousands were staging their protest in the historic Austurvollur square. A group known as the Raddir fólksins vowed to protest every Saturday to obtain the resignation of the government. The protests intensified in January, both on the Internet and in the square, braving the Icelandic winter. According to observers in this process of social mobilization, the role of the Internet and social networks was absolutely critical, partly because 94 percent of Icelanders are connected to the Internet, and two-thirds are users of Facebook.

On January 20, 2009, the day the parliament reconvened after a month-long holiday, thousands of people of all ages and conditions gathered in front of the parliament to blame the government for the mishandling of the economy and for its inability to cope with the crisis. They beat on drums, pots and pans, thus earning the nickname "the kitchenware revolution" or "the pots-and-pans revolution." Protesters were calling for the government to resign and for new elections to be held. Furthermore, they were also pushing for a re-foundation of the republic, which had become corrupted, in their view, by the subordination of politicians and political parties to the financial elite. And so, they asked for the drafting of a new Constitution, to replace the provisional Constitution of 1944, a temporary charter at the time of the declaration of independence from occupied Denmark, that was kept in place because it favored the interests of the political class (giving disproportionate weight to the conservative, rural provinces). The social democrats and greens responded positively to this request while the conservative coalition led by the Independence Party rejected it. As the pressure from the social networks and from the streets intensified, on January 23, 2009, early parliamentary elections were announced, and the conservative Prime Minister Geir Haarde declared that due to his poor health he would not be running for re-election. The elections resulted in a resounding defeat of the two major parties (both conservative) that, alone or in coalition, had been governing Iceland since 1927. A new coalition formed by social democrats and "redgreens" came into power on February 1, 2009. It was led by the social democratic leader Johanna Sigurdardottir, the first openly gay prime minister. Half of her cabinet members are women.

The new government went to work on three fronts: to clean up the financial mess and exact responsibilities for the fraudulent management of the economy; to restore economic growth by transforming the economic model, setting up strict financial regulations and strengthening the overseeing institutions; and to respond to the popular demand by engaging in a process of constitutional reform with full citizen participation.

The three major banks were nationalized and two of them returned to the private sector to be owned by a pool of the banks' foreign creditors, with participation of the state. Icelanders were compensated by the government for the loss of their savings. However, at the initiative of the President of the Republic, Olafur Grimson, a referendum was held to decide on the payment of the loan guarantees owed by the extinct banks to the British and Dutch depositors and their governments. Ninety-three percent of Icelanders voted not to pay the $US5.9 billion debt owed to the UK and the Netherlands. Of course, this prompted a series of lawsuits still being sorted out in the courts. Iceland is facing a long legal battle to settle the foreign debt. The banks tried to avoid litigation by offering to pay with the sale of their assets, but the outcome of the negotiation is still pending at the time of this writing.

The new government proceeded with legal action against those responsible for the crisis. Speaking at the convention of the Social Democratic Party on May 30, 2011, Prime Minister Johanna Sigurdardottir stated, in the clearest possible terms, that:

> The overpaid crowd, the "banksters," and the big property elites will not be allowed to gobble up the coming economic growth ... Their debauched party was held under the Independence party's neoconservative fanfare. The quality of life Icelanders have in the future, will, on the other hand, be built on equality.

Accordingly, leading figures of the banking sector were arrested in Reykjavik and London to respond to the charges against their unlawful financial management. And former Prime Minister Haarde was brought to trial under the accusation of mismanagement of public funds and yielding to the influence of pressure groups.

As expected, economic experts warned against the dire consequences of nationalizing the banks, controlling capital flows and refusing to pay foreign debt. However, after Iceland reversed its economic policies, asserting government control, the economy bounced back in 2011 and 2012, outperforming most economies of the European Union. After experiencing negative growth in 2009 and 2010, GDP increased by 2.6

percent in 2011 and was projected to increase by 4 percent in 2012. Unemployment dropped from 10 percent in 2009 to 5.9 percent in 2012, inflation was reduced from 18 percent to 4 percent and Iceland's financial standing improved in CDS ratings from 1,000 points to 200 points. Although the economy is still subject to the possibility of future crises, as is the whole of the European economy, its outlook was upgraded by Standard & Poor's in late 2011 from negative to stable. Government bond issues in 2011 were oversubscribed by international investors. In fact, according to Bloomberg in 2011, it cost less to insure Icelandic debt than sovereign debt in the eurozone. The attitudes of Icelanders toward the future became more positive by mid-2011, particularly among the most educated segments of society.

How was the new democratic government able to rescue the country from a major economic disaster in such a short span of time?

First, it did not promote the kind of drastic austerity measures that were implemented in other European countries. Iceland signed a "social stability" pact to protect citizens from the effects of the crisis. Thus public employment was not significantly reduced, and public spending kept domestic demand at a reasonable level. The government had sufficient revenue to keep spending and to buy back internal financial assets because it did not have to repay the banks' foreign debt, as mandated by the referendum. Furthermore, while compensating the bank customers for their losses, priority was given to deposit holders over bond holders. This contributed to keep liquidity in the economy, facilitating the recovery.

Second, the devaluation of the Króna, which fell by 40 percent, had a very positive impact on fish sales, aluminum exports and tourism. Furthermore, as imports became more expensive, local businesses picked up some of the consumer demand, facilitating the creation of an unprecedented number of start-up firms, which more than compensated for the disappearance of companies in financial services, construction and real estate.

Third, the government established control of capital flows and foreign currency, preventing the flight of capital from the country.

However, the Icelandic revolution, while provoked by the economic crisis, was not only about restoring the economy. It was primarily about a fundamental transformation of the political system that was blamed for its incapacity to manage the crisis, and its subordination to the banks. This is in spite of, or perhaps because of, the fact that Iceland is one of the oldest democracies in the world. The Althing (its representative assembly still in place nowadays under a different form) was established before the year 1000. And yet, after experiencing the cronyism and aloofness of the political class, Iceland plunged into the same crisis of legitimacy as most countries in the world. Only 11 percent of citizens trusted the parliament, and obviously only 6 percent trusted the banks. Trying to win back people's trust, the government called for an election that was held by popular demand, honoring its promise of engaging in a constitutional reform with the broadest feasible citizen participation. A unique constitutional process was put in place, and actually implemented. The parliament appointed a constitutional committee that convened a national assembly of 1,000 randomly selected citizens. After two days of deliberation, the assembly concluded that a new Constitution should be drafted and suggested some of the principles that should be paramount in the constitutional text. Following action, in spite of the criticism from the conservative opposition parties, the parliament then organized a popular election to designate a 25 member Constitutional Assembly Council (CAC). All citizens were entitled to candidacy, and 522 of them contested the 25 seats. The election was held in November 2010 with the participation of 37 percent of the electorate. However, the Supreme Court voided the election for technical legal reasons. To circumvent the obstruction, the parliament exercised its right to appoint the 25 citizens elected in this process to the constitutional council in charge of drafting the new constitution. The CAC sought the participation of all citizens via the Internet. Facebook was the primary platform for debate. Twitter was the channel to report on the work in progress and to respond to queries from citizens. YouTube and Flickr were used to set up direct communication between citizens and the council members, as well as to participate in debates taking place throughout Iceland.

The CAC received online and offline 16,000 suggestions and comments that were debated on the social networks. It wrote 15 different versions of the text, to take into consideration the results of this widespread deliberation. Thus, the final constitutional bill was literally produced through crowdsourcing. Some observers have labeled it a wiki-constitution (www.wired.co.uk./news/archive/2011-08/01/iceland-constitution).

After months of deliberation online and among its members, the council approved a draft of the constitutional bill by a vote of 25 to 0. On July 29, 2011, the CAC delivered to the parliament a bill containing 114 articles in 9 chapters. While the parliament debated some minor points and changed some language of the text, the left-wing majority overran the objections of the conservative opposition, and the bill was only slightly amended. The government decided that it should be submitted to a vote of citizens at large, and vowed to respect the popular decision in the final approval that is the prerogative of the parliament. A vote on the constitutional bill was scheduled for the same day as the presidential election, June 30, 2012.

If approved, the new Icelandic Constitution would enshrine philosophical principles, social values and political forms of representation that are prominent in the demands and the vision of the social movements that surged around the world in 2011. It is worthwhile to highlight some elements of this text (to see a draft of the Constitution in its English translation, visit http://www.politics.ie/forum/political-reform/173176-proposed-new-icelandic-constitution.html).

The preamble of the Constitution proclaims the fundamental principle of equality:

> We, the people of Iceland, wish to create a just society with equal opportunities for everyone.

The representative political principle of "one person, one vote" is emphasized, as this is the key in Iceland, as in many other countries, to avoiding the confiscation of popular will by political engineering. The text states that:

> The votes of voters everywhere in the country shall have equal weight.

To break the monopoly of political parties, it is established that voters will be free to vote for parties or for individual candidates on different slates.

The principle of free access to information is strongly affirmed:

> The law shall ensure public access to all documents collected or processed by public entities.

This effectively would end government secrecy and make more difficult hidden political maneuvering, as all government and parliamentary meetings should have records and these records could be accessed by anyone. Furthermore:

All persons shall be free to collect and disseminate information.

There is a limitation of the number of terms politicians, and particularly the president, can serve. The right for citizens to initiate legislation and to call for referendums on specific issues is recognized.

The public interest in the management of the economy is asserted:

Iceland's natural resources that are not in private ownership are the common and perpetual property of the nation . . . The utilization of the resources shall be guided by sustainable development and the public interest.

And the respect of nature is paramount:

Iceland's nature is the foundation of life in the country . . . The use of natural resources shall be managed to minimize their depletion in the long term with respect for the rights of nature and future generations.

That the Constitution of a country could explicitly reflect principles that, in the context of global capitalism, are revolutionary shows the direct link between a process of genuinely popular crowdsourcing and the content resulting from such a participatory process. It should be remembered that the consultation and elaboration took place in four months as requested by the parliament, belying the notion of the ineffectiveness of participatory democracy. Granted, Iceland has only 320,000 citizens. But the defenders of the experience argue that with the Internet and with full Internet literacy and unrestricted access, this model of political participation and crowdsourcing of the legislative process is scalable.

The reference that the Icelandic revolution came to be for European social movements battling the consequences of a devastating financial crisis is explained by its direct connection to the main issues that induced the protests.

Icelanders insurged, as did people in all other countries, against a brand of speculative financial capitalism that destroyed people's livelihood. But their outrage came from the realization that the democratic institutions did not represent the interests of citizens because the political class had become a self-reproducing cast that was catering to the interests of the financial elite, and to the preservation of their monopoly over the state.

This is why the primary target of the movement was the government in place, and the political class at large, although they offered a chance for the new government to legitimize its actions by following the people's will, as expressed in the public space offered by the Internet. The government responded by enacting effective economic policies leading to economic recovery in sharp contrast to many European economies that were burdened by misplaced austerity policies that aggravated the recession in the continent. The key differentiating factor between Iceland and the rest of Europe is that the Icelandic government made the bankers pay for the costs of the crisis, while relieving people from its hardship as much as possible. This is in fact one of the key demands from protesters throughout Europe. The results of this approach were positive both in economic terms and in terms of social and political stability.

Furthermore, Icelandic citizens fully realized their project of transformation of the political system by elaborating a new Constitution whose principles, if enacted, would ensure the practice of true democracy and the preservation of fundamental human values. In this particular sense it was indeed a true revolutionary experiment whose example, with all its limitations, has inspired a new generation of pragmatic idealists at the forefront of the social movements against the crisis. Indeed, in some posts on the Internet reflecting on Iceland's constitutional experience, there is reference to the Corsican Constitution of 1755 that is considered to be one of the sources of inspiration for the Constitution of the United States (www.nakedcapitalism.com/2011/10).

The first draft of the Constitution of Corsica was written by Jean Jacques Rousseau, at the request of the founders of the short-lived republic. While seeking to establish the principles on which the Constitution should be based, he wrote:

The power derived from population is more real than derived from finance, and is more certain in its effects. Since the use of manpower cannot be concealed from view, it always reaches its public objective. It is not thus with the use of money, which flows off and is lost in private destinations; it is collected for one purpose and spent for another; the people pay for protection, and their payments are used to oppress them. That is why a state rich in money is always weak, and a state rich in men is always strong (Rousseau, J.J., "Constitutional Project for Corsica," drafted 1765, Edinburgh, Thomas Nelson and Sons, retrieved from Liberty Library, www.constitution.org/jjr/corsica.htm).

The echo of this contrast between the poverty of finance and the richness of people reaches across history to the many squares where citizens envision new constitutional projects. In this sense, the making of the new Icelandic Constitution could well play the inspiring role for twenty-first century democracy that Corsica played for the proclamation of liberty in the United States.

The project of Constitutional reform was proposed to the citizens at large in a Referendum in October 2012. Fifty percent of the voters participated in the non-binding consultation, and 67 percent of them approved the new Constitutional text. However, according to Icelandic legislation, enforced by the Constitutional Court, reform of the Constitution requires two successive parliamentary votes with one election being held between the two votes. That forced the social democratic/green majority to wait until the following election before they could submit the new Constitution to the vote in parliament. The election was held on April 27 and it was a complete disaster for the reformist coalition, which lost half of its votes and half of its seats. A rightist coalition, formed by the same parties that had led Iceland to a complete collapse, was returned to power. Among the causes for this extraordinary reversal of public opinion were the austerity policies implemented responsibly by the social democratic government in order to restore the economy; the pro-European Union stand of the governing coalition, in contrast to the nationalistic, xenophobic attitude of traditional Icelandic parties; and the resentment of the majority of the population against their deep indebtedness as a result of the mortgage crisis and the inefficiency of the government in resolving the debt crisis. But perhaps the main source of discontent was the cognitive dissonance between the hopes of the social movement and the grim reality of institutional politics, a recurrent theme in the history of social movements. As a result, the new parliament tabled the project of constitutional reform and one of the most daring experiments in constitutional democracy became yet another faded dream.

However, if the crisis of political legitimacy continues to expand throughout the world, and if citizens everywhere keep looking for inspiration in their search for real democracy, the cultural and technological bases for the deepening of representative democracy might have been laid out in a small country made of ice and fire on a North Atlantic island.

## SOUTHERN WIND, NORTHERN WIND: CROSS-CULTURAL LEVERS OF SOCIAL CHANGE

The precursors of networked social movements present, after close examination, striking similarities in spite of their sharply contrasted cultural and institutional contexts.

Both revolts insurged against the consequences of a dramatic economic crisis, although in Tunisia this was not as much due to a financial collapse as to the plundering of the country's economy by a clique rooted in the predatory state. Moreover, people felt powerless because of the obvious intertwining of the business oligarchs and the political class, be it democratically elected or dictatorially imposed. I am certainly not assimilating the Icelandic democracy, fully respectful of liberty and civil rights, to the torturing dictatorship of Ben Ali and his thugs. But from the perspective of citizens in both countries, the governments in place, and even politicians at large, did not represent their will because they had merged with the interests of the financial elite, and they had put their own interests above the interests of the people. The democratic deficit, although in vastly different proportions, was present in both countries, and it was a major source of discontent at the roots of the protests. The crisis of political legitimacy combined with the crisis of speculative capitalism.

There is also an interesting common feature in these two countries. They are both highly homogeneous in ethnicity

and in religion. Indeed, Iceland, because of its historical isolation, is used as a laboratory by genetic researchers looking
for a homogeneous genetic heritage. As for Tunisia, it is the
most ethnically homogeneous country of the Arab world,
and Sunni Muslims represent the overwhelming proportion of the population. Thus, it will be significant to assess
the impact of cultural and ethnic heterogeneity in other
countries over the characteristics of social movements by
comparing them to the baseline represented by these two
countries.

Similarities extend to the practices of the movements
themselves. Both were triggered by a dramatic event (financial collapse in Iceland, the self-immolation of Mohamed
Bouazizi in Tunisia). In both cases, mobile phones and social
networks on the Internet played a major role in spreading
images and messages that mobilized people in providing a
platform for debate, in calling for action, in coordinating
and organizing the protests, and in relaying information and
debate to the population at large. Television also played a
role, but always used Internet and mobile phones to feed its
images and information.

In both cases, the movement went from cyberspace to
urban space, with the occupation of the symbolic public
square as material support for both debates and protests,
from chanting slogans in Tunis, to banging pans and pots in
Reykjavik. A hybrid public space made of digital social networks and of a newly created urban community was at the
heart of the movement, both as a tool for self-reflection and
as a statement of people's power. Powerlessness was turned
into empowerment.

From this empowerment came the strongest similarity
between the movements in Tunisia and Iceland: their meaningful success in achieving institutional change. Democracy
was established in Tunisia. A new constitutional order,

enlarging the boundaries of representative democracy, was achieved in Iceland, and a new set of economic policies was implemented. The process of mobilization leading to political change transformed civic consciousness. This is the reason why both movements became role models for the social movements that, inspired by them, emerged thereafter in the landscape of a world in crisis searching for new forms of living together.

It is the purpose of this book to investigate the extent to which the key features identified in these two movements are equally present as critical factors in movements arising in other social contexts. Because if they are, we may be observing the rise of new forms of social transformation. And if they are modified in their practice because of differences in context, we may suggest some hypotheses on the interaction between culture, institutions and movements, the key question for a theory of social change. And, for its practice.

## NOTES

1  The best analysis I know of the Tunisian revolution is by Choukri Hmed (2011). Some key elements of my own analysis are based on his. A detailed account is the one by Viviane Bettaieb (2011). On the role of Internet social networks, television and mobile phones in the Tunisian protests, see Wagner (2011) and Lotan et al. (2011).

2  An insightful and well-documented analysis of the Icelandic revolution can be found in Gylfason et al. (2010) and Gunnarson (2009). On the importance of the role of social networks on the Internet in the dynamics of the social movement, see Bennett (2011) and Garcia Lamarca (2011). On the financial crisis and economic policies in Iceland, see references.

## REFERENCES AND SOURCES

### On the Tunisian revolution

Beau, N. and Tuquoi, J.P. (2002) *Notre ami Ben Ali: l'envers du miracle tunisien*. La Decouverte, Paris.

Bettaieb, V. (2011) *Degage-La revolution tunisienne. 17 december 2010–14 Janvier 2011*. Editions du Layeur, Paris.

Cherni, A. (2011) *La revolution tunisienne: s'emparer de l'histoire*. Al Bouraq, Paris.

De Leon, J.C. and Jones, C.R. (eds.) (2011) *Tunisia and Egypt: Unrest and Revolution*. Global Political Studies, Novinka, New York.

Elseewi, T.A. (2011) A revolution of the imagination. *International Journal of Communication*. [Online] Vol. 5: 1197–206. Available at: <http://ijoc.org/ojs/index.php/ijoc/article/view/1237/596>.

Haloui, Y. (2011) *Life in Revolution: Resistance and everyday life in the Tunisian revolution*. Lambert Academic Publishers, Saarbrücken.

Hatzenberger, A. (2011) L'hiver à Tunis et le printemps. *Les Temps Modernes*, May–July: 21–25.

Hmed, C. (2011) "Si le peuple un jour aspire à vivre, le destin se doit de répondre": Apprender à devenir révolutionnaire en Tunisie. *Les Temps Modernes*, May–July: 4–20.

Laurent, J. (2011) Points d'inflexion des revoltes arabes. *Les Temps Modernes*, May–July: 63–84.

Lotan, G., Graeff, E., Ananny, M., Gaffney, D., Pearce, I., and boyd, d. (2011) The revolutions were tweeted: Information flows during the 2011 Tunisian and Egyptian revolutions. *International Journal of Communication*, [Online] Vol. 5: 1375–405. Available at: <http://ijoc.org/ojs/index.php/ijoc/article/view/1246>.

Newsom, V.A., Lengel, L., and Cassara, C. (2011) Local knowledge and the revolutions: A framework for social media information flow. *International Journal of Communication*, [Online] Vol. 5: 1303–12. Available at: <http://ijoc.org/ojs/index.php/ijoc/article/view/1245/607>.

Piot, O. (2011) *Dix jours qui ebranlerent le monde arabe*. Les Petits Matins, Paris.

Wagner, B. (2011) "I have understood you": The co-evolution of expression and control on the internet, television and mobile phones during the Jasmine Revolution in Tunisia. *International Journal of Communication*, [Online] Vol. 5: 1295–303. Available at: <http://ijoc.org/ojs/index.php/ijoc/article/view/1174/606>.

## On the Icelandic revolution

*Web resources*

Bennett, N. (2011) Iceland's crowdsourced constitution – a lesson in open source marketing. [Online] Available at: <http://socialmediatoday.com/nick-bennett/305690/icelands-crowdsourced-constitution-lesson-opensource-marketing> [Accessed on January 9, 2012].

Boyes, R. (2009) Age of Testosterone comes to end in Iceland. *The Times*, [Online] February 7. Available at: <http://www.timesonline.co.uk/tol/news/world/europe/article5679378.ece> [Accessed on January 9, 2012].

Brown, M. (2011) Icelanders turn in first draft of crowd-sourced constitution. *Wired News*, [Online] August 1. Available at: <http://www.wired.co.uk/news/archive/2011-08/01/iceland-constitution> [Accessed on January 9, 2012].

Constitution Society. (1994) *Constitutional Project for Corsica*. [Online] Available at: <http://www.constitution.org/jjr/corsica.htm> [Accessed on January 9, 2012].

Crawford, S. (2011) Digital Governance: from Iceland to New York City. *Center for Democracy and Technology*, [blog]

August 1. Available at <www.cdt.org/blogs/018digital-governance> [Accessed on January 9, 2012].

DryIslandia. (2011) *El impulsor de la revolución islandesa, manda un mensaje de apoyo a los españoles*. [video online] Available at: http://www.youtube.com/watch?v=cBAgEUCCdq8&feature=player_embedded [Accessed on January 9, 2012].

Finbar10. (2011) Proposed New Icelandic Constitution. Politics.ie, [forum] October 16. Available at: <http://www.politics.ie/forum/political-reform/173176-proposed-new-icelandic-constitution.html> [Accessed on January 9, 2012].

Fontaine, P. (2011) Occupy Reykjavík begins, police clear out protesters camping in front of Parliament. *The Reykjavík Grapevine*, [Online] October 31. Available at: <http://www.grapevine.is/Home/ReadArticle/Occupy-Reykjavik-Begins> [Accessed on January 9, 2012].

Garcia Lamarca, M. (2011) Learning from Iceland's "Kitchenware Revolution." *The Polis Blog* [blog] June 22. Available at: <http://www.thepolisblog.org/2011/06/learning-from-icelands-kitchenware.html> [Accessed on January 9, 2012].

Gunnarson, V. (2009) Iceland's Rainbow Revolution. *The Reykjavík Grapevine*, [Online] February 2. Available at: <http://www.grapevine.is/Features/ReadArticle/icelands-rainbow-revolution> [Accessed on January 9, 2012].

Gylfason, T. (2010) Iceland's special investigation: The plot thickens. [Online] Available at: <http://www.voxeu.org/index.php?q=node/4965> [Accessed on January 9, 2012].

Gylfason, T. (2011a) Crowds and constitutions. [Online] Available at: <http://voxeu.org/index.php?q=node/7090> [Accessed on January 9, 2012].

Gylfason, T. (2011b) From crisis to constitution. [Online] Available at: <http://www.VoxEU.org/index.

php?q=node/7077> [Accessed on January 9, 2012].

Landamore, H. (2014) We, All the People. Five lessons from Iceland's failed experiment in creating a crowdsourced constitution. *Future Tense*, [Online] July 31. Available at: <http://www.slate.com/articles/technology/future_tense/2014/07/five_lessons_from_iceland_s_failed_crowd sourced_constitution_experiment.html> [Accessed on November 17, 2014].

Siddique, H. (2011) Mob rule: Iceland crowdsources its next constitution. *The Guardian*, [Online] June 9. Available at: <http://www.guardian.co.uk/world/2011/jun/09/iceland-crowdsourcing-constitution-facebook/print> [Accessed on January 9, 2012].

## On Iceland's financial crisis

*Journal articles*
Wade, R. and Sigurgeirsdottir, S. (2010) Lessons from Iceland. *New Left Review*, 65: 5–29.

*Reports*
Hreinsson, P., Tryggvi, G., and Sigríður, B. (2009) *Causes of the Collapse of the Icelandic Banks – Responsibility, Mistakes and Negligence* (Special Investigation Commission Report) (Act No. 142/2008) Althingi: Icelandic Parliament.

*Web references*
Barley, R. (2011) Investors reward Iceland's steady progress. *The Wall Street Journal*, [Online] June 10. Available at: <http://online.wsj.com/article/SB1000142405270230425 9304576375340039763606.html> [Accessed on January 9, 2012].

Central Intelligence Agency. (2011) *The World Fact Book: Iceland*. [Online] Available at: <https://www.cia.gov/library/

publications/the-world-factbook/geos/ic.html> [Accessed on January 9, 2012].

IceNews. (2011) Spain adopts Iceland's Kitchenware Revolution idea. *IceNews*, [Online] May 21. Available at: <http://www.icenews.is/index.php/2011/05/21/spain-adopts-icelands-kitchenware-revolution-idea/> [Accessed on January 9, 2012].

Jiménez, D. (2011) Islandia se mueve ante la crisis. *Noticias Positivas*, [Online] March 21. Available at: <http://www.noticiaspositivas.net/2011/03/21/islandia-se-mueve-ante-la-crisis/> [Accessed on January 9, 2012].

Lamant, L. (2011) A gentle cure for the crisis. Presseurop.eu, [Online] April 8. Available at: http://www.presseurop.eu/en/content/article/590821-gentle-cure-crisis [Accessed on January 9, 2012].

Neate, R. (2011) Iceland's former premier denies criminal negligence over banking crisis. *The Guardian*, [Online] June 7. Available at: <http://www.guardian.co.uk/business/2011/jun/07/iceland-former-premier-trial-banking-crisis> [Accessed on January 9, 2012].

Roos, J. (2011) Democracy 2.0: Iceland crowdsources new constitution. Roarmag.org, [Online]. Available at: <http://roarmag.org/2011/06/iceland-crowdsources-constitution-investors-spain-greece/> [Accessed on January 9, 2012].

Sibert, A. (2010) Love letters from Iceland: Accountability of the Eurosystem. [Online] Available at: <http://voxeu.org/index.php?q=node/5059> [Accessed on January 9, 2012].

Valdimarsson, O.R. (2011) Icelanders reject foreign depositor claims, forcing year-long court battle. *Bloomberg*, [Online] April 11. Available at: <http://www.bloomberg.com/news/2011-04-07/icelanders-may-reject-icesave-accord-in-april-9-referendum.html> [Accessed on January 9, 2012].

Wienberg, C. and Valdimarsson, O.R. (2011) Iceland president defends pre-crisis tours promoting bank model. *Bloomberg*, [Online] April 14. Available at: <http:// www.bloomberg.com/news/2011-04-14/iceland-president-defends-pre-crisis-tours-promoting-bank-model.html> [Accessed on January 9, 2012].

# THE EGYPTIAN
# REVOLUTION

The 25 January Revolution (*Thawrat 25 Yanayir*), which in 18 days dethroned the last Pharaoh, arose from the depth of oppression, injustice, poverty, unemployment, sexism, mockery of democracy, and police brutality.[1]

It had been preceded by political protests (after the rigged elections of 2005 and 2010), women's rights struggles (harshly suppressed as in the Black Wednesday of 2005) and workers' struggles, such as the strike in the textile mills of Mahalla-al-Kubra on April 6, 2008, followed by riots and occupation of the city in response to the bloody repression against the striking workers. From that struggle was born the 6 April Youth Movement,[2] which created a Facebook group attracting 70,000 followers. Waleed Rashed, Asmaa Mahfouz, Ahmed Maher, Mohammed Adel,[3] and many other activists of this movement played a significant role in the demonstrations that led to the occupation of Tahrir Square on January 25. They did it together with many other groups that were formed in backroom conspiracies, while reaching out on the

Internet. Most prominent among these initiatives was the network created around the Facebook group "We are all Khaled Said," named in the memory of the young activist beaten to death by the police in June 2010 in an Alexandria cybercafé after he distributed a video exposing police corruption.[4] The group, set up by Wael Ghonim, a young Google executive, and AbdulRahman Mansour, was joined by tens of thousands in Egypt and around the world (Ghonim 2012). These groups, and others, called for supporters on Facebook to demonstrate in front of the Ministry of Interior to protest against the police brutality that had terrorized Egyptians for three decades. They chose January 25 because it was National Police Day.

However, the actual spark that ignited the Egyptian revolution, prompting protests on an unprecedented scale, was inspired by the Tunisian revolution, which added the hope of change to the outrage against unbearable brutality. The Egyptian revolution was dramatized, in the wake of the Tunisian example, by a series of self-immolations (six in total) to protest the rise of food prices that left many hungry. And it was conveyed to the Egyptian youth by one of the founders of the 6 April Youth Movement, Asmaa Mafhouz, a 26-year-old business student from the University of Cairo.

On January 18 she posted a vlog on her Facebook page, showed her veiled face, and identified herself by name before stating:

> Four Egyptians set themselves on fire . . . People, have some shame! I, a girl, posted that I will go down to Tahrir Square to stand alone and I'll hold the banner . . . I am making this video to give you a simple message: we are going to Tahrir on January 25th . . . If you stay home, you deserve all that's being done to you, and you will be guilty before your nation

and your people. Go down to the street, send SMSs, post it
on the Net, make people aware.

Someone uploaded the vlog to YouTube, and it was virally
diffused by thousands. It came to be known throughout the
Middle East as "The Vlog that Helped Spark the Revolution"
(Wall and El Zahed 2011). From Internet networks, the call
to action spread through the social networks of friends, family
and associations of all kinds. The networks connected not only
to individuals but to each individual's networks. Particularly
important were the fan networks of soccer teams, mainly al-Ahly
as well as its rival Zamolek Sporting, who had a long history of
battling the police.[5] Thus, on January 25, tens of thousands converged in Cairo's symbolic central square of Tahrir (Liberation)
and, resisting the attacks of the police, occupied the square and
transformed it into the visible public space of the revolution.
In the following days, people from all conditions, including the
urban poor, religious minorities (Copt Christians were highly
present in the movement, alongside Islamists and secular protesters) and a large proportion of women, some with their
children, used the safe space of the liberated square to stage
their demonstrations by the hundreds of thousands, calling for
the resignation of Mubarak and the end of the regime. It is estimated that over two million people demonstrated in Tahrir at
different points in time.[6] Friday, January 28 came to be known as
the Friday of Rage, when a violent effort by the central security
police to put down the demonstrations was met with determination by the protesters who seized control of areas of the city and
occupied government buildings and police stations, at the price
of hundreds of lives and thousands of wounded people. Similar
events took place in Egypt at large, as many other cities, particularly Alexandria, joined the protest. Fridays – this one and
many others – have a special meaning in the Egyptian revolution as well as in other uprisings around the Arab world because

it is the day of congregational prayer (also known as *Jummah*), and it is a holiday, and people congregate in the mosques, or outside the mosques. This does not necessarily mean that these were religious movements inspired by the Friday sermons. In Egypt, this was not the case, but it was an appropriate time/space to meet other people, to feel the strength and the courage of being together, and so Fridays became the weekly moment to rekindle the revolution. Throughout the year of continuing struggle with the successors of Mubarak, the new rulers of the Supreme Council of the Armed Forces (SCAF), Fridays, with their symbolic tags, became the lightning moments of mass protests usually leading to violent repression by the military police: Friday of Anger (January 28), Friday of Cleaning (April 8), Second Friday of Anger (March 27), Friday of Retribution (July 1), Friday of Determination (July 7), the march of hundreds of thousands against SCAF (July 15), etc.

Thus, Internet networks, mobile networks, pre-existing social networks, street demonstrations, occupations of public squares and Friday gatherings around the mosques all contributed to the spontaneous, largely leaderless, multimodal networks that enacted the Egyptian revolution. In the assessment of Allagui and Kuebler: "If we learned political leadership and coalition building from the Russian Revolution, and popular initiative from the French Revolution, the Arab Revolutions in Tunisia and Egypt demonstrated the power of networks" (2011: 1435).

## SPACE OF FLOWS AND SPACE OF PLACES IN THE EGYPTIAN REVOLUTION

There is no question that the original spaces of resistance were formed on the Internet, as traditional forms of protest were met with utmost ferocity by a police that had been torturing with impunity (occasionally subcontracted by the

CIA for anti-terrorist operations) for as long as the thugs could remember. It is also clear that the calls to demonstrate on January 25, and then on successive dates, were sent via Facebook, to be received by an active following made up of youth for whom social networks and mobile phones were a central part of their way of life.

At the end of 2010, an estimated 80 percent of Egyptians had a cell phone, according to research firm Ovum. About a quarter of households had access to the Internet as of 2009, according to the International Telecommunications Union. But the proportion was much higher among the 20- to 35-year-old demographic group of Cairo, Alexandria and other major urban centers, who, in their majority, be it from home, school or cybercafés, are able to access the Internet. In less than two years after Facebook launched its Arabic version in 2009, the number of users tripled, reaching 5 million users by February 2011, of which 600,000 were added in January and February, the months leading up to the start of the revolution. Once the message sent over the Internet reached an active, technology savvy, large group of young Egyptians, mobile phone networks expanded the message to a broader segment of the population.

Thus, social media networks played an important role in the Egyptian revolution. Demonstrators recorded the events with their mobile phones, and shared their videos with people in the country at large and around the world via YouTube and Facebook, often with live streaming. They deliberated on Facebook, coordinated through Twitter, and used blogs extensively to convey their opinion and engage in debates.

An analysis of the Google trends in Egypt during the days of the revolution shows the growing intensity of searches related to the events, peaking on the day of the first demonstration, January 25, and the following days (see figure 1).

Aouragh and Alexander emphasize the relevance of

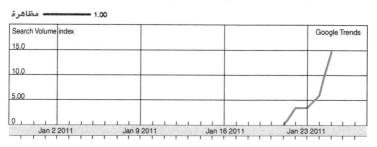

*Figure 1 Google trends in Egypt during the days of the revolution*

Internet spaces as spheres of dissidence, alongside other spheres of dissidence, such as those formed in the "new quarters" of the urban poor. Noha Atef, an activist interviewed during the revolution, points to the specific role of online-based mobilization:

> To have a space, an on-line space, to write and talk to people, to give them messages which will increase their anger, this is my favorite way of on-line activism ... When you ask people to go and to demonstrate against the police, they were ready because you had already provided them with materials which made them angry (Aouragh and Alexander 2011: 1348).

An analysis of a large data set of public tweets in Tahrir Square during the period of January 24–29 shows the intensity of Twitter traffic and provides evidence that individuals, including activists and journalists, were the most influential tweet originators, rather than the organizations present at the scene. In other words, Twitter provided the technological platform for multiple individuals to rise as trendsetters in the movement. On the basis of their observation, Lotan et al.

concluded that "the revolutions were indeed tweeted" (2011: 1401).

Thus the activists, as some put it, planned the protests on Facebook, coordinated them through Twitter, spread them by SMSs and webcast them to the world on YouTube. Indeed, videos of security forces treating the protesters brutally were shared via the Internet, exposing the violence of the regime in unedited form. The viral nature of these videos and the volume and speed with which news on the events in Egypt became available to the wider public in the country and in the world was key to the process of mobilization against Mubarak.

The role of pre-existing offline social networks was also important, as they helped facilitate the canvassing of pamphlets in the digitally excluded slums, and the traditional forms of social and political gatherings in the mosques after the Friday prayers. It was this multimodality of autonomous communication that broke the barriers of isolation and made it possible to overcome fear by the act of joining and sharing.

Yet, the fundamental social form of the movement was the occupation of public space. All of the other processes of network formation were ways to converge on the liberation of a given territory that escaped the authority of the state and experimented with forms of self-management and solidarity. This is why Tahrir Square was attacked repeatedly to evict the occupiers, and why it was re-occupied again and again, at the cost of pitched battles with the security forces, every time the movement felt the need to step up the pressure, first against the dictatorship, and then against the military government that appeared determined to stay in power for as long as it would need to protect its business bounty.

This communal solidarity created in Tahrir Square became a role model for the Occupy movements that would spring up in the world in the following months. This solidarity was expressed in a variety of social practices, from the self-management of the logistics of daily life during the occupation (sanitation, food and water supply, medical care, legal assistance, communication) to gestures such as the protection of the square by Christian Copts during the siege of November 21 while Muslims were in their Friday prayers.

Moreover, by creating a public space where the movement could openly exist in its diverse reality, the mainstream media could report on the protests, give a face to their protagonists and broadcast to the world what the revolution was about. As in all Arab uprisings, Al Jazeera played a major role in communicating in Arabic to the Egyptian population and to the Arab audiences at large that the unthinkable was actually happening. It contributed to a powerful demonstration effect that fed the unfolding of the uprisings in the Arab countries. While Western mainstream media lost interest in daily reporting on Egypt once Mubarak was removed from power, Al Jazeera continued to connect the Egyptian protesters to the Egyptian and Arab public opinion. The quality of Al Jazeera reporting, conducted at great risk by its journalists, was supported by the station's openness to citizen journalism. Many of the feeds and information that it broadcast came from activists on the ground and from ordinary citizens that were recording history-making with their cell phones. By broadcasting live, and by keeping a permanent focus on developments in the public space, professional mainstream media created a certain mantle of protection for the movement against violent repression, as the international supporters of Mubarak first, and of SCAF later tried to avoid embarrassment vis-à-vis global public opinion because of unjustified repressive actions of their protégés. The connection between the Internet's social media, people's social networks, and mainstream media was made possible because of the existence of an occupied territory that anchored the new public space in the dynamic interaction between cyber-space and urban space. Indeed, activists created a "media camp" in Tahrir, to gather videos and pictures produced by the protesters. In one instance, they collected in a few hours 75 gigabytes of images from people in the streets. The centrality of this hybrid public space was not limited to Cairo's Tahrir Square. It was replicated in all major urban centers in which hundreds of thousands of demonstrators mobilized at different points in time during the year: Alexandria, Mansoura, Suez, Ismailia, Tanta, Beni Suez, Dairut, Shebin-el-Kan, Luxor, Minya, Zagagig, and even the Sinai peninsula where reports indicate that Bedouins battled the police for weeks, and then by themselves secured the borders of the country. The Internet revolution does not negate the territorial character of revolutions throughout history. Instead, it extends it from the space of places to the space of flows.

## STATE'S RESPONSE TO AN INTERNET-FACILITATED REVOLUTION: THE GREAT DISCONNECTION

No challenge to the state's authority is left unanswered. Thus, in the case of the Arab revolutions, and in Egypt, there was outright repression, media censorship and shutdown of the Internet.

Repression cannot be sustained against a massive movement supported by communication networks under global media attention unless the government is fully unified and can operate in cooperation with influential foreign powers. Because these conditions were not met in Egypt, the regime tried both violent repression and suppression of the Internet. So doing, it attempted to do what no regime had dared before: the great disconnection, switching off Internet access in the whole country as well as mobile phone networks.[7]

Because of the significance of this event for the future of Internet-based movements, and because it actually echoes the implicit or explicit wishes of most governments around the world, I will dwell with some detail on what happened, how it happened, and, most importantly, why it failed.

Beginning on the first day of protests, the Egyptian government censored the media inside Egypt and took measures to block social media websites, which had helped to call for the protest and spread news about the events on the ground. On January 27, it blocked text messaging and BlackBerry messaging services. On the nights of January 27 and 28, the Egyptian government blocked Internet access almost entirely. There was not a central switch button to be activated. The government used a much older and more efficient technology. It placed successive telephone calls to the four biggest Internet service providers – Link Egypt, Vodafone/Raya, Telecom Egypt, and Etisalat Misr – and ordered them to turn off the connections. ISP's employees accessed each one of the ISP's routers, which contained lists of all the IP addresses connected through that provider, and deleted most or all of those IP addresses, thus cutting off anyone who wanted to access them from within or outside of the country. So, each ISP did not have to physically turn off their computers; they simply had to change the code. Some 3,500 individual BGP routes were withdrawn.[8] For two more days, Noor Data Networks, connecting Cairo's stock exchange, was still functioning. When it went offline, 93 percent of the Internet traffic in or from Egypt was eliminated. The shutdown was not total because some small ISPs, particularly in academic institutions, kept working. Web connections used by the government and military were also working, using their own private ISPs. A few Egyptian users were still able to access the Internet through old dial-up connections. The European-Asia fiber optic routes through

Egypt were operational, but they could not be accessed from Egypt.

However, the most important obstacle governments face when trying to shut off the Internet comes from the vigilance of the global Internet community, which includes hackers, techies, companies, defenders of civil liberties, activist networks such as Anonymous, and people from around the world for whom the Internet has become a fundamental right and a way of life. This community came to the rescue of Egypt as it did with Tunisia in 2010 and Iran in 2009. Furthermore, the ingenuity of Egyptian protesters made reconnection possible within the movement, and between the movement and Egypt and the world at large.

In fact, the revolution was never incommunicable because its communication platforms were multimodal. Al Jazeera was crucial in its continuing reporting on the uprising against the regime. The movement was kept informed by images and news received from Al Jazeera, fed from reports by telephone on the ground. When the government closed its satellite connection, other Arab satellite television networks offered Al Jazeera the use of their own frequencies. Furthermore, other traditional communication channels like fax machines, ham radio and dial-up modems helped to overcome the blocking of the Internet. Protesters distributed information about how to avoid communication controls inside Egypt. Activists provided instructions for using dial-up modems and ham radios. ISPs in France, Sweden, Spain, the US, and other countries set up pools of modems that accepted international calls to channel information to and from the protesters. Companies waived fees for people to connect free of charge. The Manalaa blog gave advice to Egyptians about how to use dial-up by using a mobile phone, Bluetooth and a laptop. The advice was posted to many blogs and diffused virally.

The most important means of circumventing the blackout

was the use of telephone landlines. They were not cut because countries nowadays cannot function without telephony of some kind. Using landlines, activists in Egypt reached telephone numbers abroad that would automatically forward the messages to computer networks provided by volunteers, such as those of TOR (The Onion Router network), which forwarded the messages back to Egypt by a variety of means. Using networks such as HotSpot Shield, Egyptian internauts could access proxies (alternative Internet addresses beyond the control of the government). Companies such as the French NDF offered free connection to the global Internet via a telephone call to a number in Paris. Engineers from Google and Twitter designed a speak-to-tweet program that automatically converted a voicemail message left on an answering machine accessed by a landline into a tweet. The message was then sent out as a tweet with the hashtag of the state from where the call came. Since Twitter accounts in Egypt were blocked, Twitter created a new account – @twitterglobalpr – dedicated to the speak-to-tweet system in Egypt. An international hacker organization, Telecomix, developed a program that automatically retrieved messages by phone from Egypt and forwarded them to every fax machine in the country. Many fax machines were managed from the universities that were often used as communication centers. From the universities' faxes, messages were distributed to the occupied sites. Telecomix worked on receiving and decoding amateur radio messages, sent on frequencies recommended by the group of activists. Thus an old-fashioned technology became instrumental in overcoming government censorship. Altogether, these different means added to the formation of a dense, multimodal network of communication that kept the movement connected within Egypt and with the world at large. Activists published a manual of instructions on communicating by different channels, and any information that would be forwarded by any of the multiple channels still available would be distributed by leaflets printed and handed out by people gathered in the occupied squares and demonstrations.

On February 1, Internet access in Egypt was restored. Egyptian Internet service providers (ISPs) reconfigured their core routers, letting upstream providers and other networks re-establish data pathways. The speed with which the networks reconnected (in about half an hour, Internet in Egypt was up and running) shows that rather than physically plugging in cables, Egypt's ISPs simply let other networks' routers know about their availability using BGP or "border gateway protocol." Thus, neither the disconnection nor the reconnection was physical. There was simply a matter of re-writing the code for the routers, once the government authorized the ISPs to operate again.

But why did the government restore the Internet while the movement was still in full swing? The first reason was to contribute, under some pressure from the United States, to a "return to normal," following Mubarak's announcement that he would not seek re-election in September. An army spokesman appeared on television to ask protesters to return home and help "bring stability back to the country." There were also economic reasons. According to the Organisation for Economic Co-operation and Development (OECD), the five-day shutdown of Internet access in Egypt resulted in a loss of about US$90 million in revenue due to blocked telecommunications and Internet services, which account for around US$18 million per day; about 3 or 4 percent of Egypt's annual GDP. But this estimate did not include loss of business in other sectors affected by the shutdown such as e-commerce, tourism and call center services. Indeed, IT outsourcing firms in Egypt account for revenues of 3 million dollars a day, and this activity had to be interrupted during the Internet disconnection. Tourism, a fundamental sector in the Egyptian economy, was severely affected by the shutdown. Furthermore, foreign direct investors would be unable to operate in a country that would cut off the Internet for a prolonged period. In short, the Internet is the lifeline of the interconnected global economy, and so its disconnection can only be exceptional and for a limited period of time.

But the fundamental reason for the restoration of the Internet is that its shutdown was ineffective in stopping the movement. On the one hand, as argued above, the blackout was circumvented in many ways with the help of the world's Internet community. On the other hand, it was too late to have a paralyzing effect on the protest movement. Urban networks had taken over the role that Internet networks had played in the origins of the protest. People were in the streets, media were reporting, and the whole world had become aware of a revolution in the making. Indeed, the revolutionary potential of the Internet can only be tamed by permanent control and surveillance, as China attempts to do on a daily basis. Once a social movement has reached a certain threshold of size and impact, closing the Internet is neither possible nor effective. In the Internet Age, tyrants will have to reckon with people's autonomous communication capacity. Unless the Internet is constantly blocked or ad hoc mechanisms are ready to operate, as in China; once the movement has extended its reach from the space of flows to the space of places, it is too late to stop it, as many other networks of communication are set up in multimodal forms.

## WHO WERE THE PROTESTERS, AND WHAT WAS THE PROTEST?

Bread, Freedom, and Social Justice were the main themes of the revolution, in the words of the demonstrators that took to the streets in January 2011. They wanted to bring down Mubarak and his regime, called for democratic elections, and asked for justice and redistribution of wealth. Most protesters were young, and many were college students. But this is not a biased representation of the urban population, as two-thirds of Egyptians are under the age of 30, and as the rate of unemployment among college graduates is 10 times higher than among the less-educated. Indeed, the majority of the labor force takes part in informal activities as a means of survival, so that to be truly unemployed is a luxury few can afford. The poor, who account for at least 40 percent of the population, must participate in some income-generating activity, however meager the income may be, or they would starve. But while the movement was largely enacted by an impoverished middle class longing for freedom and human rights, segments of the urban poor, desperate as a result of rising food prices, joined in. And industrial workers, with or without union support, staged a number of powerful strikes, particularly intense in Suez, leading to the occupation of the city for a few days. Some reports indicate that fear of the movement extending to the industrial labor force was a factor in influencing the business-wary army generals to sacrifice the dictator on the altar of their own profits. The so-called pro-Mubarak masses, epitomized in the picturesque and ruthless charge of the camels on Tahrir occupiers on February 1, were in most cases connected to the *balgatiya* (gangs of thugs paid by the police) (Elmeshad and Sarant 2011). The real support for the regime was to be found among the hundreds of thousands of bureaucrats, central security forces, policemen, informers, thugs, and thieves, whose livelihood depended on the patronage networks of the dictator, his sons, and their cronies. However, all of these beautiful people had to share power with the Egyptian army, which still held some prestige among the population, as it had incarnated the nationalist movement that established modern Egypt and led the Arab world in the wars against Israel.

It was precisely the economic power struggle between the army and Gamal's boys (the businessmen protected by Mubarak's son and heir apparent) that created the conditions for a decisive split within the ruling elites and prompted the downfall of Mubarak, his family and their clique. The army is at the heart of a vast business empire that anchors the wealth and growth potential of the old, national Egyptian capital. The internationalization of business promoted by Gamal Mubarak since 2000, with the full support of American, British, and French political leaders, threatened directly its control of the economy. Thus, when the moment came, they were not ready to sacrifice their national legitimacy and their profitable business to support an aged dictator and a potentially dangerous successor. So, they refused to open fire against the demonstrators and, in due course, arrested the Mubaraks and their accomplices. By assuming full power, the Supreme Council of the Armed Forces (SCAF) tried to appease and deactivate the revolutionary movement, draping itself in the mantle of revolution to make sure that as every-thing changed, everything would remain the same. However, this revolution was not a military coup. It originated from a popular uprising. And so, the more SCAF wanted to limit its measures to cosmetic changes, the more the movement pressured the new authorities, demanding retribution and prosecution of those responsible for the killings of pro-testers and of those who had robbed the national wealth. They stepped up demands for political freedom, democratic elections and a new Constitution. The whole of 2011 wit-nessed a relentless confrontation between the SCAF and the movement, while old and new political parties positioned themselves for the elections. Elections for the Constituent Parliament did take place, starting on November 28 and going on for several weeks. But it was finally accepted by SCAF only after a series of bloody confrontations between the movement and the military throughout the year, with 12,000 civilians sentenced in military courts, about 1,000 protesters killed and tens of thousands injured. But even during and after the elections, repression continued, people were imprisoned, the independent media were attacked, dissidents were tried and sentenced by military courts, Egyptian and foreign NGOs were harassed or prohibited, and dozens of demonstrators were killed in Tahrir and elsewhere. And yet, the movement did not budge in their determination to achieve full democratization of the country. The defence of the occupation of Tahrir Square, of free communication on the Internet, and of media independence, continued to be the ramparts for the conquest of freedom in a country suffering from dramatic economic and social problems.

The future of democracy is not clear, as the victory of moderate Islamists of the Muslim Brotherhood (reborn as the Freedom and Justice Party, with 45 percent of the vote), together with the 25 percent of the vote obtained for the more strictly Islamic coalition of Nour,[9] raised doubts among the Western powers about the support to be given to a democracy that could slip away from their control. With the Egyptian army receiving US$1.3 billion annually in discretionary income from the United States, the Egyptian revolution may have to confront a military counter-revolution if the movement oversteps the geopolitical limits that it has been prescribed. However, the paths of revolution are always surprising, and some of the key struggles taking place in post-Mubarak Egypt have to do less with geopolitical strategies and class interests than with the cultural transformation of the society, starting with the conquest of new autonomy by women.

## WOMEN IN REVOLUTION

Women played a major role in the Egyptian revolution. The vlogs (there were four in total) that Asmaa Mahfouz posted on Facebook in January and February 2011 were influential in sparking the movement and meaningful in terms of their content and style. She was a young woman addressing, in her own name, and with her own face, the people of Egypt, and particularly men; playing the card of patriarchalism with skillful irony in asking men to join her, a girl!:

> Whoever says women shouldn't go to the protests because they will get beaten, let him have some honor and manhood, and come with me on January 25th ... If you have honor and dignity as a man, come and protect me, and other girls in the protest.

In short, you are not a man if you do not act as men are supposed to be: courageous, protective and willing to confront the security forces to defend freedom, dignity and honor. Because:

> ... I am going down to Tahrir Square and I will stand alone and I will hold up a banner ... I even wrote my number so maybe people will come down with me. No one came except three guys! Three guys. Three guys, three armored cars of riot police and tens of balgatiya ... I am making this video to give you a simple message: we are going to Tahrir on 25 January.

People ultimately did come. And on January 26 she posted a new vlog:

> The people want to bring down the regime! ... The most
> beautiful thing about [the protests] is those who worked on
> this were not politicians at all. It was all of us, all Egyptians.

Later, she invoked God, for Muslims or Christians, and cited
chapter 13, verse 11 (Surat Ar-Ra'd) of the Quran: God says
he will "not change the condition of a people until they
change what is in themselves."

Her influence and moral authority were precursors of
what many women bloggers would do during the revolution
and what many women would suffer during the demonstrations and the attacks on Tahrir. Blogger Nawara Nagu
posted on January 21 a video of a young activist saying, "Do
you see this girl? She is going to demonstrate." And she did,
as did thousands of others.

Many women, young and old, many with headscarves and
others dressed in Western-style clothing, were present in
Tahrir and other occupied spaces, some of them with their
children. In many cases they led the demonstrations. They
participated in the security committees and managed the
field hospitals. On March 8, International Women's Day,
women's rights activists marched in Tahrir asking for the end
of discrimination by the state and the end of violence against
women (Elwakil 2011). Some of the marchers were attacked
by a large group of men.

Women were also active participants in the public debate,
and there were numerous women bloggers reporting from
the ground. It did not go unnoticed by the military regime.
Leil Zahura Mortada, a blogger reporting from Tahrir, was
abused because of her denunciations. On August 14, Asmaa
Mahfouz was arrested and ordered to face a military trial,
although she was released after widespread public protests against her indictment. Women were targeted, beaten
and often killed during the demonstrations and assaults on

Tahrir. Sally Zahran was beaten to death in one of the protests. During January and February, at least 15 women were killed. Many women arrested in the square were subjected to virginity tests, which members of the military government openly acknowledged and justified in a CNN interview, on the grounds that these women were whores. Samira Ibrahim, a 25-year-old, filed a lawsuit against the military and obtained a court ruling making the virginity tests equivalent to sexual assault.[10] On December 19, 2011, during a new assault on Tahrir, a young woman was beaten, stripped and left unconscious, wearing only a blue bra. Women who tried to help her were attacked by the police. The video of this barbaric act of sexist violence was diffused throughout the world and prompted universal outrage, particularly among women. It came to be known as the video of the "blue bra girl." The following day, tens of thousands of women demonstrated in Tahrir, Alexandria and around Egyptian university campuses against the military violations of women's rights. From balconies, office workers clapped and cheered. Referring to the head of SCAF, they displayed a banner that read "Tantawi is the supreme commander of harassment and violation of honor." After this march, SCAF was compelled to release a hypocritical "apology to the women of Egypt."

The awakening of Egyptian women during the revolution is one of the main fears of a deeply patriarchal society, and is triggering a wave of violence against women that may increase over time. Furthermore, while women have participated side by side with men in the revolution, even calling for their protection, many of the male protesters feel uncomfortable with the agency of women, and have not helped to defend them against the targeted sadistic violence of the military police.

Indeed, in spite of their prominent role in the revolution, throughout 2011 women were all but excluded from

government positions, and were confined to the last positions in the political party candidacies, so that there were
only eight women among the 498 elected members of the
new parliament.[11] The program of the main political force
resulting from the elections, the Freedom and Justice Party,
bans women from being elected president of the country.[12]

It is no wonder that a report of the Egyptian Center for
Women's Rights could write at the end of 2011: "Is El-Tahrir
Square will remain synonym to 'the freedom, justice, and
equality'?! Or the revolution will eat/sacrifice its children
and the forefront of them the women?!" (Komsan 2011: 2).[13]

It appears that there is a revolution within the revolution
brewing in the Egyptian uprising, as a generation of educated
women (who represent the majority of college graduates)
confront the ancestral limits of men's definition of what a
revolution should be.

## THE ISLAMIC QUESTION

The parliamentary elections of 2011 confirmed the resilience of Islamic political forces in Egypt. The old Muslim
Brotherhood survived decades of repression from nationalist,
military regimes and, renamed as the Freedom and Justice
Party, obtained a majority of seats in the parliament. It benefitted from strong organization, political experience and a
certain aura of resistance against the regime in large segments of the population. The more strictly Islamist coalition
of Noor, dominated by the Salafists, secured 25 percent of
the vote. This is a clear indication of the widespread sympathy for Islamism among the population at large. Indeed,
in practically all Arab countries, there is a potential Islamic
political majority that was held in check by force from
nationalist authoritarian leaders backed by the army and the
Western powers. Arab nationalism, invoking the anti-colonial

nation-state, in spite of rhetorical religious references when the need arose, and Islamism, invoking the *ummah* (universal community of believers beyond the nation) and the *Sharia* (law inspired by God, not by the state), have been locked in a confrontation that evolved toward the defeat of nationalism in people's minds when it became subordinated to foreign powers and when corruption and brutality became the distinctive features of these regimes.

Islamism was widely seen by many in Egypt and elsewhere as a force of regeneration of politics, of hope for social justice, and of restoration of moral values. The unconditional support of foreign powers for Arab military regimes was precisely predicated on their fear of Islamism as a threat to oil supply and Israel's security. Thus, as expected, processes of democratization in the Arab world usually result in the hegemony of Islamism in the political system, as secular, progressive political forces have limited appeal beyond the small segments of Westernized elites. Yet, for Islamists to come to power, with the consent of the army and without the opposition of the secular segments of the revolutionary movement, they had to moderate their religious standing. And they have done so. The program of the Freedom and Justice Party, and the public statements of its leaders, accept the principles of democracy, and focus on addressing the immense social and economic problems of the country. They do not oppose the notion of a secular state. At the same time, it is the stated goal of the party to govern, if they ever come to power, according to the Sharia law, but they emphasize that the meaning of this orientation is misunderstood in the West. It does not mean, in their view, to impose a theocracy, and they explicitly reject the Iranian model (Adib and Waziri 2011).[14] It simply means that they will find inspiration for their policies in the Quran, in the same way, they argue, European Christian Democrats try to follow

Christian principles in the conduct of public affairs. This has serious implications for women and Copts, as the Freedom and Justice Party will not accept either as president of the country. However, even in this matter, they would still accept women or Copts in the government cabinet, a policy that is a long way from strict Muslim orthodoxy.[15] Furthermore, in foreign policy the Brothers have stated their commitment to respecting the existing treaties between Egypt and Israel, a "must" condition from the perspective of the United States, the supervisory power in the country, via the Egyptian army on its payroll (Adib and Waziri 2011).[16]

In sum, for the Muslim Brotherhood, Islam and democracy are fully compatible, as shown in the example of Turkey, albeit they concede that contexts are different, and they do not identify with Erdogan. While the Muslim Brotherhood has been often accused of being opportunistic, in reality they have had no other choice. Neither the army nor its Western sponsors will accept a radical Islamic state in Egypt. Thus, any consolidation of a democratic regime in Egypt will imply a moderate Islamic government at the helm. A different matter is the significant groundswell of support for the Salafists, whose uncompromising stand on the primacy of Sharia over civilian power could evolve into a full-scale confrontation against both the army and the secular wing of the revolutionary movement. If the economic situation continues to deteriorate, the religious fundamentalist way out of a Westernized regime could open a new chapter in the process of political change in Egypt.

However, while trying to understand the Egyptian revolution, it should be clear that neither in the origin nor in the process of transformation of the 2011 revolution was there any dominance of Islamism or Islamic themes. To be sure, Islamists from all tendencies, and particularly young Islamists, actively participated in the demonstrations, in the occupation of Tahrir and other public places, and in the deliberation over the Internet. But there were no direct religious confrontations (the attack on the Copts was a police provocation), and there was respectful sharing of the goals and practice of the revolution. During the 18 days that launched the revolution, the Muslim Brotherhood called for the departure of Mubarak, but always referred to the movement as the source of legitimacy of the protest. It was of course an intelligent tactic, as the call for democracy and parliamentary elections could well position the Brothers to access power on the grounds of popular support. Yet, it remains that neither the Brotherhood nor the Salafists were successful in controlling or leading the movement. They were a part of the movement, but they were not the movement. The Egyptian revolution was not and is not an Islamic revolution, even if it may have created the conditions for a democratic way toward an Islamic-dominated polity in the country. The networks formed around Islamism networked with networks constituted around the goals of political freedom and social justice, all converging toward the struggle for democracy, first against Mubarak and then against the SCAF, whose bloody repression to the movement could not stifle a revolution spoken in multiple voices.

## "THE REVOLUTION WILL CONTINUE"

The Supreme Council of the Armed Forces attempted to capture the revolution for its own benefit by using even harsher repression than the Mubarak regime, once it became clear that the movement that toppled the dictatorship, in its multifaceted composition, would not accept a change of rulers without a change of rules. The military even tried to impose a document (known as the Selmi document from the name of the deputy prime minister) as a guideline for the Constitution to be elaborated in 2012 by the new parliament, before the parliament was elected. It basically gave full control of the state and limitless autonomy to the Armed Forces. The uproar against this blatant attack on future democratic institutions unified all components of the movement in their opposition, including the Muslim Brotherhood, which for the first time had broken up openly with the generals. On November 18, a massive protest against SCAF took place in Tahrir. On November 19, Central Security forces, the elite of former Mubarak's police, attacked Tahrir Square, occupied only by a small group of people. Media and the Internet came to the rescue and thousands rushed to defend the liberated public space. It followed a five-day pitched battle in the streets of Cairo that left at least 42 people killed and 3,000 wounded. The prime minister resigned, but he was replaced by a former Mubarak minister. It became clear that the military council incarnated a new form of dictatorship, and the movement switched from the old unifying slogan of "Down with the Mubarak regime" to "Down with military rule." Women marched under a banner proclaiming "You Won't Intimidate Us." Fear had been overcome forever. Networks of outrage had multiplied with the savage repression against all forms of criticism of the new powers: in the media, in the streets and in the military courts, with women being particularly targeted. On January 20, 2012, Joda Elsadda, from the Women's Media Center, wrote:

> The current slogan is "the revolution will continue" because the job is not done. We may have deposed Mubarak, but the regime, led by the SCAF, is still intact. In the early days of the revolution, the military appeared to side with the people; today the people are against the SCAF and military rule. Why? Because the SCAF is trying to reinstate the old regime and people have lost faith in its ability to transition Egypt to a democratic future (2012: 1).

While the army was a far more formidable adversary than Mubarak himself, the strength of the movement was much greater than one year earlier, because the networks of solidarity and mobilization were now in place, and active, on the Internet, in the squares, in the streets, in a blossoming civil society, and in a diverse, and vital, new political sphere, with multiple parties. One year of deception and repression had not weakened the determination of a movement that had begun to envision a revolution capable of ushering in real democracy.

## UNDERSTANDING THE EGYPTIAN REVOLUTION

The Egyptian revolution of 2011 altered power relationships in the country, brought down the Mubarak dictatorship and continued to fight with determination the reincarnation of oppression in the form of a military regime. To understand how it could happen after decades of ruthless domination and the repeated crushing of the resistance that took place in many instances, we have to go back to the theory of power and counterpower presented at the onset of this book.

Power is exercised by a combination of coercion and intimidation with persuasion and consensus building. The monopoly of violence is a necessary condition for holding power, but not a sufficient one in the long run. It requires the construction of legitimacy, or of acceptance and resignation, in people's minds. In modern Egypt the power of the state (the decisive agency in the country) was originally based on selective legitimacy and targeted repression. The rise of Nasserism, as the harbinger of Arab nationalism, provided a mantle of legitimacy to a populist regime, and to an army geared for the decisive battle with Zionism. Yet, at the same time nationalism was determined to suppress the main alternative source of legitimacy: Islamic influence, politically represented by the Muslim Brotherhood, and a few influential Islamic intellectuals, some of whom, like Sayyid Qtub, were executed. They were the enemy, and they were prosecuted to the end, while official religious leaders were co-opted into the regime. Repression worked as long as it was concentrated on one particular segment of polity. But legitimacy was eroded by military failure and the fall of Nasser, and more importantly by the inability of a statist economy to adapt to the new environment of economic globalization. Moreover, whatever development was generated was appropriated by the regime's crony capitalists, by the top brass of the military, and by high-level government bureaucrats. Widespread poverty and the deterioration of living standards for an increasingly educated middle class prompted many youth to turn to Islamism, both in its moderate and radical versions. Elections were introduced as an image-making ploy to satisfy the new, Western allies of the regime, but each time that independent candidates (Islamic or secular) had some success, they were dismissed or curtailed in their voice and in their vote. In the first decade of the twenty-first century, the monopoly of violence, and the actual use of violence with total impunity, became the main pillar sustaining the regime.

But there is more complexity to be accounted for. Power is multidimensional. Each one of the dimensions (economic, political, military, ideological, cultural) is enacted by specific networks of power. Yet, for power to be sustainable, it is essential that several of the key networks network with each other, with the help of switchers that establish the connection. In the case of Egypt, the military was always the key network of power but it remained autonomous while holding decisive power in the state. Mubarak was the chief of the prestigious air force, and as such he became the switcher between the state and the Armed Forces, and took control of the bureaucracy and of the NDP, the official party. The state generated its own network of bureaucracies (including the police) through which power was exercised over society. Economic power was in the hands of business elites that were traditionally dependent on the state and on the military, although in the last decade, globalized businesses, including foreign companies, built their own connections to the regime, gaining autonomy because of their international reach. Religious power was integrated and/or repressed depending on its level of submission to the state. Media were censored and controlled, although multiple private satellite television channels provided an opening that would become decisive in the crisis of the regime. The other fundamental network to which the state had to connect was the geopolitical network. After the fall of Nasser and the assassination of Sadat, the influence of the Soviet Union all but disappeared. Mubarak added to his switching capacities a privileged connection to the United States. This was a fundamental source of stability for the dictatorship both in terms of fake democratic credentials, and in its ability to withstand economic difficulties and domestic challenges.

This complex network of power networks is what the social protesters and political opponents of the regime had to face in 2005, in 2008, and in 2010, with the ensuing outcome of their submission by force. Any semblance of legitimacy or consensus had disappeared among the overwhelming majority of Egyptians. But fear was instilled in their minds, and in the minds of the few opponents who dared to use institutional openings to counter the dictator. No organized opposition could match the formidable repressive machine networked with all domestic and international sources of power in a maze of intertwined economic, geopolitical, political and personal interests.

Then, the revolution happened, without warning and

strategy, as the first calls for demonstrations were not different from those that took place in previous years, only to be easily dissolved by thugs and police. Why? Because fear had been overcome by large numbers. How? And why then? People overcome fear by being together. And they were, in the Internet social networks and in the urban networks formed in the squares. But to come together in throngs they needed a strong motivation, a mobilizing force. Outrage induces fearless risk-taking, and there was extreme outrage against police abuse, against hunger rising in the country and against the desperation that led people to immolate themselves. However, outrage had been there for quite a long time. The key difference was that another potent, positive emotion was present: Hope. Tunisia epitomized the hope for change. It showed that it was possible to topple a well-entrenched regime if everybody would come together and fight uncompromisingly, to the end, regardless of the risks. The Internet provided the safe space where networks of outrage and hope connected. Networks formed in cyberspace extended their reach to urban space, and the revolutionary community formed in public squares this time successfully resisted police repression, and connected through multimedia networks with the Egyptian people and with the world. Tahrir was the switcher that linked together the multiple networks of counterpower in spite of their diversity. Under the pressure of grassroots resistance and international public opinion, the switches connecting the networks of power were turned off, one after another, from the central connector, the dictator and his clique at the top of the state. First, and foremost, the army regained its autonomy trying to preserve remnants of its legitimacy and to recover control of the country by disconnecting the dictator and the police from the military network. The business elites split, with domestic groups siding with the army, a major business group in itself, against the growing threat of globalized business led by Gamal's boys. While the state media remained until the last minute in the hands of the censors, segments of the media, particularly private television channels, global satellite channels and Internet companies, disconnected themselves from the media networks that were appendages of state power. The political networks of the state (and particularly the official party) lost any capacity to influence people without the backing of decisive force, and so they remained in the state but isolated from key sources of economic, military, or cultural power.

Most importantly: the geopolitical network, dominated by the United States, switched off its connection with Mubarak's network to strengthen its privileged connection with the military network. Obama's Cairo speech calling the Arab world to embrace and mobilize for democracy, and Hillary Clinton's speech in January 2010 arguing for the democratizing role of the Internet in the world, could not be openly contradicted by continuing support for a shaken dictator. Thus, the last critical switching off, the one from the geopolitical network, left Mubarak's state disconnected from any significant source of power, other than its central security forces and the camelback brigade of the *bagatiya*.

By connecting networks of counterpower, the protesters became powerful enough to induce the disconnection between major networks of power, weakening the system of domination and making violence an increasingly difficult means of keeping the country under control. This is why the military network, and its connected geopolitical network, tried to regain legitimacy by apparently moving toward democratic elections, legalizing Islamic political forces, promising a new constitution, and prosecuting the dictator and a few individuals of his immediate clique. However, the military quickly moved to switch all the networks of power, including the new network of parliamentary politics, around its command and control capacities, thus voiding in practice the promise of democracy. As the networks of counterpower remained fully active, and since they had broadened their connections internationally and nationally, the military went back to stern repression as a way of political life. Indeed, 2011 was a much more bloody and repressive year than any of the preceding years under Mubarak. Accordingly, the military lost the last of their legitimacy, and set the stage for a long, protracted battle between the networks of power and counterpower formed in the process of the Egyptian revolution.

## NOTES

1 For a detailed account of the background and events of the January 2011 revolution in Egypt, see Mona El-Ghobashy, "The praxis of the Egyptian Revolution," in MER258, Middle East Research and Information Project (2011), <www.merip.org/mer/mer258/praxis-egyptian-revolution>.

2 Official website for the 6 April Movement (in Arabic): <http://6april.org>. Esraa Abdel Fattah Ahmed Rashid was one of the co-founders of the movement who later split from the group. See PBS's Frontline "Inside April 6th Movement" for further details: <http://www.pbs.org/wgbh/pages/frontline/revolution-in-cairo/inside-april6-movement/>.

3 In summer of 2009, Adel traveled to Serbia to study non-violent strategies for revolution. "What Egypt learned from the students who overthrew Milosevic" by Tina Roseberg for *Foreign Policy* (<http://www.foreignpolicy.com/articles/2011/02/16/revolution_u?page=full>) and PBS's Frontline Profile page on the 6 April Movement from

"Revolution in Cairo" documentary <http://www.pbs. org/wgbh/pages/frontline/revolution-in-cairo/inside- april6-movement/>.

4 On the "Silent Revolution" envisioned by "We are All Khaled Said" group members: "Reclaiming Silence in Egypt" by Adel Iskandar, *Egypt Independent*, July 22, 2010, <http://www.egyptindependent.com/node/58021>.

5 The significant role of al-Ahly soccer club fans in the protests against Mubarak was not forgotten by the cen- tral security police. On February 1, 2012, in a game in Port Said between the local team and al-Ahly, hun- dreds of armed thugs, posing as fans of the Port Said team attacked the players and fans of al-Ahly without any opposition from the police present in the stadium. Seventy four people were killed and hundreds wounded. The obvious complicity of the old Mubarak's police, and the permissiveness of the military regime in the aggres- sion, led to violent demonstrations in Cairo on February 2 and 3, with thousands charging police buildings brand- ing the flag of al-Ahly. Several people were killed and hundreds wounded.

6 There were some tensions among Copts and radical Islamic groups during the occupation in Tahrir square. But the sharing of risks and goals in the movement created an atmosphere of tolerance and cooperation between Muslims, Copts and seculars. For instance, on February 6, 2011, a multi-faith mass was celebrated in Tahrir, with thousands of believers attending. There was, however, one major incident of violence against the Copts on October 9, during a demonstration by Copts in front of the state television building to protest against media reporting, and asking for the resignation of Tantawi, head of the Supreme Council of the Armed Forces, with the result of 25 demonstrators killed and

200 wounded. The media tried to portray the attack as conducted by Islamists, but reliable sources pointed out the police responsibility in planning the attack to stir sectarian violence. On November 21, while Muslims in Tahrir were in their Friday prayers, Copts kept guarding the square against potential attackers, in a clear sign of inter-religious solidarity.

7  Egypt's great disconnection was an entirely different situation from the limited Internet manipulation that took place in Tunisia, where only specific routes were blocked, or Iran, where the Internet stayed up in a rate-limited form designed to make Internet connectivity extremely slow. Disconnecting the Internet in Egypt was relatively easy, compared with what would be necessary in democratic countries. In Egypt there were only four major ISPs, each of which had relatively few routers connecting them to the outside world. A similar shutting down of the Internet in the United States would have to deal with many different companies. And while Egypt can legally disable telecom companies by decree, US regulations limit the federal government's power to intervene in communication channels. However, we should be aware that members of the US Congress have proposed making plans for a "kill switch" that would shut down the Internet at the push of a button in the case of a "cybersecurity emergency."

8  BGP (border gateway protocol) is the protocol at the heart of the Internet's routing mechanism, and is used by routers to share information about the paths data traffic uses to "hop" from one network to another as it moves from a source to its destination.

9  Al-Nour Party official website, "FAQ" (<http://www.alnourparty.org/page/answer>) and "Who we are" (<http://www.alnourparty.org/about>).

10  Flock, E. (2011) Samira Ibrahim is the woman behind Egypt's ban of virginity tests. *The Washington Post.* <http://www.washingtonpost.com/blogs/blogpost/post/samira-ibrahim-is-the-woman-behind-egypts-ban-of-virginity-tests/2011/12/27/gIQACKNgKP_blog.html>.

11  Moore, H. (2012) Experts weigh in on low female representation in parliament. *Daily News Egypt.* <http://www.thedailynewsegypt.com/egypt-elections-2011/experts-weigh-in-on-low-female-representation-in-parliament.html>.

12  *Egyptian Independent.* (2011) Brotherhood sticks to ban on Christians and women for presidency. <http://www.egyptindependent.com/node/352738>.

13  Komsan, N.A. (ed.) (2011) Press Release: Women's Status Report of 2011: The Egyptian Women between the Wings of the Revolution and Stripping the Reality. *The Egyptian Center for Women's Rights.* <https://docs.google.com/viewer?url=http%3A%2F%2Fwww.ecwronline.org%2Fenglish%2Fpress%2520reless%2F2011%2FPress%2520Release-%2520English-%2520Women's%2520Status%2520Report%25202011.pdf>.

14  Adib, M. and Waziri, H. (2011) The Brotherhood in their first TV appearance: "We are not opportunists and reject the Iranian Model." *Al-Masry Al-Youm.* <http://www.almasry-alyoum.com/article2.aspx?ArticleID=288427>.

15  *Egyptian Independent.* (2011) Muslim Brotherhood to establish "Freedom and Justice Party." <http://www.egyptindependent.com/node/325599>.

16  Adib, M. and Waziri, H. (2012) The Brotherhood: "We respect all the treaties signed Between Egypt and Israel." *Al-Masry Al-Youm.* <http://www.almasry-alyoum.com/article2.aspx?ArticleID=288347>.

REFERENCES AND SOURCES

*Note*: The titles of texts originally written in Arabic and used as sources have been translated into English for the convenience of the reader. The referred texts are in Arabic.

## On the background and events of the Egyptian revolution

6 April Youth Movement (Official Site). (2011) <http://6april. org/>.

Al Jazeera, Arabic. (2011a) Egyptian protests continue and high death toll. <http://www.aljazeera.net/news/pages/585df5cd-4ee1-46d3-ae2e-bb82d15221ce>.

Al Jazeera, Arabic. (2011b) Dead and wounded: Demonstrations in Egypt. <http://aljazeera.net/news/pages/9b5f8d6d-afed-4584-a502-cabf184ec070>.

Al Jazeera, Arabic. (2011c) Round up: Developments in Egypt. <http://aljazeera.net/news/pages/fc20dc11-146b-4081-b745-a1222bba2953>.

Al Jazeera, Arabic. (2011d). Mobilization of two million in Tahrir Square. <http://www.aljazeera.net/news/pages/b35ad6ba-80e2-4105-a310-35b980547b04>.

Al Jazeera, English. (2011) Timeline: Egypt's Revolution. <http://www.aljazeera.com/news/middleeast/2011/01/20 1112515334871490.html>.

Al-Khalsan, M. (2011) The Army and the economy in Egypt. *Jadaliyya*. Available at: <http://www.jadaliyya.com/pages/index/3732/the-army-and-the-economy-in-egypt>.

Cook, S.O. (2011) *The Struggle for Egypt: from Nasser to Tahrir Square*. Oxford University Press, Oxford.

El-Gobashy, M. (2011) The praxis of the Egyptian Revolution. *Middle East Report*, Spring edition (volume 41) (MER258).

Elmeshad, M. and Sarant, L. (2011) Violence erupts as pro-Mubarak forces pour into Tahrir. *Al Masry Al Youm.* <http://www.almasryalyoum.com/node/308110> (Arabic).

Ghonim, W. (2012) *Revolution 2.0: The Power of the People is Greater than the People in Power. A Memoir.* Houghton-Mifflin-Harcourt, Boston, MA.

Hosni Mubarak announced that he would step down and hand over power to the Supreme Council of Armed Forces. (2011) *Al Arabiya.* <http://www.alarabiya.net/articles/2011/02/11/137168.html>.

Kouddous, S.A. (2012) Tahrir one year later: The fight for Egypt's future. *The Nation*, [Online]. Available at: <http://www.thenation.com/article/165735/tahrir-one-year-later-fight-egypts-future>.

Shatz. A. (2012) Whose Egypt? *London Review of Books*, January [Online]. Available at: <http://www.lrb.co.uk/v34/n01/adam-shatz/whose-egypt>.

PBS Frontline. (2011a) Inside April 6th Movement. *Revolution in Cairo.* <http://www.pbs.org/wgbh/pages/frontline/revolution-in-cairo/inside-april6-movement>.

PBS Frontline. (2011b) "Day to Day" Timeline. <http://www.pbs.org/wgbh/pages/frontline/revolution-in-cairo/day-to-day>.

## On the interaction between Internet networks, social networks, and public space in the process of the revolution

Allagui, I. and Kuebler, J. (2011) The Arab Spring and the role of ICTs. *International Journal of Communication.* [Online] Vol. 5: 1435–42. Available at: <http://ijoc.org/ojs/index.php/ijoc/article/view/1392/616>.

Aouragh, M. and Alexander, A. (2011) The Egyptian

experience: Sense and nonsense of the Internet Revolution. *International Journal of Communication*. [Online] Vol. 5: 1344–58. Available at: <http://ijoc.org/ojs/index.php/ijoc/article/view/1191/610>.

Eltantawy, N. and Wiest, J.B. (2011) Social media in the Egyptian Revolution: reconsidering resource mobilization theory. *International Journal of Communication*. [Online] Vol. 5: 1207–24. Available at: <http://ijoc.org/ojs/index.php/ijoc/article/view/1242/597>.

Harlow, S. and Johnson, T. (2011) Overthrowing the protest paradigm? How the New York Times, Global Voices and Twitter covered the Egyptian Revolution. *International Journal of Communication*. [Online] Vol. 5: 1359–74. Available at: <http://ijoc.org/ojs/index.php/ijoc/article/view/1239/611>.

Iskander, E. (2011) Connecting the national and the virtual: Can Facebook activism remain relevant after Egypt's January 25 uprising? *International Journal of Communication*. [Online] Vol. 5: 1225–37. Available at: <http://ijoc.org/ojs/index.php/ijoc/article/view/1165/598>.

Lotan, G., Graeff, E., Ananny, M., Gaffney, D., Pearce, I., and boyd, d. (2011) The revolutions were tweeted: Information flows during the 2011 Tunisian and Egyptian revolutions. *International Journal of Communication*. [Online] Vol. 5: 1375–405. Available at: <http://ijoc.org/ojs/index.php/ijoc/article/view/1246>.

Rinke, E.M. and Röder, M. (2011) Media ecologies, communication culture, and temporal-spatial unfolding: Three components in a communication model of the Egyptian regime change. *International Journal of Communication*. [Online] Vol. 5: 1273–85. Available at: <http://ijoc.org/ojs/index.php/ijoc/article/view/1173/603>.

Russell, A. (2011) Extra-national information flows, social

media, and the 2011 Egyptian uprising. *International Journal of Communication*. [Online] Vol. 5: 1375–405. Available at: <http://ijoc.org/ojs/index.php/ijoc/article/view/93/630>.

Wall, M. and El Zahed, S. (2011) "I'll Be Waiting for You Guys": A YouTube Call to Action in the Egyptian Revolution. *International Journal of Communication*. [Online] Vol. 5: 1333–43. Available at: <http://ijoc.org/ojs/index.php/ijoc/article/view/1241/609>.

## On media in the Egyptian Revolution

Iskandar, A. (2012) A year in the life of Egypt's media: A 2011 Timeline. *Jadaliyya*. <http://www.jadaliyya.com/pages/index/3642/a-year-in-the-life-of-egypts-media_a-2011-timeline>.

## On women in the Egyptian Revolution

Abdel-Fattah, B. (2012) Egyptian women victims of the revolution and the election. *Al Jazeera, Arabic*. <http://www.aljazeera.net/NR/EXERES/4A52E5A7-B70A-4CD6-B64A-83B12CADC5CA.htm>.

Carr, S. (2011) Women march against SCAF brutality, hope for a nascent movement. *Al-Masry Al-Youm*. <http://www.almasryalyoum.com/en/node/559926>.

Egyptian Center for Women's Rights, Arabic. <http://www.ecwronline.org/>.

Egyptian Center for Women's Rights, English. <http://www.ecwronline.org/english/index.html>.

Elsadda, H. (2012) Exclusive Egypt – the revolution will continue. *The Women's Media Center*. Available at: <http://www.womensmediacenter.com/feature/entry/egypt-the-revolution-will-continue>.

Elwakil, M. (2011) Women's demo outlines controversial demands. *Egypt Independent*, March 8. <http://www.egyptindependent.com/node/344981>.

Komsan, N.A. (ed.) (2011) The Egyptian women between the wings of the revolution and stripping the reality. Press Release: The Status of Egyptian Women in 2011. *The Egyptian Center for Women's Rights*. Available at: <http://www.ecwronline.org/english/press%20reless/2011/Press%20Release-%20English-%20Women's%20Status%20Report%202011.pdf>.

## On political Islamism in Egypt

Adib, M. and Waziri, H. (2011a) The Brotherhood Renewed Demands for Mubarak's Departure and For a Peaceful Transition of Power. *Al-Masry Al-Youm*. <http://www.almasry-alyoum.com/article2.aspx?ArticleID=287453>.

Adib, M. and Waziri, H. (2011b) The Brotherhood in their first TV appearance: "We are not opportunists and reject the Iranian Model." *Al-Masry Al-Youm*. <http://www.almasry-alyoum.com/article2.aspx?ArticleID=288427>.

Adib, M. and Waziri, H. (2012) The Brotherhood: "We respect all the treaties signed between Egypt and Israel." *Al-Masry Al-Youm*. <http://www.almasry-alyoum.com/article2.aspx?ArticleID=288347>.

Al-Nour Party, Arabic site. (2012a) <http://www.alnourparty.org>.

Al-Nour Party, Arabic site. (2012b) Who we are. <http://www.alnourparty.org/about>.

Al-Nour Party, Arabic site. (2012c) FAQ. <http://www.alnourparty.org/page/answer>.

Ashour, A. (2011) Islamist parties in Turkey. *AL-AHRAM*. <http://weekly.ahram.org.eg/2011/1072/op42.htm>.

Bokhari, K. and Senzai, F. (2011) The many shades of Islamist.

*The Huffington Post.* <http://www.huffingtonpost.com/kamran-bokhari/the-many-shades-of-islami_b_1102063.html>.

*Egypt Independent.* (2011) Muslim Brotherhood to establish "Freedom and Justice Party." <http://www.egyptindependent.com/node/325599>.

El-Shobaki, Amr. (2011) Where does the Brotherhood's strength lie? *Egypt Independent.* <http://www.egyptindependent.com/node/470381>.

Freedom and Justice Party ("hurryh"), Arabic site. <http://www.hurryh.com>.

Freedom and Justice Party, English site. <http://www.fjponline.com>.

Iskander, A. (2010) "We are All Khaled Said" group members: Reclaiming silence in Egypt. *Egypt Independent.* <http://www.egyptindependent.com/node/58021>.

Muslim Brotherhood, Arabic site. <http://www.ikhwanonline.com>.

Muslim Brotherhood, English site. <http://www.ikhwanweb.com>.

Party Platforms 2011. (2011) <http://www.fjponline.com/articles.php?pid=80>.

## On the relationship between Arab nationalism and political Islam

See my analysis on the issue, which provides the backdrop for the interpretation presented here:

Castells, M. (2010) *The Power of Identity.* Blackwell, Oxford, pp. 13–23.

See also:

Carre, O. (2004) *Le nationalisme arabe.* Payot, Paris.

Keppel, G. (2008) *Beyond Terror and Martyrdom: the Future*

*of the Middle East*. Harvard University Press, Cambridge, MA.

Roy, O. (2007) *Secularism Confronts Islam*. Columbia University Press, New York.

# DIGNITY, VIOLENCE, GEOPOLITICS:

## THE ARAB UPRISING AND ITS DEMISE[1]

The Arab world is today witnessing the birth of a new
world, which tyrants and unjust rulers strive to oppose. But
in the end, this new world will inevitably emerge ... Our
oppressed people have revolted, declaring the emergence
of a new dawn in which the sovereignty of the people, and
their invincible will, will prevail. The people have decided
to break free and walk in the footsteps of civilized free
people of the world.

> Tawakkol Karman, statement on the occasion of
> receiving the 2011 Nobel Peace Prize for her work
> on peace and justice in Yemen and among Arab
> women at large.[2]

In the wake of the Tunisian and Egyptian revolutions, Days
of Rage (*Youm al-Ghadab*) surged across the Arab world in
2011: January 7 in Algeria, January 12 in Lebanon, January
14 in Jordan, January 17 in Mauritania, January 17 in Sudan,
January 17 in Oman, January 27 in Yemen, February 14

in Bahrain, February 17 in Libya, February 18 in Kuwait, February 20 in Morocco, February 26 in the Western Sahara, March 11 in Saudi Arabia, March 18 in Syria. In a few instances (Saudi Arabia, Lebanon, Kuwait, and the United Arab Emirates, where little happened in fact), the protest fizzled out for a variety of causes.[3] In others, uprisings were quelled by a mixture of repression and concession from the regimes (Morocco, Jordan, Algeria, Oman), although the ashes of the movements are still hot and could be rekindled at any moment. In Bahrain, a Saudi Arabia-backed savage repression crushed in blood a massive, peaceful movement largely made out of the Shia population in the "Bloody Thursday" of February 17. In Yemen, Libya, and Syria, initially peaceful movements were met with utmost violence from the dictatorships, degenerating in civil wars that transformed these countries into battlefields where geopolitical contenders fought to assert their influence. Indeed, foreign direct military intervention was decisive in Libya and foreign geopolitical influence became an essential factor in the evolution of the Syrian uprising. These various movements emerged from causes specific to each country, and evolved according to the conditions of their contexts and to the idiosyncrasies of each revolt. However, they were all spontaneous uprisings stimulated by the hope inspired by the success of the Tunisian and Egyptian revolutions, conveyed by images and messages arriving from the Internet and from Arab satellite television networks. Without any doubt, the spark of indignation and hope that was born in Tunisia and had brought down the Mubarak regime, bringing in a democratic Tunisia and a proto-democratic Egypt, extended quickly to other Arab countries, following the same model: calls on the Internet, networking in cyberspace and calls to occupy urban space to put pressure on the government to resign and open a process of democratization, from the Pearl

Roundabout in Bahrain to "Change Square" in Saana, or squares in Casablanca and Amman. States all over the Arab world reacted in different ways, from slight liberalization to bloody repression, out of fear of losing power. The interaction between the protests and the regimes depended on internal and geopolitical conditions.

To be sure, there were deep-seated grievances among a population that had been submitted to political oppression and kept in dire economic conditions for decades, without a chance to claim their rights under the threat of arbitrary violence from the state.[4] Furthermore, the majority of these countries' populations were composed of people under 30 years of age, many of them relatively educated, and most of them unemployed or underemployed. These youth were familiar with the use of digital communication networks, as the penetration of mobile phones exceeded 100 percent in half of the Arab countries, with most others over the 50 percent mark, and many in the urban centers had some form of access to social media (Howard 2011). Moreover, they felt daily humiliation in their lives, void of opportunities in their society and participation in their polity. They were ready to rise for their dignity, a more potent motivation than anything else. Some had done so in the last decade, only to be met with violence, imprisonment and often death. Then, the spark of outrage and the light of hope came to them simultaneously. The hope was provided by other Arab youth, like themselves, who had risen up in other countries, particularly in Egypt, known in the Arab cultural imagination as *um al-dunya* ("mother of the world"). The spark resulted from specific events in each country: self-immolations and symbolic martyrdoms as a form of protest, images of police torture and beatings of peaceful demonstrators, assassinations of human rights advocates and popular bloggers. These were no Islamists, or leftist revolutionaries, although anyone

with a project to change society eventually participated in
the movement. Initially they were of a middle class background,[5] albeit usually an impoverished middle-class, and
many were women. They were later joined by poor people
hit by inflation and unable to buy their daily food staples as a
result of policies of economic liberalization and the subjuga-
tion of their countries to increased food prices in the world
market.[6] Dignity and bread were the original drivers of most
movements, together with housing demands in the case
of Algeria. But asking for bread meant actually to reverse
economic policies, and to end corruption as a way of governance. The assertion of dignity became a cry for democracy.
Thus all movements became political movements, asking for
democratic reforms.

The evolution of each movement largely depended on
the reaction of the state. When governments showed some
semblance of accommodation to their demands, and hinted
at political liberalization, movements were channeled into
a process of democratization of the state within the limits
of maintaining the essence of elite domination. Thus King
Abdullah II in Jordan sacked his prime minister and dismissed
his cabinet (the target of the protest against economic policies), establishing mechanisms of consultation with citizens,
particularly with representatives of the Bedouin tribes. King
Mohammed VI of Morocco proposed a few democratizing
amendments in the Constitution, including a transfer of the
power to appoint members of parliament to the prime minister. The amendments were approved by referendum in July
2011 with 98.5 percent voting in favor. He also freed dozens
of political prisoners and held new elections on November
25, 2011 that saw the victory of Islamist candidates (most
of them moderate), as in all other free elections held in the
Arab world in recent years.

However, when the regimes resisted the demands for

political reform and resorted to sheer repression, the movements shifted from reform to revolution and engaged in a process of overthrowing the dictatorships. In such process, the interplay of internal factionalism and geopolitical influences led to bloody civil wars whose differential outcome is redefining the politics of the Arab world in the coming years.

## VIOLENCE AND THE STATE

When states are challenged in their power, they respond according to their institutional rules, be they democratic, dictatorial, or a mix of both. When they fail to integrate the demands or projects of their challengers without jeopardizing the fundamentals of the power relationships they embody, they resort to their ultimate essence: their monopoly of violence in their sphere of action. Their willingness to use extreme violence depends on the extent of their legitimacy, the intensity of the challenge they have to face, and their operational and social capacity to use violence. When movements are determined enough to keep up their relentless pressure on the state regardless of the violence they endure, and the state resorts to extreme violence (tanks against unarmed demonstrators), the outcome of the conflict depends on the interplay between political interests in the country and geopolitical interests related to the country.

In Yemen, a fractured state, in a barely unified nation, split under the assault of a massive, variegated movement, with one part of the army siding with the demonstrators in their demand concerning the resignation of dictator Ali Abdullah Saleh. The tribal nature of Yemen, and the secessionist movements in the North and the South, led to a stalemate between Saleh, backed by Saudi Arabia, and the democratic movement calling for a new constitution and true democracy. The suspected presence of Al Qaeda, with greater intensity than in any other country, prompted the US to extreme caution, so that in spite of some rhetoric of support for the movement, the American diplomacy left the Saudis in charge of a controlled political transition. In February 2012, under a brokered agreement, Saleh stepped down after three decades in power, and his vice president, Abd Rabbuh Mansur al-Hadi, ran for an election that he won with 99.8 percent of the vote . . . to be continued.

In Libya, the nation-state, while incarnating the messianic pan-Africanist project of its charismatic founder, expressed in reality the domination of Western tribes over Eastern tribes. Ruthless suppression of any attempt from the Bengazhi elites or from subdued tribes to claim their share of the bounty of oil and gas, mainly found in the Eastern desert, led to the concentration of power in Gaddafi's family, their tribal supporters and a small circle of the elites in the Western areas of the country. Power was exercised by the control of a well-equipped, well-trained praetorian guard, backed when necessary by mercenaries from other countries. Thus, there was not a real national army that could embody the institutions of the nation independently of the designs of the dictator and his clique. The Libyan state was largely a patrimonial state. This meant that, on the one hand, large segments of the population, particularly in the East, were excluded from the riches of energy revenues. On the other hand, the clientelistic networks organized around the patronage system of the leader were extensive and treated with generosity. The regime had a certain social base, supported by tribal divisions, fears and animosities that the leader played skillfully against one another for his own benefit. Most of the youth of Libya were disaffected politically vis-à-vis the regime, but in Tripoli they had greater economic opportunities than their counterparts in Egypt. Under these conditions, the demonstrations that started on

February 17 in Bengazhi, following calls in social media and
through mobile phone networks, had only limited repercus-
sions in Tripoli, and expressed both democratic aspirations
and a regional and tribal rebellion against the authoritarian,
patrimonial state. As such they were backed by one segment
of the armed forces with links to the East, and were protected by these armed units when Gaddafi tried to crush the
movement by force. Thus, the rebellion quickly escalated to
a civil war: by February 20, only three days after the beginning of the movement, the rebels had occupied Bengazhi and
other towns in the East, and by February 23 they had taken
Misrata, midway to Tripoli. The movement improvised a
civilian administration in Bengazhi with the cooperation of
most of the local bureaucrats, while enthusiastic ragtag mili-
tias, mounted on pickup trucks, hastily armed and without
any combat experience, marched toward Tripoli only to be
doomed in their unequal confrontation with a well-prepared
private army, commanded by Gaddafi's sons with supe-
rior firepower. Hours before Gaddafi could implement his
announced intention to occupy Benghazi and search and kill
all of the rebels house by house, 20 French bombers stopped
the assault and internationalized the Libyan conflict, draping
the NATO intervention under the UN flag. Geopolitics took
over. Obama's deep reluctance to engage in any form of military action was partly overcome by the insistence of Hillary
Clinton, Susan Rice, and some members of the presidential
team such as Samantha Power, to protect the rebels from
massacre, perhaps remembering the terrible consequences of
President Clinton's inaction in Rwanda. More decisive was
the role played by France, the UK, and Italy in the intervention, in order to secure the control of Libyan oil and gas, a
critical supply for Western Europe. Russia and China were
caught off guard and out-maneuvered by NATO in a lesson
they would never forget. Since my main interest here is not

about war games but about the fate of social movements, what appears clearly is that once the movement engages in military violence to counter military violence, it loses its character as a democratic movement to become a contender, sometimes as ruthless as its oppressors, in a bloody civil war. And any civil war may become an opportunity for geopolitical actors to increase their real estate, under whatever ideological mantle, just in case their competitors would be tempted to take advantage of the vacuum of power created in the aftermath of regime collapse. In a certain sense, civil wars not only kill people, they also kill social movements and their ideals of peace, democracy and justice.

The poignant contradiction between social movements and violence was also acutely present in the Syrian uprising, one of the most potent, determined social movements to shake up the Arab world. It too was ignited by the explosive coincidence of hope and outrage. Hope: the example of Egypt, a historical reference for Syrians. Outrage: on February 27, 2011, in the Southern city of Daraa, 15 children, aged 9 to 14, were arrested. Their crime? Inspired by the images from other countries, they wrote on walls of the city "*As-shaab yureed askot an-nizam*" ("The people want to overthrow the regime"). They were jailed and tortured. When their parents protested in the streets they were shot and a few were killed. When a funeral was held for them, the mourners were shot and many were killed. Bashar Al-Assad thought that he could simply follow the lessons of his father when he crushed the Muslim Brotherhood rebellion in the city of Hama in 1982 by shelling the entire town with over 20,000 people killed. It was different this time. People had their networks among themselves and with the world. In Damascus, four women, three human rights lawyers and one blogger, called over the Internet for a "Family Vigil for Prisoners" to be held in front of the Ministry of Interior on

March 16. Only 150 persons came, and they were beaten and
jailed. But calls to demonstrate against the regime's brutality
then came from Daraa, Homs, Hama, Damascus, Baniyas,
and many other towns, and on March 18 tens of thousands
of people marched nationwide, confronting with their hands
and their will the police and the thugs shooting at them. No
one came to their rescue. They were not asking for it; they
refused the notion of foreign intervention. But they wanted
the world to know. Their original demands were about low-
ering food prices, stopping police brutality and putting an
end to political corruption. They wanted political reform.
Assad replied with vague promises of constitutional reform
in the parliament, dismissing the governor of Daraa, sack-
ing his cabinet, lifting the ban on *niqab* for teachers, closing
the only casino in the country and giving Syrian nationality
to Kurds, among other concessions. Yet, in the perception
of the people, these limited gestures could not offset the
extreme violence unleashed by the regime, which escalated
to the use of combat troops and tanks against unarmed demonstrators. The movement became uncompromising: people
wanted to overthrow the regime; Assad should go. Then,
after six months, 5,000 dead, and tens of thousands injured
and imprisoned, the movement evolved toward a combination of demonstrations, occupations of urban space, and
limited armed resistance. People started to arm themselves,
a few military units deserted and formed a mysterious Free
Syrian Army, of unknown origin and allegiance, and a civil
war began. This time, however, it was not like in Libya. The
dictator had some social support, particularly among the business elites of Damascus and Aleppo, and among the minority
Alawites, who are the ethnic base of the Baath Party and of
the state's leadership. Some social groups were influenced by
Assad's propaganda and were afraid of the possibility that an
Islamist takeover could curtail their religious freedom; a fear

that Assad instilled, and provoked, including by setting up car bombs and blaming the Islamists. Moreover, the core of the dictatorship is the Baath Party, which controls a powerful, modern army that takes orders only from the party leaders, led by the Assad family. Thus the fracture in the society did not permeate into the state that remained, at least for the first year of the movement, unified around the party. Yet, the decisive factor in the fate of the Syrian revolution was its geopolitical environment, as Syria occupies a key position in the entangled power games of the Middle East. Russia and China have supported wholeheartedly the dictatorship and were not ready to repeat the Libyan scenario. Thus, they blocked any military action from the UN and warned NATO and the US against intervention, while supporting negotiations. Russia has its only military base outside Russia in Tartus, a Syrian naval base, and sells considerable amounts of weapons to Assad, its last ally in the Arab world. China is a supporter of Iran, its main supplier of oil, and Iran is the protector of Assad. On the other hand, Saudi Arabia, together with Qatar and Jordan, is engaged in a major fight with Shia Iran over Syria, to claim the power for its majority Sunni population and to undermine a fundamental position for its archrival Iran for influence in the region. Informed circles considered that, in 2012, the Free Syrian Army was in fact bankrolled and trained by the Saudis who had called openly in the Arab League for intervention in Syria. At the time of this writing, Kofi Annan was leading a United Nations mission to engage in political negotiations in Syria, where the movement continued to occupy the streets, in spite of shelling, and an uneven combat went on between army troops and armed rebels. Yet, here again, regardless of the outcome of this process in political terms, one of the most extraordinary democratic movements of the Arab uprising would become entangled in the maneuvers of a fragmented political opposition, in the realignments of power in the corridors of the state, and in the web of geopolitical strategies, losing its grip on the promise of democracy that people had defended with their lives. However, freedom and autonomous deliberation continue in the occupied squares and in the digital networks where the movement was born. There is no going back for the Syrian people, who did not yield to sectarian confrontation, and did not accept dictatorship under different names in their determination to choose their right to be.

## A DIGITAL REVOLUTION?

As in Tunisia and as in Egypt, most of the Arab uprisings started with organization, debate, and calls to rise up on the Internet, and continued and formed in the urban space. Thus, Internet networks provided a space of autonomy from where the movements emerged under different forms and with different results depending on their social context. As in all of the other cases of social movements I studied in this volume, there is also a raging debate in the media and in academia about the precise role of digital networks in these movements. Fortunately, in the case of the Arab uprisings, we can rely on a rigorous assessment of their role on the basis of social science research, thanks to the work that Philip Howard, Muhammad Hussain, and their collaborators have been conducting on this matter for some time. I will summarize here their main findings because I think they have put to rest a meaningless debate about the causal role of social media on social movement. Of course technology does not determine social movements or for that matter any social behavior. But Internet and mobile phone networks are not simply tools, but organizational forms, cultural expressions, and specific platforms for political autonomy. Let's look at the evidence collected and theorized by Howard, Hussain, and their team.

First of all, in his book *The Digital Origins of Dictatorship and Democracy: Information Technology and Political Islam* (2011), written before the Arab uprisings, Philip Howard, on the basis of a comparative analysis of 75 countries, either Muslim or with significant Muslim populations, finds that, while framed by a number of contextual factors, the diffusion and use of ICTs favor democratization, strengthen democracy and increase civic involvement and autonomy of the civil society, paving the way for the democratization of state and also for challenges to dictatorships. Furthermore, involvement of civic young Muslims was favored by Internet use. He wrote: "Countries where civil society and journalism made active use of the new information technologies subsequently experience a radical democratic transition or significant solidification of their democratic institutions" (2011: 200). Particularly significant, before the Arab Spring, was the transformation of social involvement in Egypt and Bahrain with the help of ICT diffusion. In a stream of research conducted in 2011 and 2012 after the Arab uprisings, Howard and Hussain, using a series of quantitative and qualitative indicators, probed a multi-causal, statistical model of the processes and outcomes of the Arab uprisings by using fuzzy logic (Hussain and Howard 2012). They found that the extensive use of digital networks by a predominantly young population of demonstrators had a significant effect on the intensity and power of these movements, starting with a very active debate on social and political demands in the social media *before* the demonstrations' onset. In their words:

> Digital media had a causal role in the Arab Spring in that they provided the fundamental infrastructure of a social movement unlike the others that have emerged in recent years in these

countries. In the first few weeks of protest in each country, the generation of people in the streets – and its leadership – was clearly not interested in the three major models of political Islam ... Instead, these mostly cosmopolitan and younger generations of mobilizers felt disenfranchised by their political systems, saw vast losses in the poor management of national economies and development, and most importantly, a consistent and widely shared narrative of common grievances – a narrative which they learned about from each other and co-wrote on the digital spaces of political writing and venting on blogs, videos shared on Facebook and Twitter, and comment board discussions on international news sites like Al Jazeera and the BBC.

The Arab Spring is historically unique because it is the first set of political upheavals in which all of these things [alienation from the state, consensus among the population in the protest, defence of the movement by the international public opinion] were digitally mediated ... It is true that Facebook and Twitter did not cause revolutions, but it is silly to ignore the fact that the careful and strategic uses of digital media to network regional publics, along with international support networks, have empowered activists in new ways that have led to some of the largest protests this decade in Iran, the temporary lifting of the Egyptian blockade on Gaza, and the popular movements that ended the decades long rule of Mubarak and Ben Ali. Digital media had a causal role in the Arab Spring in the sense that it provided the very infrastructure that created deep communication ties and organizational capacity in groups of activists before the major protests took place, and while street protests were being formalized. Indeed, it was because of those well-developed, digital networks, that civic leaders so successfully activated such large numbers of people to protest.

In every single case, the inciting incidents of the Arab Spring were digitally mediated in some way. Information infrastructure, in the form of mobile phones, personal computers, and social media were part of the causal story we must tell about the Arab Spring. People were inspired to protest for many different, and always personal reasons. Information technologies mediated that inspiration, such that the revolutions followed each other by a few weeks and had notably similar patterns. Certainly there were different political outcomes, but that does not diminish the important role of digital media in the Arab Spring. But even more importantly, this investigation has illustrated that countries that don't have a civil society equipped with digital scaffolding are much less likely to experience popular movements for democracy – an observation we are able to make only by accounting for the constellation of causal variables that existed before the street protests began, not simply the short-term uses of digital technologies during the short period of political upheaval.

In my words: the Arab uprisings were spontaneous processes of mobilization that emerged from calls from the Internet and wireless communication networks on the basis of the pre-existing social networks, both digital and face-to-face, that existed in the society. By and large, they were not mediated by formal political organizations, which had been decimated by repression and were not trusted by most of the young, active participants that spearheaded the movements. Digital networks and occupation of the urban space, in close interaction, provided the platform for autonomous organization and deliberation on which the uprisings were based, and created the resilience that was necessary for the movements to withstand ferocious assaults from state violence until the moment that, in some cases, out of a self-defence instinct, they became a counter-state.

There was another meaningful effect of the movements' presence on the Internet networks that has been pointed out to me by Maytha Alhassen: artistic political creativity. The movements, particularly in Syria, were supported by the innovative graphic design of avatar images, mini-documentaries, YouTube web series (such as Beeshu), vlogs, photographic montages and the like. The power of images, and creative narrative-activated emotions, both mobilizing and soothing, created a virtual environment of art and meaning on which the activists of the movement could rely to connect with the youth population at large, thus changing culture as a tool of changing politics.

Political blogs, in the time before the uprisings, were essential in creating, in many countries, a political culture of debate and activism that contributed to the critical thinking and rebellious attitudes of a young generation that was ready to revolt in the streets. The Arab uprisings were born at the dawn of the explosion of the digital age in the Arab world, albeit with different levels of diffusion of these communication technologies in various countries. Even in countries with low levels of Internet access, the core of activists that, as a network, networked the movement and the movement with their nation and the world, was organized and deliberated on the social networking sites. From that protected space, extensive mobile phone networks reached out to society at large. And because society was ready to receive certain messages about bread and dignity, people were moved and – ultimately – became a movement.

## POST-SCRIPTUM 2014

As we now know, the Syrian revolution disintegrated in an atrocious downward spiral of multi-pronged violence as a result of the intervention of geopolitical forces and the attempt by global jihadist networks of various allegiances to take advantage of the void of power created by the war to seize the Syrian state or to create a new one in Syria and Iraq. The military and political success of ISIS, and the ineptitude of Western powers in constructing a multi-religious Iraq have planted the seeds of yet another endless war in the most unstable and strategically decisive region of the planet. The investigation presented in this book stops at the threshold of understanding this barbaric confrontation, as it would require a different set of information and a different conceptual framework.

I would simply add that the inability of authentic social movements to overcome the violence of the state, and their subsequent attempt to engage in the same kind of violence usually end up in the destruction of the social movement, and in justifying additional violence. Under such conditions, the actors, state or non-state, able to implement the highest level of violence are the winners, while people at large are the dramatic losers under all circumstances. This is to say that confronted with uncompromising violence social movements should find ways to abstain from engaging in the same destructive logic since they can never win in the confrontation. This is why social movements and revolutionary movements are not the same kind of collective actors. It may be inevitable to be drawn into the dynamic of violence. Yet, this leads to the worse possible kind of death for a social movement. Sometimes it will take extreme courage to respond to war with peace, in the hope of winning the minds of people in the country and around the world. And yet, it may be the only true defense against the barbarism practiced by states, all states, and the would-be state actors confronting them.

## NOTES

1  This chapter largely relies on the contribution of information, data gathering, and advice of journalist and
   scholar Maytha Alhassen. For her own analysis of the Arab
   uprisings, see Alhassen, Maytha and Ahmed Shihab-Eldin
   (eds.) (2012) *Demanding Dignity: Young Voices from the Arab
   Revolutions*. White Cloud Press, Ashland, OR.
2  http://www.democracynow.org/2011/12/13/the_arab_
   people_have_woken_up
3  The context of each country partly explains the cases in
   which protests were limited in 2011 (still to be seen in
   the future). Thus, in Lebanon and Algeria, the memory of
   atrocious civil wars had a paralyzing effect, although active
   protests did take place in Algeria, and were reproduced in
   January 2012. In Iraq, the painful period of war, occupation, civil war, and lingering terrorism left the population
   exhausted and yearning for peace. In Saudi Arabia, the
   limited protest that took place on March 11 was largely
   confined to the Shia minority in the Eastern part of the
   country, and so its movement was isolated from the Sunni
   majority, and easily repressed by an effective security
   apparatus. The most significant social movement in Saudi
   Arabia was the women's campaign for their right to drive,
   a movement still in process, with the potential of extending to other women's rights. In the United Arab Emirates,
   the fact that most residents are not citizens, and most citizens enjoy affluent subsidized lives creates a context in
   which the lack of liberty does not necessarily appear as a
   burden to the citizens, and is a factor of intimidation for
   the immigrants.
4  For a discussion on Arab dictatorships, see Marzouki
   (2004); Schlumberger (2007).
5  For the social background of Syrian activists, as well as a

first-hand account of the uprising, see the excellent analysis by Mohja Kahf: <http://www.jadaliyya.com/pages/index/4274/the-syrian-revolution-on-four-packs-a-day>.
6 For the impact of the rise of food prices in the world on the social situation of the Arab countries (they import more food than any other region in the world), see: <http://www.economist.com/node/21550328?fsrc=scn/tw/te/ar/letthemeatbaklava>.

## REFERENCES AND SOURCES

Council of Foreign Affairs. (2011) *The New Arab Revolts: What Happened, What it Means, and What Comes Next.* Council of Foreign Affairs, New York.

Howard, P. (2011) *The Digital Origins of Dictatorship and Democracy. Information Technology and Political Islam.* Oxford University Press, Oxford.

Hussain, M.M. and Howard, P. (2012) *Democracy's Fourth Wave? Information Technology and the Fuzzy Causes of the Arab Spring*, unpublished paper presented to the meeting of the International Studies Association, San Diego, April 1–4.

Marzouki, M. (2004) *Le mal arabe. Entre dictatures et integrisme: la democratie interdite.* L'Harmattan, Paris.

Noland, M. (2011) *The Arab Economies in a Changing World.* Peter G. Peterson Institute for International Economics, Washington, DC.

Schlumberger, O. (2007) *Debating Arab Authoritarianism: Dynamics and Durability in Nondemocratic Regimes.* Stanford University Press, Stanford, CA.

# A RHIZOMATIC
# REVOLUTION:

## *INDIGNADAS*[1] IN SPAIN[2]

February 2011. The euro-crisis is in full swing in Spain. Unemployment reaches 22 percent, with youth unemployment at 47 percent. After ignoring the severity of the crisis for a long time, under the pressure of Germany and the IMF, the Socialist government, reversing its electoral promises of 2008, is engaged in ever deeper budget cuts in health, education and social services. Priority is given to recapitalizing the financial institutions and to reducing the skyrocketing public debt for the sake of preserving Spain's membership in the eurozone. Labor unions are in disarray, and politicians and political parties are despised by a large majority of citizens. A small network of concerned citizens from Madrid, Barcelona, Jerez, and other cities create a Facebook group under the name "Platform of Coordination of Groups Pro-Citizen Mobilization." Some of them have been at the forefront of the campaign to defend a free Internet against the Sinde Law, approved by the government to impose control and censorship of Internet Service Providers (ISPs) and

Internet users. Networks such as x.net, Anonymous, and Nolesvotes were among the participants. Others were veterans from the movements for global justice. Still others, such as Estado del Malestar, Juventud Sin Futuro, Juventud en Accion, Plataforma de Afectados por la Hipoteca, and others were inspired by the struggles spreading throughout Europe against the social consequences of the rampant financial crisis, although in Spain the main criticism focused on the mismanagement of the crisis by a dysfunctional, unresponsive political system. They were encouraged by the example of Iceland: by the possibility of successfully confronting the collusion between bankers and politicians through grassroots mobilization. This platform evolved quickly into a Facebook group of debate and action under the name of "*Democracia Real Ya*" (Real Democracy Now!), which created a forum, a blog, and an email list.[3] However, as one of the initiators of DRY, Javier Toret, puts it:

> The campaign was anonymous, Democracia Real Ya was nothing. It was a conglomeration of blogs, different groups, some people that came from the Ley Sinde or the Nolesvotes groups. Democracia Real was a brand that did not have anyone behind it, there were no people behind it.[4]

The group was based on a decentralized network with autonomous nodes in different cities. In some cases, such as in Barcelona, they met in person every Sunday morning. Hundreds joined the Facebook group, and some participated in the meetings. They denounced the lack of representative democracy under its current form in Spain. In their view, the main political parties were at the service of the bankers and were not responsive to the interests of citizens. Following the example of the Arab revolutions, they decided to call for action in the streets. They seized the opportunity of the municipal elections that were scheduled throughout the country on May 22, 2011. Thus, on March 2, they called for citizens to demonstrate their protest in the streets on Sunday, May 15, under the slogan "Real Democracy Now! Take the streets. We are not merchandise in the hands of politicians and bankers," and published a manifesto:

> We are normal people. We are like you: people who get up in the morning to study, to work or to look for a job, people with family and friends. People who work hard every day to live and get a better future for those we are with . . . Yet in this country most of the political class does not even listen to us. Its functions should be to bring our voice to the institutions, facilitating citizen's political participation, aiming at achieving the greatest benefit for the majority of society instead of just enriching themselves on our back, paying attention only to the instructions of the great economic powers, and maintaining a partytocratic dictatorship . . . We are people, not merchandise. I am not only what I buy, why I buy it, and for whom I buy it. For all these reasons, I am indignant. I believe I can change it. I believe I can contribute. I know together we can. Come with us. It is your right.

The call was not supported by any political party, labor unions or civil society associations, and was ignored by the media. It was diffused primarily over the Internet's social networks, Facebook, Twitter, tuenti, etc. On May 15, without any formal leadership but with a careful preparation of the demonstrations that went on for weeks, tens of thousands of people demonstrated in Madrid (50,000), Barcelona (20,000), Valencia (10,000), and 50 more cities, peacefully, without any major incident anywhere.

At the end of the demonstration in Madrid, a few dozen protesters went to the Puerta del Sol, the most symbolic square of the city, and spent the night in balmy weather to discuss among themselves what Real Democracy meant. At that point they decided they were not going to leave Puerta del Sol until they came to a consensus about the meaning of Real Democracy – a lengthy process, as it turned out. The following night, May 16, many people gathered in Barcelona's Catalunya Square. In both places they decided to occupy the square to debate the issues that had not been discussed in the meaningless campaigns of political candidates for the municipal elections to be held in a few days. They tweeted their friends. Hundreds came, who then tweeted their networks, and so thousands came. Many of them came with sleeping bags, to spend the night in the occupied space. The *acampadas* (camps) were born. Many more people came during daytime. They participated in debates, activities, and demonstrations. Commissions of all sorts sprung up spontaneously. Some took care of the logistical problems, including sanitation, water and food supply. Others set up webs, deployed Wi-Fi networks, and connected to occupied spaces around the country and around the world. Many others facilitated debates, on any theme anyone wanted to propose and for anyone who was interested. No leaders were recognized: everybody represented just her/himself, and decisions were left in the hands of the General Assembly meeting at the end of every day, and in the commissions that were formed on every issue that people wanted to act upon. Over 100 Spanish cities followed suit, triggering a massive occupy movement that spread in a few days to almost 800 cities around the world, although, interestingly enough, its impact was limited at that point in the United States. National and international media reported on the movement, albeit usually misrepresenting it. The police tried, unsuccessfully, to evict the occupiers twice. The Electoral Court declared occupations unlawful as they were interfering with the "day of reflection" before the elections, as established by the law. Yet, on the two occasions there was a threat against the occupied spaces, thousands joined in, blocking police action. Political parties were mindful of adverse consequences for their electoral prospects if they would engage in all-out police operations, and so the occupations continued, as per the decision of the assemblies, beyond election day. The movement had taken on a life of its own. It was first known as the 15-M, a name derived from the date of the first demonstration, but soon the media popularized the label of "*indignados*," which some in the movement had adopted, perhaps inspired by the title of a pamphlet ("*Indignez-vous!*") published a few months earlier by a 93-year-old French philosopher and former diplomat, Stephane Hessel, who struck a nerve among young people in Spain (more so than in France).[5] Indeed, there was a general climate of indignation in the country (as in most of the world) against politicians who cared only about themselves, and against the bankers who had wrecked the economy with their speculative maneuvers, only to be bailed out, and to receive handsome bonuses, while citizens suffered dearly from the consequences of the crisis in their jobs, salaries, services, and foreclosed mortgages. The movement went on under different forms for several months, although most of the occupations of public space ended in early July. During July, several marches started from different points in Spain and converged on Madrid on the 22nd. The marchers walked, passing through towns and villages, explaining the reasons for the protest, and were joined by many others during their journey. When they reached Madrid after hundreds of kilometers by foot, they were greeted by supportive crowds, who joined them for the final lap. On July 23 in the Puerta del Sol, a demonstration of about 250,000 people reaffirmed the determination of the movement to keep fighting for democracy and against the unfair management of the economic crisis. Actions of protest continued during August, including some attempts to reoccupy Sol in Madrid, to the point that hundreds of policemen occupied the square themselves for several days, to preempt a new occupation by the *indignadas*. At the end of August, the Socialist Party government and the opposition Partido Popular (Conservative) agreed to bow to the ultimatum from Merkel to amend the Spanish Constitution to forbid the possibility of budget deficits as a way to appease the financial markets speculating against the Spanish debt (this in fact did not work). The country was on vacation and the vote took place almost in secrecy. The *indignadas* protested in front of the parliament, calling for a referendum, and staged demonstrations in many cities, receiving some support from the trade unions and from a left-wing party that also opposed amending the Constitution under the gun of Germany. The *indignadas* carried a banner saying, "Unions, thanks for coming."

It is estimated that a minimum of 2.2 million people participated, and participation in the protests increased from May to October (Blanco 2011).

On October 15, 2011 a global demonstration, convened over the Internet at the initiative of a network of activists who met in Barcelona in early September, gathered hundreds of thousands of demonstrators in 951 cities and 82 countries around the world under the slogan "United for Global Change." There were almost 500,000 demonstrators in Madrid and about 400,000 in Barcelona.

Who were these determined protesters? While at the origin of the movement there were many university students and unemployed college graduates in the 20–35 age group (as there were in the Arab revolutions), they were joined later by people from all social backgrounds and ages, with an active participation of elderly, under direct threat of deteriorating living conditions. Moreover, the movement received the overwhelming support of the public opinion throughout 2011, with at least three quarters of the Spanish people, according to different surveys, declaring their agreement with the critiques and statements of the movement. Some sources put the degree of identification with the movement at 88 percent (see table 1).

Yet, in early 2012 there was uncertainty about the path ahead for those who "worried about our future because this is the place where we will spend the rest of our lives," as a banner in the occupied square stated. This is why the search and the debates continued on the Internet social networks, the safe space from which the movement was imagined and where new projects were and are being conceived.

## A SELF-MEDIATED MOVEMENT

While the occupation of public space was essential to make the movement visible, and to provide support to the key organizational form of the movement – the local assemblies – the origin of the movement, and its backbone through-out the protest can be traced back to the free spaces of the Internet. This is the account of Javier Toret, a psychologist and researcher on techno-politics, who was one of the first members of the network that created *Democracia Real Ya*:

> What the 15-M has shown is that people can overcome a media block. The capacity of mass self-communication and self organization online has allowed people to overcome a media block. In Barcelona there was only one media outlet that did come to the press conference we organized around the 15-M demonstrations, BTV (Barcelona TV). All the media outlets knew that the 15-M demonstrations were going to take place. We had written to them, everything had been announced via Twitter, Facebook, email lists ... but nothing

**Table 1: Public opinion toward the 15M mobilizations in Spain**

| | Percentage of the total surveyed | Scale from 1 to 10 (where 1 is completely disagree and 10 is completely agree) |
|---|---|---|
| **Metroscopia survey conducted June 1–2, 2011** | | |
| Do the 15M mobilizations inspire a sense of sympathy or rejection in you? | | |
| They inspire a sense of sympathy. | 66% | |
| They inspire a sense of rejection. | 21% | |
| Do you think the motivations for protesting are right? | | |
| Yes, they are right. | 81% | |
| No, they are not right. | 9% | |
| Which of the following opinions do you agree with most? | | |
| The 15M movement deals with problems that only affect a few people. | 11% | |
| The 15M movement deals with problems that affect the entire society. | 84% | |
| The 15M movement is politically left leaning. | 31% | |
| The 15M movement is politically right leaning. | 2% | |
| The 15M movement does not have a definite political tendency. | 58% | |
| The 15M movement deals with real problems that exist in our society. | | |
| Agree/Strongly Agree | 80% | |
| Disagree/Strongly Disagree | 15% | |
| The 15M movement is something that is widely discussed, but will soon be forgotten. | | |
| Agree/Strongly Agree | 57% | |
| Disagree/Strongly Disagree | 38% | |

The 15M movement will evolve into a political party.

| | |
|---|---|
| Agree/Strongly Agree | 21% |
| Disagree/Strongly Disagree | 69% |

The 15M movement will become radicalized and engage in violent acts.

| | |
|---|---|
| Agree/Strongly Agree | 19% |
| Disagree/Strongly Disagree | 74% |

The 15M movement will become integrated into an existing political party.

| | |
|---|---|
| Agree/Strongly Agree | 22% |
| Disagree/Strongly Disagree | 68% |

**The Cocktail Analysis survey conducted May 31, 2011**

Have you heard of the Democracia Real Ya movement, also known as the 15M movement or the movement of the Indignados?

| | |
|---|---|
| Yes | 97% |
| No | 3% |

Would you say that you agree or disagree with the Democracia Real Ya/15M movement?

| | |
|---|---|
| Agree | 88% |
| Disagree | 12% |

Do you think that the Democracia Real Ya/15M movement should continue?

| | |
|---|---|
| Yes | 83% |
| No | 17% |

On a scale of 1 to 10, where 1 is completely disagree and 10 is completely agree, what do you think of the following?

| | |
|---|---|
| The electoral law needs to be reformed. | 8.7 |
| Corruption needs to be fought by implementing rules aimed at full political transparency. | 9.3 |
| There needs to be an effective separation of political powers. | 8.6 |
| Mechanisms for effective citizen control need to be created to keep effective political responsibility. | 8.7 |

**Table 1: (continued)**

| | Percentage of the total surveyed | Scale from 1 to 10 (where 1 is completely disagree and 10 is completely agree) |
|---|---|---|
| **Simple Lógica survey conducted June 1-6, 2011** | | |
| Do you approve or disapprove of the protests that have been occurring in many plazas throughout Spain? | | |
| Approve | 73% | |
| Disapprove | 19% | |
| Do you agree with the ideas that are being defended by the movement? | | |
| Agree | 72% | |
| Neither Agree nor Disagree | 10% | |
| Disagree | 10% | |
| To what extent do you think that this movement will help improve things in Spain? | | |
| A lot | 12% | |
| Somewhat | 27% | |
| Not at all | 53% | |

*Source:*
1) Metroscopia available at www.metroscopia.es/portada.html
2) The Cocktail Analysis available at http://www.tcanalysis.com/2011/06/03/movimiento-15mdemocraciarealya-representatividad-movilizacion-social-y-canales-de-informacion/
3) Simple Lógica available at http://www.simplelogica.com/iop/iop11002.asp

appeared. Television stations ignored us completely, newspapers also ignored us. There were individual journalists who did accompany the movement, for example Lali Sandiumenge, who has a blog in La Vanguardia [http://blogs.lavanguardia. com/guerreros-del-teclado/] . . . But generally, the mainstream media either ignored, or blocked the proposal we put forth . . . What this shows is a type of movement that is postmedia. It's postmedia because there is a technopolitical reappropriation of tools, technologies and mediums of participation and communication that exist today. This is where people are today. There are a lot of people in these mediums. It's an online viral campaign that is sufficiently open for anyone to get involved and participate . . . For something to be viral online, for it to be mimetic, slogans have to resonate. For example, "we are not merchandise in the hands of bankers." This has resonated, and it has circulated. It was something that anyone could relate with. People have created videos, and all sorts of signs with these slogans. The initial slogans had wide circulation because they were anonymous and because they were common sense. Slogans were not coming from a left-leaning group that had certain ideologies. It just had a viral capacity, that was mimetic, and had the capacity to use web 2.0 tools. This caused everyone to be their own media. It caused thousands of people to be their own media distributors. That's why it's a postmedia movement. It has the capacity to overcome the media and create an event, and communicate this event . . . Some media outlets have taken the tweets or what was said in the Facebook page of Acampadasol or DRY to inform the public. This could be because with a movement that is networked, that does not have leaders, it is hard for the media to be able to tell the story of what is happening. The media initially ignored the movement, but when all of the plazas of Spain were full with people, they had no choice but to explain what was happening . . . A lot of spaces were created that functioned as media outlets, for example there were a lot of personal blogs that had good coverage of the movement. We became a collective that had the capacity to speak each one for themselves without the filters of the media. The media outlets amplified what we did, be it for better or worse. There was a lot of autonomy for each person to say what they thought and felt. The 15-M movement positioned itself against intermediaries, be it political, media, or cultural. It directly attacks the idea that someone has to do things for me. This is a paradigm shift in the relationship between citizen and governments, unions, media outlets ... If this is a movement that is being created equally by thousands of people, it creates contradictions to have one person speaking. There has been an internal debate on whether there should be spokespeople. The movement's idea is that everyone spoke for themselves. It's not a person who decides anything. This makes it hard for media outlets to cover what is happening. In 2001, when we started Indymedia, we had a saying that said: "Don't hate the media, become the media." This is what the 15-M has shown. When people join together, they become more powerful than any other media outlet. For example, on the 27 May when they hit us in the plaza Catalunya, the movement had an incredible capacity to communicate what was happening ... Everyone became a reporter even if it is for a few moments. Everyone has been at some point the primary source of the news. When you have a lot of people reporting, you have a collective account of what is happening. People can follow what is happening via streaming, online, on television, live. People who were there were tweeting, "come help us," and people came. This has permitted people to take things from a digital medium, be it at their homes, or through a cell phone and be able to move in the city.[6]

Yet, even a new medium, as powerful and participatory as the Internet's social networks, is not the message. The message constructs the medium. As Toret argues, the message went viral because it resonated with people's personal experiences. And the key message was a rejection of the entire political and economic institutions that determine people's lives. Because as one banner in Madrid said, "This is not a crisis, it is that I do not love you any more."

But how is new love found?

### WHAT DID/DO THE *INDIGNADAS* WANT?

The movement did not have a program. The main reason for this was that there never was a formal organization known as "the movement." But there were many demands approved by the assemblies in many occupations. Every possible demand, critique and proposal was present in the movement. It was certainly a movement against the bankers and speculators, and against people paying the consequences of a financial crisis they were not responsible for. A deep feeling of unfairness was boiling in the population at large and came to be expressed in the movement. They felt that the banks in trouble should not be bailed out but nationalized, just as they were in Iceland, a constant reference of the movement. They thought that the fraudulent executives should be prosecuted. They were unanimously opposed to the government's budget cuts, and asked instead for taxation of the rich and of the corporations. There was widespread denunciation of the unemployment of millions of young people who had no prospects of finding a decent job. On April 7, 2011, thousands of youth had demonstrated in Madrid following the call of "Youth Without a Future," an Internet-based campaign to defend their rights to education, work and housing. There had also been a protest against the housing crisis in general and against the shortage of affordable housing for young people in particular. One important contingent of the

15-M movement came from the youth involved in the "*V as Vivienda* (Housing)" campaign in the months preceding the movement. There were particularly virulent protests against mortgage foreclosures and evictions of elderly and families in need, who had been trapped by the banks in subprime loans that they would have to continue to pay for the rest of their lives, even after having lost their homes. There was a clear criticism of capitalism as such: "This is not a crisis, it is the system." But there were no specific proposals to either overcome capitalism or restore economic growth. The reason was that many in the movement opposed the very notion of growth for the sake of growth. Environmental concerns were paramount. The opposition to a consumption-driven society was running deep. So, while the criticism of capitalism in general and of the kind of financial capitalism that led to the crisis in particular was shared almost unanimously, there was no consensus about which kind of economy would provide jobs, housing and decent living conditions to everybody in ways that were environmentally sustainable and ethically just. This is not to say that the movement was incapable of generating very specific, highly sophisticated policy proposals. In fact, there was a wealth of such proposals that were elaborated and debated in assemblies and commissions. Yet, since the movement was not organized to agree on any detailed program, there were multiple proposals from various people in various places, and so they were as diverse as the movement's composition.

However, in spite of the vast array of critiques and demands on economic and social issues, my deep conviction, from my own observation, is that this movement was essentially political. It was a movement for the transformation of pseudo-democracy into real democracy. In spite of the fact that the original call from Real Democracy Now! was later diluted in the ocean of demands and dreams present in the movement, and that Real Democracy Now! was the trigger but not the movement itself, its original manifesto was the implicit or explicit common core of the *Indignadas* movement. Yes, the crisis was an expression of the capitalist system, and the banks were the culprits. But politicians of all affiliations, parties, parliaments and governments were accomplices of the bankers whose interests they defended above those of the citizens they represented. There was a general opinion in the movement that politicians lived in their own, closed, privileged world, indifferent to people's needs, manipulating the elections and the electoral law to perpetuate their power as a political class. "They do not represent us" is probably the most popular and certainly the most fundamental slogan from the movement. Because if there is no real representation, there is no democracy, and the institutions have to be reconstructed from the bottom up, as they were in Iceland. Starting with the judiciary, fully politicized, and part of the system of reciprocal support between bankers, politicians and the high levels of the Magistracy.

This rejection of the current form of democracy has deep consequences in the project of the movement because it implies that elections and parties are useless and irrelevant to defending citizens' interests and values. Thus the movement was indifferent to electoral participation as long as there was not a deep reform of the system, starting with the reform of the electoral law that had been tailored to the convenience of the largest parties through a system of non-proportional representation favoring the majority vote getters (the D'Hondt method). In positive terms, the movement agreed to move to different models of participatory democracy, starting with deliberative democracy over the Internet to ensure a fully conscious participation of citizens in the process of consultative decision-making. The forms of deliberation and decision-making in the movement itself, which I will discuss below, aimed explicitly to prefigure what political democracy should be in society at large. Fully aware of the difficulty of affecting politics and policies within the limits of existing institutions, the movement, in its large majority, positioned itself in the long haul. It was not a matter of creating a program to be approved in the next election, since they did not recognize any political party as their interlocutor. In the view of the movement, a long march had to be undertaken from the negation of the system to the reconstruction of the institutions that would express people's will through the process of raising consciousness and participatory deliberation.

This is why the project(s) of the movement can be better found in the discourse of its actors, rather than in specific demands, which only represented the momentarily predominant view in the local assemblies that voted on them.

## THE DISCOURSE OF THE MOVEMENT

The *Indignadas* is a movement of multiple, rich discourses. Imaginative slogans, punchy terms, meaningful words and poetic expressions constituted a language ecosystem expressive of new subjectivities. Although I cannot speak of one single discourse, there are a number of terms, connotating ways of thinking, that appeared regularly in the slogans and debates that took place, both in the camps and on the Internet.

Eduardo Serrano (2011) constructed, on the basis of his observation, a list of key terms widely present in the discourse of the movement, characterizing each term by both its implications and its cancellations. His analysis, whose terms I have translated, is presented in table 2, providing a profile of the movement in its orientations as revealed in its discourse.

What is evident in this analysis is the depth of the cultural transformation embodied in this movement. Although

**Table 2: Implications and cancellations of meaning in the shared terms of discourse in the *Indignados* movement**

| Term | Implies | Cancels |
|------|---------|---------|
| **Common** | Self-management of community, shared space | Restricted property, dichotomy of public/private, seizing of power by a few |
| **Consensus by Assembly** | Decisions result from interaction between different proposals, respect of all ideas, non-linear process of decision-making, no vote but synthesis, qualitatively superior outcome of the decision-making process | Opposition consensus/dissent, averaging propositions, linear decision-making, outcome inferior to the quality of the original proposals debated |
| **Anybody** | Singularity, anonymous citizens | Everybody, totality |
| **Future-less** | Right now | Delayed fulfillment, separation between means and goals |
| **No bosses** | Self-regulation, distributed network, full involvement of everybody (as in the Internet interaction), anonymity, rotation of responsibilities | Assignment of rigid social roles, pre-definition of subjects, command and submission |
| **Non-representation** | Participation, direct democracy, politics of expression | Delegation |
| **Non-violence** | Legitimacy, exemplarity, actual self-defence, intangible field of force by de-legitimizing violence from others | Efficacy of violence, tyranny of the testosterone |
| **Respect** | Reciprocity, dignity, self-limitation, true citizenship | Security, enemy |

Table 2: (continued)

| Term | Implies | Cancels |
|---|---|---|
| Money-less | Wealth is not monetary, disconnection with the financial system, local currencies, decommodification | Economy of scarcity, financial tyranny, inevitable austerity, zero sum games |
| Fearless | Together we can, you are not alone, the crisis can be overcome (as in Iceland), creativity | Fatality, paralysis |
| Slowness | Co-evolution, processes of gradual maturation | 'Fast life' subordination of life to the acceleration of capital |

*Source:* Eduardo Serrano, 2011. El poder de las palabras: glosario de términos del 15M. [online] Available at: <http://madrilonia. org/2011/06/el-poder-de-las-palabras-glosario-de-terminos-del-15m/> [Accessed 8 February 2012]. My translation.

partly prompted by the precarious lives of millions of young people (54 percent in the age group 18–34 still were living with their parents because of lack of housing and work), the discourse of the movement expresses the rise of a new economic and political culture: an alternative economic culture, which our research team studied in Barcelona in 2009–12. It is expressed in everyday life practices that emphasize the use value of life over commercial value and engage in self-production, cooperativism, barter networks, social currency, ethical banking and networks of reciprocal solidarity. The economic crisis helped to extend the appeal of this alternative economic culture to a significant proportion of the population of Barcelona. These practices were present in the lives of thousands of people, precisely in the same age group as most of the *indignadas* (20–35) for quite some time. It was the search for a meaning of life that explains why a majority of the Barcelona population would prefer to work less even if this meant being paid proportionally less (Conill et al. 2012a, 2012b). The movement extended the values present in this alternative economy project to the formation of an alternative political project. In both cases, the construction of autonomy of the individual and the networking of these autonomous individuals to create new, shared forms of life are paramount motivations.

A sample of popular slogans express this dream of freedom and democracy in the movement's own words: "Another politics is possible," "People united function without parties," "The revolution was in our hearts and now it flies in the streets," "We carry a new world in our hearts," "I am not anti-system, the system is anti-me."

How can this political transformation be achieved? By being together, by thinking together, by pursuing the struggle, by calling the majority to join the movement: "Love to the world is what moves revolutionaries. Join us!" There will be difficulties, but it is worthwhile: "The barricade closes the street but opens the way," "Sorry for the inconvenience, we are changing the world." And a warning to the powers that be: "If you steal our dreams, we will not let you sleep."

However, the most critical issue for the movement has been how to put into its own practice the principles of democracy that they had proposed for society at large.

REINVENTING DEMOCRACY IN PRACTICE:
AN ASSEMBLY-LED, LEADERLESS MOVEMENT

There was no formal decision, but everybody agreed in practice, from the onset of the movement. There would be no leaders in the movement, either locally or nationally. For that matter, not even spokespersons were recognized. Everyone would represent him/herself, and no one else. This drove the media crazy, as the faces of any collective action are necessary

ingredients in the media's storytelling technique. The source
of this ancient, anarchist principle, usually betrayed in history, was not ideological in the case of this movement,
although it became a fundamental principle, enforced by the
large majority of the movement's actors. It was present in
the experience of Internet networks in which horizontality
is the norm, and there is little need for leadership because
the coordination functions can be exercised by the network
itself through interaction between its nodes. The new subjectivity appeared in the network: the network became the
subject. The rejection of leaders was also the consequence
of the negative experiences that some of the veteran activists had suffered in the movement for global justice and in
the various radical organizations of the extreme left. But
it resulted as well from the deep distrust of any organized
political leadership after observing the corruption and cynicism that characterized governments and traditional parties.
This search for authenticity by a new generation that came
into politics by rejecting *realpolitik* defines fundamentally the
movement, although this was at times criticized within the
movement itself, by unreconstructed militants, as *"buenismo"*
(naïve goodness). Yet, the claim for legitimacy in constructing a new form of politics could only be credible if practiced
in the daily activity of the movement.

The organizational concretion of this principle was to
give all power of decision-making for matters that would
imply the whole collective to the General Assembly that
would represent the people camping in a given location, as
well as anyone joining the camp at the time of the assembly. Assemblies would usually meet daily, except when an
emergency meeting had to be called. The number of participants varied with the size of the encampment, but in Madrid
and Barcelona attendance would range from hundreds to
two or three thousand in special moments. Decisions of the

assembly held merely symbolic power, as each person was always free to make her own decision. But the main issue was how to reach a decision. In many of the camps, the movement tried to reach a decision by consensus, conversing and debating until everybody would agree, after arguments and counter-arguments were exchanged politely and respectfully (for hours). To avoid excessive noise and interruptions, a hand language was adopted (adapted from the deaf language) to signal approval and disapproval, or to ask the speaker to wrap it up. Assemblies were moderated by volunteers who rotated regularly in these roles, not so much to prevent the rise of leaders as to care for the exhaustion derived from such a task. Although the debates did not have the acrimony often found in discussions within social movements in most cases that our team observed, there was a collective pressure exercised by the participants against any attempt by ideologues and self-proclaimed leaders to use the assembly for their propaganda. After many days of experience, some in the movement began to debate the need to reach a collective decision on specific proposals by a simple majority vote, after integrating as many different contributions as possible. Indeed, the principle of decision by consensus allowed some minority groups to block any decision by engaging in obstruction to impose a pre-conceived position. The movement re-learned old historical lessons, such as the importance of recognizing the rights of minorities without submitting to their blackmail.

The contradiction between deliberation and efficient implementation was addressed by creating multiple commissions that would enact the general orientations derived from the assembly into specific initiatives. In fact, the commissions were fully autonomous, and they also had to deliberate different proposals to reach agreement on what was to be done. Furthermore, anyone could propose the creation of a commission on a specific topic, from agro-ecological initiatives to child care or the reform of the electoral law. Some were functional, to take charge of the needs of the movement (sanitation, security, communication, etc.). Others focused on elaborating proposals on different issues to be submitted to the assembly. Still others would organize action to put some of these proposals into practice, such as the commission to block housing evictions. Commissions would remain active as long as there were people attending them, so they would appear and disappear depending on the evolution of the movement. In the case of Barcelona, those that lasted longer were the commissions reflecting on the forms of the movement, elaborating strategies on how to implement principles of participatory democracy in the practice of the movement.

However, the possibility for the movement to organize this new polity was materially dependent on the occupation of public space: on the existence of camps that, even if only a small minority would stay overnight, provided the setting for the counter-society that materialized the dreams of real democracy. Yet, it was clearly impossible to maintain such occupation indefinitely. This was not only due to logistical problems and harassment by the police, but also to the process of degradation of life in the camp. Homelessness is a dramatic reality in Spanish cities like everywhere in the world. Only a fraction of homeless people have serious psychiatric problems, but this fraction is highly visible, and many of them ended up in the camps where they felt protected. This created a major problem in the movement, in Spain as in almost every occupation I have experienced in other countries. On the one hand, the image that the presence of the homeless in the camp projects to the 99 percent (who are the reference of the movement) makes it impossible for people at large to identify with the *indignadas* camps. On the other hand, very few people among the occupiers would be ready to forbid the presence of anyone in the encampment, as this would contradict the inclusive principles of the movement.

Yet, the most important problem that the movement faced in continuing with the occupation of public space is that, over time, only full-time activists could actually participate in the assemblies and manage the day-to-day tasks of the movement. They were usually young men without family responsibilities, jobless, and increasingly devoted almost exclusively to the movement. The more the occupations would continue, the more the movement would become identified with a tiny minority of activists, hardly representative of the citizenry they wanted to mobilize. This is why after six or eight weeks, on average, most of the assemblies voted to lift the camps and continue the movement in other forms. A few opted to stay in the squares but they became an easy target for the police, who ultimately removed all occupations by mid-August.

In many towns, the movement decided to decentralize its action to the neighborhood level, and organize assemblies at the local level, representing the interests of the residents according to the same pattern of democratic deliberation and decision-making. Commissions continued to be formed spontaneously to conduct campaigns or to simply elaborate proposals that would be diffused over the Internet, and discussed in different forms and venues. Yet, the key organizational principles – refusal of elected leaders, sovereignty of the assemblies and spontaneity and self-management of the commissions – continued to operate everywhere. So did the same problems of functionality and efficiency that had plagued the movement, inducing a deep reflection on what was the meaning of efficiency and achievement in a collective practice aiming to change lives, in addition to achieving demands and defending rights.

## FROM DELIBERATION TO ACTION:
## THE QUESTION OF VIOLENCE

A popular hacker slogan says "Do not propose, do!" This is what the movement attempted. It started by voicing its indignation in street demonstrations, the oldest form of collective action. Thereafter, by occupying public space in many cities around the country, it affirmed its determination to stand up to the arrogance of power that had responded to the protest with a combination of disdain and police operations. The question quickly arose about the ways and means of affecting the goals of the movement. Since there was total distrust in the political system, the movement did not issue any advice about what to do in the elections, not even whether to abstain or cast a blank ballot. Everybody was free to follow her own assessment on tactical voting decisions. With formal politics absent from the movement's horizon, it had to resort to other forms of action. There were numerous street demonstrations, as well as marches crisscrossing Spain and Europe. There were also a number of actions against injustice: physically blocking evictions from homes whose mortgages had been foreclosed; protecting immigrants harassed by the police; refusing to pay for the subway to protest against excessive fare hikes; engaging in civil disobedience in different forms and demonstrating in front of government buildings, European Commission offices, bank headquarters, rating agency services, and the like. Yet, from the early stages of the movement it was clear that the main action concerned raising consciousness among its participants and in the population at large. The assemblies and commissions were not gatherings to prepare revolutionary actions: they were not a means, but a goal in themselves. Coming together to fully realize the inequity of the system, to dare to confront it from the safety of a shared space, on the Internet and in the squares, was the most meaningful form of action of the movement. If there was a long march to be undertaken, it was critical to share feelings and knowledge among occupiers themselves and with people at large. The first assemblies were very emotional: people were able to freely express themselves, receive attention and feel respected. I personally witnessed an old woman calling home from a bench near the assembly of Catalunya Square in Barcelona, reporting, almost in tears, that she had actually spoken in the meeting and that they had listened to her. She added: "never before in my life, this was the first time I spoke in public." Just saying loudly and collectively what everybody had been keeping inside for years was a liberating gesture that made the movement more expressive than instrumental in the short term. Since we know that emotions are the drivers of collective action, this could in fact be a key for future social change, a major issue that I will discuss below.

For the movement to go further in non-institutional action, engaging fully in civil disobedience, it had to dare to deal with the possible consequences of confrontation: the possibility of violence. By occupying public space, protesters exposed themselves to police repression. There were several violent police actions in different cities. A particularly vicious one took place in Barcelona on May 27. A combined operation between the Catalan government police (under orders from councillor Felip Puig, from the nationalist party) and the Municipality police (under orders of Socialist councilwoman Assumpta Escarp) attacked in the early morning the camp of Plaza Catalunya with the pretext of cleaning the square. Occupiers sat peacefully and refused to leave. They were clubbed repeatedly for six hours, with the result of 147 injured, scores of them seriously. The scene, with people being bloodied mercilessly without opposing resistance, was streamed live on the Internet and broadcast on TV, inducing massive, renewed indignation. In the afternoon, over 20,000 people came in solidarity and reoccupied the square while the police withdrew. Feeling strong with such a display of support, some in the Barcelona movement decided to step up the offensive by blocking the entrance to the Catalan parliament on June 11, the day the MPs would meet to vote on the budget cuts they had prepared. Several hundred demonstrators tried to block the entrance and they insulted, pushed, and threw paint on some of the parliamentarians. The police had infiltrated the demonstrators, disguised as protesters, and some observers considered this a provocation. A violent police repression ensued, ending with people injured, arrested and later charged and brought to trial. These incidents were distorted and widely reported in the media, portraying the movement as radical and violent. Many thought this was the end of the movement. In fact, these demeaning tactics backfired. A few days later, on June 19, the movement called for a demonstration in protest of police violence and in support of its demands, which attracted 200,000 people in the streets of Barcelona. The movement survived the acid test of its popularity. Yet, a debate surged within the movement about the role of self-defence, including physical defence, as a form of action. After all, some argued, violence is in the system: it is in systematic police brutality against the youth; it is in the torture that, according to some judicial sentences, the police practices occasionally; it is in the refusal of decent jobs and affordable housing for the youth; and it is in the unresponsiveness of government and parliamentarians to citizens' serious grievances. And yet, it was reaffirmed as an axiom of the movement that non-violence was essential. First, because violence, amplified in the media, even when not provoked by the protesters, would alienate the support of the population. But more fundamentally, opposing violence, under all its forms, and regardless of the origin, is a basic principle of the new culture of peace and democracy that the movement wants to propagate. Thus, civil disobedience is appropriate, including some daring forms such as blocking buildings by sitting in entranceways, or chaining bodies to gates. But it is never okay to engage in active violence or even respond to violent attacks from the police. The question of violence was debated in the assemblies, and received always the same answer from the large majority of the movement. To engage in violence, even if justified, contradicts the very essence of what the movement is about, and goes back to the old tactics of revolutionary actions that gave up ethical integrity for the sake of expressing rage, becoming in the process the same evil as the one they were opposing.[7] The *Indignadas* was and is a peaceful movement whose courage allowed for the de-legitimization of violent repression, thus achieving a first and major victory in the citizens' hearts.

## A POLITICAL MOVEMENT AGAINST THE POLITICAL SYSTEM

If we were to identify a unifying goal of the movement, it is the transformation of the political democratic process. Many different versions of democracy, and how to achieve it, were envisioned. One of the most popular themes was the reform of the electoral law, to make it proportional, and to make feasible an adequate representation of political minorities. But there were also proposals for mandatory referendums, for consultation and participation in decision-making both locally and over the Internet. Control of corruption, term limits for elected officials, salary caps, privilege elimination (including the lifting of judicial immunity for MPs) and a flurry of measures to clean up and open up the political system were debated and proposed in assemblies and commissions. The notion was that without truly democratic political institutions, any progressive policies or decisions adopted would not be implemented, as politicians would not be responsible to their citizens, and would continue to serve the powers that be. Thus, this was a political movement, but a non-partisan political movement, with no affiliation with or sympathy for any party. It was ideologically and politically plural, even if in its ranks there were individuals of many ideologies, as well as a majority of young people with little prior political experience and a total distrust of organized politics. However, if the movement was political, its intent was not to work through the institutional system, since the large majority considered the institutional rules of representation to have been manipulated. Thus, even if some reforms were proposed, it was more of a pedagogic exercise to connect with the population at large than a real hope of changing the political system. Creating a party, or parties, to express the aspirations of the movement was never considered. Yes, other politics would be possible, but not yet, and not through the channels established by those who wanted to limit within narrow boundaries the process of democratic representation.

Political parties did not know how to deal with the movement. In practice they were hostile and used police repression, with varying degrees of violence, against occupation of public space. They were particularly incensed by the attempts to block the parliament, going even so far as to denounce these actions as a fascist attack on democracy. At the same time, particularly for the Socialists and for the United Left (ex-Communists), the massive mobilizations appeared to be a chance to re-supply their meager contingents, since the young generation had given up any hope of being represented by the traditional parties. The Socialists, the government party at the onset of the movement, declared somewhat ambiguous verbal support during

the electoral campaign for some of the demands of the movement, but did not follow up after its crushing defeat in the
elections of November 2011. The conservative party, Partido
Popular, after a cautious attitude during the electoral period
so as not to alienate any constituency, insulted the *indignadas*
once it came into power, labeling them as "a mixture of radical revolutionaries, violent anarchists and naïve followers."
The United Left did express some sympathy and attracted
votes as a result of this benevolent attitude. It appeared
purely tactical to most in the movement, since they knew
there was a deep distrust in the Communist tradition against
any movement without leaders or program, a libertarian
brand that was historically at odds with the vanguard role of
the party. In sum, there was almost total exteriority between
the movement and the political system, both organizationally
and ideologically.

However, even if the movement did not care at all about
the electoral process (other than intervening in the debates to
raise consciousness among citizens), and dismissed the election results as irrelevant for the future of democracy, it did
appear to have had an impact on the elections. There were
two elections in Spain in 2011: municipal elections on May
22 – precisely the elections that were used by the nascent
movement to trigger its critique of democracy – and parliamentary elections on November 20. There are few rigorous
studies on the electoral impact of the movement at the time
of this writing. However, there are a number of observa-
tions that are relevant for our analysis. The study of Jimenez
Sanchez (2011) on the municipal elections shows that there
was the largest increase of blank and nullified votes since
1987, with an increase of 37 percent and 48 percent respec-
tively from the prior municipal election in 2007. There
was also an increase in the vote for the United Left. These
trends were correlated with the cities where the movement

had the strongest presence. Conservatives, Moderate Catalan nationalists and Basque pro-independence candidates also increased their votes. The combined impact of these votes negatively affected the Socialist Party, which lost 19 percent of its votes in 2007, suffering the most serious defeat in municipal elections of its history, losing in particular the municipality of Barcelona that it had governed for three decades.

The parliamentary elections of November 20 were a resounding victory for the Partido Popular (PP), which obtained an absolute majority in terms of seats in the parliament. This was considered by the conservatives, as well as their supporting media, as a rejection of the values of the movement by the silent majority of voters. In fact, a closer look at the election results tells a different story (Molinas 2011). The key factor in the election was the collapse of the Socialist Party, which lost 4,300,000 votes compared to the prior election in 2008, while the Partido Popular won only 560,000 more votes than in 2008. The remaining votes went to minor parties that, with one exception, increased their votes substantially. Indeed, with the number of votes it obtained in 2011, the Partido Popular would have lost the election in 2004 and in 2008. It was the loss of the Socialists, not the victory of the conservatives, that gave the PP control of the parliament because of the distorted electoral law in favor of majority vote getters. Thus, although this analysis has to be confirmed with future studies, it seems that the main impact of the movement in the political system was to inflict major, lasting damage to the Socialist PSOE, the party that, in most elections, had dominated Spanish politics since 1982. This was not a deliberate strategy on the part of the movement. It was the consequence of a spontaneous reaction of withdrawal from the young electorate that made possible the Socialist victory in 2004, in the wake of the

movement against the Iraq war, and against the manipulation of information on terrorist attacks by the Conservative
Prime Minister Aznar (Castells 2009: 349–61). The conservative vote was not affected by the movement because of
the fidelity of conservative voters to their party, and their
general ideological distrust of popular protests. Indeed, parties such as the Socialists, which have based their historical
legitimacy around claims of representing workers and civil
society rather than the business and social elites, are dependent on their electoral base believing that they can still count
on them. Since it became clear, through the protest of the
movement, that the Socialist government was more interested in bailing out banks and following Merkel's instructions
than helping the youth and preserving the welfare state,
political disaffection against the system concentrated on the
Socialists. They lost most of the institutional power they
held around the country, and most observers believe that it
will take a long time, if ever, for them to recover from this
crushing defeat. The United Left (ex-Communists) consid-
erably improved their electoral results, more than tripling
their seats. However, this impressive display of Communist
resilience actually translated into 11 seats in a parliament of
350. Indeed, what the elections show is that the new politics,
present in the movement, and the old politics, present in the
institutions, are disconnected in the minds of citizens who
will ultimately have to decide if they dare to reconcile their
feelings with their vote.

## A RHIZOMATIC REVOLUTION[8]

After months of intense activity, of mobilizing hundreds of
thousands in the streets, of camping by the thousands, of
networking around the world with similar movements, the
measurable impact of the *Indignadas* in Spain appeared to be

scant: few of their proposals have become policy, their main political impact was to contribute to the quasi-destruction of the Socialist Party, and their dreams remained dreams.

A number of actions opposing evictions or denouncing institutional abuses found sympathy in the public opinion, but were not able to change the greed of landlords, the cold determination of lenders to execute their contracts, or the bureaucratic application of law and order by the authorities. Yes, there were, and there are, hundreds of autonomous assemblies in cities and neighborhoods around the country that meet with variable periodicity. There is relentless buzz on the Internet – debates, ideas, projects – but no coordination between the different voices of the movement. But a certain uneasiness became pervasive among the most active components of the movement.

On December 19, 2011, the Commission of the international extension of the Acampada Sol in Madrid made a symbolic decision: they declared themselves "on strike" from their activity and in a situation of "indefinite active reflexion." The reason:

> The 15-M is losing participation, we see it in the demonstrations, in assemblies, in the neighborhoods, in activities, in the Internet. . . . This is the time to stop and ask ourselves some deep questions . . . Have we forgotten to listen to each other? Are we reproducing the forms of old activism that have been shown to be useless because they exclude so many people? . . . The success of the movement depends of being again the 99% . . . We live in a unique historical moment when we can change the world, and we cannot miss it . . . We hope to be able to get out of our assemblies, to join each other again, without the constraints of our commissions and working groups, to breathe fresh air again and build a common path. A path that could allow us to recover the

force we had and that shook up those above (<http://www.
actasmadrid.tomalaplaza.net/?p=2518, my translation>).

This was a clear manifestation of the self-reflexive character of
a movement that was reinventing politics and would not yield
to the temptation of becoming another political force while
refusing to accept the marginality of a critical voice without
influence in society at large. The question for many was: what
is next? Proposals started to circulate, one of them targeting
May 12, 2012 as a day for a coordinated global action to rekindle the struggle against an unjust social order. But there was a
prior question to be considered: what has this movement, the
largest autonomous mobilization in Spain in many years, been
able to accomplish? The most direct answer is that the true
transformation was taking place in people's minds. If people
think otherwise, if they share their indignation and harbor
hope for change, society will ultimately change according to
their wishes. But how do we know that such a cultural change is
actually happening? A very rough approximation can be derived
from opinion polls gauging the Spanish population's attitude
regarding the movement (*Zoom Politico* 2011; Metroscopia several surveys 2011; Simple Lógica 2011). Since the first survey
in May 2011 to the latest at the time of this writing, conducted
in November 2011 and accessed on January 18, 2012, consis-
tently about three quarters of Spaniards were in sympathy with
the movement and shared its main ideas concerning the critique of the political system, the responsibility of the banks in
the crisis, and a number of other themes. Seventy-five percent
considered the movement a source of regeneration of democracy. However, 53.2 percent of respondents did not think that
the movement had helped to change the situation: the crisis
continued, and nothing changed in politics as usual (<http://
www.simplelogica.com/iop/iop11002.asp>). Indeed, this was a
fair assessment of the situation.

Thus, the movement clearly voices the feeling and opinion of people at large. It is not a marginal protest, and refuses
to be enclosed in a radical, ideological ghetto. Its ideas diffuse and are accepted by most people because they connect
with the movement's frustration. But the ways to link these
feelings with action, leading to material change in people's
lives and social institutions, are still to be explored. Because
this is exactly what new politics is. This sincere search undertaken by most in the movement is still a work in progress.

However, there is also a meaningful debate in some of
the movement's circles. This is the critique of what many
call a "productivist vision of social action." If nothing concrete is accomplished, there is failure. They argue this is the
reproduction of the capitalist logic in the evaluation of the
movement. By internalizing the productivity imperative, they
actually engage in a self-defeating perspective in relation to
the original goals of deep social transformation. Because if
a precise outcome has to be obtained, then there is no way
out of the need for a program, a strategy, an organization
and an action plan going from A to B. These are all of the
things that the *indignadas* have refused because they know
by experience or they feel by intuition where they lead: to a
new form of delegated democracy and to surrendering the
meaning of life to economic rationality. So, a serene feeling
of patience settled in many activists. Let us rebuild ourselves,
they said, from the inside out, not waiting for the world to
change to find the joy of living in our daily practice. It is
winter now, and spring will come. Spring is the season of life
and revolution. We will be there. There will be moments:
moments of crisis, moments of struggle, moments of sorrow,
moments of heroism, and exhilarating moments when new
avenues open up and millions join out of their own desire,
not because they have alienated their freedom to whatever
flag was raised on their behalf. For a deep, self-reflexive cur-

rent in the movement, what matters is the process, more than the product. In fact, the process is the product. Not that the ultimate product (a new society) is irrelevant. But this new society will result from the process, not from a pre-conceived blueprint of what the product should be. This is the true revolutionary transformation: the material production of social change not from programmatic goals but from the networked experiences of the actors in the movement. This is why inefficient assemblies are important, because these are the learning curves of new democracy. This is why commissions exist and die depending not on their effectiveness but on the commitment of people contributing their time and ideas. This is why non-violence is a fundamental practice, because a non-violent world cannot be created out of violence, let alone revolutionary violence. Because they think this non-productivist logic in the movement is the most important mental transformation, they accept the slowness of the process, and they place themselves in the long haul, because slowness is a virtue: it allows for self-reflection, makes it possible to correct mistakes, and provides space and time to enjoy the process of changing the world as a prelude to celebrating the new world in the making. "We are slow because we go far" was one of the most popular banners in the movement. In this long journey, the tempos alternate: sometimes accelerating, and then calming down in other moments. But the process never stops, even if it remains unseen for a while. There are roots of the new life spreading everywhere, with no central plan, but moving and networking, keeping the energy flowing, waiting for spring. Because these nodes are always connected. There are nodes of Internet networks, locally and globally, and there are personal networks, vibrating with the pulse of a new kind of revolution whose most revolutionary act is the invention of itself.

NOTES

1  There is some debate within the Spanish movement about its labeling. Most people in the movement simply talk about "the movement." The most frequent name used in the movement is the "15-M," a neutral term simply designating the date of the first large demonstration that ushered in the protest throughout Spain on May 15, 2011. I have retained the name of *"Indignadas"* because this is the term most often used in Spain and around the world among people at large to designate the Spanish movement, after the initial name circulating on the Internet – #spanishrevolution – ceased to be used. *Indignadas* was largely used by the media because it is a catchy term. Some activists do not like it because it refers only to indignation, and not to the positive, propositional dimension of the movement, but this double character is clear in the text of my analysis. In my observation, most people sympathizing with the movement in Spain would refer to the *"indignados,"* because this term echoed their own feelings. Finally, I have used the name *Indignados/as* systematically in feminine to follow the cultural habit of the movement, to reverse the traditional male-dominated connotation of language.

2  The study presented in this chapter is largely based on fieldwork research, participant observation, and interviewing by our research team on alternative cultures at the Open University of Catalonia, Barcelona, a team formed by Amalia Cardenas, Joana Conill, and myself. Amalia and Joana did most of the fieldwork and interviewing. We also followed the movement through reports and accounts on the Internet. Two interviews have been essential for my understanding of the movement, conducted by Amalia Cardenas and Joana Conill in February 2012. One with

Javier Toret, and another with Arnau Monterde, both self-reflexive activists in the movement, who played a significant role in the origins of *Democracia Real Ya*. My own prior conversations with Javier and Arnau were also key sources of ideas and analysis. Other sources of information, both in print and on the web, are cited in the references, without being attributed to any specific statement, as they have been mixed in my narrative.

3  On the origins of *Democracia Real Ya*, and the subsequent development of the movement in Barcelona, I have relied on the excellent analysis by Monterde (2010–11).

4  Interview and translation by Amalia Cardenas, Barcelona, February 2012.

5  The pamphlet by Hessel (2010) was translated in Spanish and widely read by many in Spain in the months prior to the movement. It has sold over three million copies worldwide. Most activists do not acknowledge his direct influence, attributing it to the media obsession to find sources of inspiration from outside the movement itself. However, I found in most cases a deep respect and appreciation for the stern denunciation of the system by someone of a much older generation, even if its reference to the values of the French Resistance in War World II did not really connect with the movement. In fact, Hessel called for the necessity of leadership if the movement were to succeed, in clear dissonance with the philosophy of the movement. Yet, there was a tender affection for this dignified man appealing to the defence of principles that were being sullied by European governments. His main contribution was probably to find a word that could resonate.

6  Javier Toret, Barcelona, February 2012, interview and translation by Amalia Cardenas.

7  In 2012, a number of demonstrations, particularly in Barcelona, were followed by violent confrontations

between the police and small groups of youth burning garbage containers and breaking windows of banks and shops. Although the origin of these actions remains unclear, there is certainly a propensity among some youth, outraged by their living conditions, without any positive response to their claims, to engage in violence. These violent actions are magnified by the media and used by the authorities to de-legitimize the movement, going as far as denouncing the rise of urban guerrillas, an obvious exaggeration if we consider the international experience of what urban guerrillas are. Yet, while this particular movement is overwhelmingly non-violent, there is an ambiguity among actors of social change throughout history concerning the question of violence, including Karl Marx: "Force is the midwife of every society which is pregnant with a new one. It is itself an economic power." *Capital*, cited in Bruce Lawrence and Aisha Karim (eds.) (2007) *On Violence: A Reader*. Duke University Press, Durham, NC, p. 17. This volume is an excellent compendium of debates about violence in the processes of social change.

8 The concept of rhizomatic revolution was suggested to me by Isidora Chacon. According to Wikipedia, a rhizome is "a characteristically horizontal stem of a plant that is usually found underground, often sending out roots and shoots from its nodes ... If a rhizome is separated into pieces, each piece may be able to give rise to a new plant."

## REFERENCES

Bennasar, S. (2011) *La primavera dels indign@ts*. Meteora, Barcelona.

Calvo, K., Gomez-Pastrana, T., and Mena, L. (2011) Movimiento 15M: quienes son y que reivindican? *Zoom*

*Politico*, 4/11: 4–17. Laboratorio de Alternativas: Salamanca.

Castells, M. (2009) *Communication Power*. Oxford University Press, Oxford.

The Cocktail Analysis. (2011) *Movimiento #15M/Democracia Real Ya: Representatividad, movilizacion y canales de informacion*. Madrid: The Cocktail Analysis (www.tcanalysis.com, accessed January 18, 2012).

Conill, J., Cardenas, A., Castells, M., and Servon, L. (2012a) Another life is possible: the rise of alternative economic cultures. In Castells, M., Caraca, J., and Cardoso, G. (eds.) *Aftermath. The Cultures of the Economic Crisis*. Oxford University Press, Oxford.

Conill, J., Cardenas, A., Castells, M., Servon, L., and Hlebik, S. (2012b) *Otra vida es posible: practicas economicas alternativas en la crisis*. Ediciones UOC Press, Barcelona.

Fernandez-Planells, A. and Figueras, M. (2012) *Plaza en red. Características del seguimiento informativo de la @acampadaBCN por parte de los/las jóvenes participantes en Plaza Cataluña*. (Informe). Available at: <http://hdl.handle.net/10230/16284>.

Hessel, S. (2010) *Indignez-vous!* Indigene, Montpellier.

Jimenez Sanchez, M. (2011) Influyo el 15M en las elecciones municipales? *Zoom Politico*, 4/11: 18-28. Laboratorio de Alternativas, Salamanca.

Lawrence, B. and Karim, A. (eds.) (2007) *On Violence: A Reader*. Duke University Press, Durham, NC.

Metroscopia. (2011) Opinion de los Espanoles ante el 15 M. June 22, 2011.

Molinas, C. (2011) La izquierda volatil sigue decidiendo pero . . . *El Pais*, November 22.

Monterde Mateo, A. (2010–11) *Movimients moleculars a la ciutat-xarxa, produccio de noves subjectivitats connectedes y emergencia dels "commons."* Un preludi del 15M. Barcelona: Universitat Oberta de Catalunya, Master Thesis del

Programa de Master en Societat de la Informacio i el Coneixement (unpublished).

Serrano, E. (2011) *El poder de las palabras*. Madrilonia.org (blog), June.

Simple Lógica. (2011) *Indices de opinión publica sobre el movimiento 15 M*, Madrid. Available at: <http://www.sim plelogica.com/iop/iop11002.asp> [Accessed January 18, 2012].

Taibo, C. (2011) *El 15-M en sesenta preguntas*. Los libros de la Catarata, Madrid.

Various Authors. (2011a) *Nosotros los Indignados*. Destino, Barcelona.

Various Authors. (2011b) *Las voces del 15-M*. Del Lince, Barcelona.

Various Authors. (2011c) *La rebelion de los indignados*. Popular, Madrid.

Velasco, P. (2011) *No nos representan. El Manifiesto de los Indignados en 25 propuestas*. Temas de Hoy, Madrid.


**Web resources**

*Evolution of the movement*

15October.net. (2011) October 29 #Robinhood global march. [Online] Available at: <http://15october.net/> [Accessed February 25, 2012].

AcampadaBcn. (2011) Documents. [Online] Available at:    <http://acampadabcn.wordpress.com/documents/> [Accessed February 28, 2012].

Acampadasol. (2011) Cómo fue #acampadasol, texto para difusión internacional. [Online] Available at: <http://mad rid.tomalaplaza.net/2011/07/16/como-fue-acampadasol-texto-para-difusion-internacional/> [Accessed February 25, 2012].

Antibanks. (2011) September 17th everywhere. [Online] Available at: <http://antibanks.takethesquare.net/2011/08/15/september-17th-everywhere/> [Accessed February 25, 2012].

Bcnhubmeeting. (2011) 15SHM statement. *Bcnhubmeeting*, [blog] September 18. Available at: <http://bcnhubmeeting.wordpress.com/> [Accessed February 25, 2012].

Blanco, J. L. (2011) Análisis estadístico del movimiento 15M: ¿Cuántos y quiénes se han manifestado?. *Ciencia explicada*, [blog] October 26. Available at: <http://www.ciencia-explicada.com/2011/10/analisis-estadistico-del-movimiento-15m.html> [Accessed January 18, 2012].

Bretos, D. (2011) Democracia Real Ya convoca una manifestación internacional para el 15 de octubre. *Nación Red*, [Online] May 30. Available at: <http://www.nacionred.com/sociedad-civil-digital/democracia-real-ya-convoca-una-manifestacion-internacional-para-el-15-de-octubre> [Accessed February 25, 2012].

Buentes, P. (2011) ¿Como se gestó el 15M? [Online] Available at: <http://storify.com/pablobuentes/que-es-y-como-se-gesto-el-movimiento-15m> [Accessed February 25, 2012].

Democracia Real Ya. (2011) Datos de participación oficiales de DRY. [Online] Available at: <http://www.facebook.com/notes/democracia-real-ya/datos-de-participaci%C3%B3n-oficiales-de-dry/139427826133836> [Accessed February 25, 2012].

De Soto, P. (2011) Los mapas del 15M al 15O. *Periodismo Humano*, [blog] October 15. Available at: <http://tomalapalabra.periodismohumano.com/2011/10/15/los-mapas-del-15m-al-15o/> [Accessed February 25, 2012].

Fernández-Savater, A. (2011) Apuntes de AcampadaSol. Publico.es *Fuera de lugar blog*, [blog] June 9. Available at: <http://blogs.publico.es/fueradelugar/531/apuntes-de-acampadasol-8> [Accessed February 25, 2012].

Galarraga, N. (2011) 951 ciudades en 82 países (por ahora) se suman a la protesta planetaria del 15-O. *El País*, [Online] October 14. Available at: <http://politica.elpais.com/politica/2011/10/13/actualidad/1318509855_468846.html> [Accessed February 25, 2012].

Kaosenlared. (2011) Inside 15M: 48 horas con l@s indignad@s. [video online] Available at: <http://www.portaloaca.com/videos/documentales-/3194-documental-inside-15m-48-horas-con-ls-indignads.html> [Accessed February 25, 2012].

Lenore, Victor. (2011) 15 datos que explican el 15M. Madrilonia.org, [blog] September 19. Available at <http://madrilonia.org/2011/07/15-datos-que-explican-el-15m/> [Accessed February 25, 2012].

Letón, H. and Sanz D. (2011) ¿Quién es quién en las protestas de la red?. *Diagonal Web*, [Online] May 4. Available at: <http://www.diagonalperiodico.net/Quien-es-quien-en-las-protestas-de.html> [Accessed February 25, 2012].

Noor, O. (2011) Espagne labs: Inventer la démocratie du futur. *Owni*, [Online] June 6. Available at: <http://owni.fr/2011/06/06/espagne-labs-inventer-la-democratie-du-futur/> [Accessed February 25, 2012].

Personal sources of Joana Conill (2011).

Saleh, S. (2011) El núcleo del 15-M acuerda irse el domingo. *El Pais*, [Online] June 8. Available at: <http://www.elpais.com/articulo/madrid/nucleo/15-M/acuerda/irse/domingo/elpepiespmad/20110608elpmad_1/Tes> [Accessed February 25, 2012].

Sánchez, J. (2011) El 15M rompe otro tópico y llena Madrid en verano. *Periodismo Humano*, [Online] July 25. Available at: <http://periodismohumano.com/sociedad/el-15m-rompe-otro-topico-y-llena-madrid-en-verano.html> [Accessed February 25, 2012].

Sandiumenge, L. (2011) La calle (y la red) es nuestra. La Vanguardia.com *Los guerros del teclado*, [blog] May 2. Available at: <http://blogs.lavanguardia.com/guerreros-del-teclado/2011/05/02/la-calle-y-la-red-es-nuestra/> [Accessed February 25, 2012].

Taylor, A. (2011) Occupy Wall Street Spreads beyond NYC. *The Atlantic*, [Online] October 7. Available at: <http://www.theatlantic.com/infocus/2011/10/occupy-wall-street-spreads-beyond-nyc/100165/> [Accessed February 25, 2012].

Versus Sistema. (2011) ¿Qué ha pasado con la Spanish Revolution?. *Versus Sistema*, [blog] September 23. Available at: <http://www.versussistema.com/2011/09/%C2%BFque-ha-pasado-con-la-spanish-revolution/> [Accessed February 25, 2012].

Wikipedia. (2011) Protestas en España de 2011–2012. Available at: http://es.wikipedia.org/wiki/15M [Accessed February 28, 2012].

## On violence

Hotmatube. (2011) ¿Quiénes son los violentos?. [video online] Available at: <http://www.youtube.com/watch?v=pbhuEVgU9mI&feature=player_embedded> [Accessed February 25, 2012].

Teclista. (2011) Quince de mayo no tuvimos miedo. [video online] Available at: <http://vimeo.com/29544229> [Accessed February 25, 2012].

## On Internet in the camps

*Map of interactions*

BifiUnizar. (2011) Interacciones entre usuarios 15m. [video online] Available at: <http://15m.bifi.es/index.php> [Accessed February 25, 2012].

*Twitter in the occupied squares*

15October.net, 2011. Reports. [Online] Available at: <http://map.15october.net/> [Accessed February 25, 2012].

Algo grande. (2011) Clasificación de las acampadas por el volumen de su conversación. *Algo grande*, [blog] May 23. Available at: <http://algogrande.org/seccion/analisis/> [Accessed February 25, 2012].

Comscore. (2011) El tiempo en la Red crece en España un 17% en mayo, influido por los acontecimientos nacionales e internacionales. [Press release] July 7, 2011. Available at: <http://www.comscore.com/esl/Press_Events/Press_Releases/2011/7/comScore_Releases_Overview_of_European_Internet_Usage_for_May_2011> [Accessed February 25, 2012].

Congosto, M. L. (2011) Evolución de la propagación del 15M en la plaza de Twitter. *Barri blog*, [blog] May 21. Available at: <http://www.barriblog.com/index.php/2011/05/21/evolucion-de-la-propagacion-del-15m-en-la-plaza-de-twitter/> [Accessed February 25, 2012].

**On media and the movement**

Ibarrondo, J. (2011a) Medios de comunicación y 15-M: un avispero fuera de control. *Diagonal Web*, [Online] July 14. Available at: <http://www.diagonalperiodico.net/Medios-de-comunicacion-y-15-M-un.html> [Accessed February 25, 2012].

Ibarrondo, J. (2011b) Medios de comunicación y 15M. *Análisis Madrid 15M*, [blog] July 18. Available at: <http://analisismadrid.wordpress.com/2011/07/18/medios-de-comunicacion-y-15m-juan-ibarrondo/> [Accessed February 25, 2012].

Público.es. (2011) Los manifestantes de "Occupy Wall Street" son como los nazis. Público.es, [Online]

October 5. Available at: <http://www.publico.es/inter
nacional/399995/los-manifestantes-de-occupy-wall-stre
et-son-como-los-nazis> [Accessed February 25, 2012].

## On leadership

Balblogger, R. (2011) Cómo se hace una asamblea en Wall
Street. *Tuamiguelturrayyoafiladelfia*, [blog] October 12.
Available at: <http://tuamiguelturrayyoafiladelfia.blogspot.
com/2011/10/como-se-hace-una-asamblea-en-wall.html>
[Accessed February 25, 2012].

## General sources

15m.cc. (2011) Project. [Online] Available at: <http://
www.15m.cc/> [Accessed February 25, 2012]. (Set of
documents and interviews available on the web with free
licenses. It is a documentary project in the making.)
Centro de documentación Ciudadana. (2011) Available at:
<http://www.archive.org/details/centrodedocumentaci
onciudadana> [Accessed February 25, 2012].

## Websites of the movement

Acampadabcn. (2011a) [Online] Available at: <http://acam
padabcn.wordpress.com/> [Accessed February 25, 2012].
Acampadabcn. (2011b) Actes de l'Assemblea. [Online]
Available at: <http://acampadabcn.wordpress.com/docu
ments/actes-de-lassemblea-general/> [Accessed February
25, 2012].
#Acampadasol. (2011) Available at: <http://madrid.tomal
aplaza.net/> [Accessed February 25, 2012].
Acampadatrs. (2011a) Available at: <http://acampadatrs.net/>
[Accessed February 25, 2012].

Acampadatrs.(2011b)Acampadatrs–Pads.[Online]Availableat: <http://agora.acampadatrs.net/es/node/3/content/pads> [Accessed February 25, 2012].

Acampadatrs. (2011c) Agora. Available at: <http://agora. acampadatrs.net/> [Accessed February 25, 2012].

Análisis Madrid. (2011) Available at: <http://analisismadrid. wordpress.com/> [Accessed February 25, 2012].

Democracia Real Ya. (2011) Available at: <http://www. Democracia Real Ya.es/> [Accessed February 25, 2012].

Marchapopularindignada. (2011) Available at: <http:// marchapopularindignada.wordpress.com/>      [Accessed February 25, 2012].

N-1. (2011) Available at: <https://n-1.cc/> [Accessed February 25, 2012]. This is a critical source; it reports on internal documents and interactions in the movement not available anywhere else.

Occupy Wall Street. (2011) Available at: <http://occupywallst. org/> [Accessed February 25, 2012].

Tomalaplaza.net. (2011a) Actas de #acampandasol. Available at: <http://actasmadrid.tomalaplaza.net/> [Accessed February 25, 2012].

Tomalaplaza.net. (2011b) Grupo Pensamiento. Available at:      <http://madrid.tomalaplaza.net/category/grupos-de-trabajo/pensamiento/> [Accessed February 25, 2012].

# OCCUPY WALL STREET:

## HARVESTING THE SALT OF

## THE EARTH

### THE OUTRAGE, THE THUNDER, THE SPARK

There was outrage in the air. At first, suddenly, the real estate market plunged. Hundreds of thousands lost their homes, and millions lost much of the value they had traded their lives for. Then, the financial system came to the brink of collapse, as a result of the speculation and greed of its managers. Who were bailed out. With taxpayers' money. They did not forget to collect their millionaire bonuses, rewarding their clumsy performance. Surviving financial companies cut off lending, thus closing down thousands of firms, shredding millions of jobs and sharply reducing pay. No one was held accountable. Both political parties prioritized the rescue of the financial system. Obama was overwhelmed by the depth of the crisis and quickly set aside most of his campaign promises – a campaign that had brought unprecedented hope for a young generation that had re-entered politics to revitalize American democracy. The hardest was the fall. People

*[handwritten marginal note:]* THEY / WERE / PRAISED

became discouraged and enraged. Some began to quantify
their rage. The share of US income of the top 1 percent of
Americans jumped from 9 percent in 1976 to 23.5 percent
in 2007. Cumulative productivity growth between 1998 and
2008 reached about 30 percent, but real wages increased
only by 2 percent during the decade. The financial industry
captured most of the productivity gains, as its share of profits increased from 10 percent in the 1980s to 40 percent in
2007, and the value of its shares increased from 6 percent to
23 percent in spite of employing only 5 percent of the labor
force. Indeed, the top 1 percent appropriated 58 percent of
the economic growth in this period. In the decade preceding
the crisis, hourly real wages increased by 2 percent while the
income of the richest 5 percent increased by 42 percent. The
pay of a CEO was 50 times higher than that of the average
worker in 1980, and 350 times more in 2010. These were
no longer abstract figures. There were faces, too: Madoff,
Wagoner, Nardelli, Pandit, Lewis, Sullivan. And they were
interspersed with politicians and government officials (Bush,
Paulsen, Summers, Bernanke, Geithner, and, yes, Obama)
who were rationalizing people's pain and arguing for the
need of saving finance to save people's lives. Moreover, the
Republican Party went on a vengeful offensive to bring
down a popular president who came to power advocating
for an active role of government in improving the welfare of
society. The electoral success of this suicidal strategy allowed
the Republican dominated Congress to block most reform
initiatives, thus aggravating the crisis and increasing its social
costs. The first expression of popular outrage was the rise of
the Tea Party, a mixture of populism and libertarianism that
offered a channel of mobilization to a variety of indignant
opposition to government in general and to Obama in particular. Yet, when it became clear that it was bankrolled by
Koch Industries, among other corporations, and captured by

the right of the Republican Party as stormtroopers to be sacrificed in the final stage of the electoral process, it lost appeal for many of its participants. Diehard Tea Partiers became militants of a manipulated cause: to undo government, so to free the hands of corporate business. A sense of despair set throughout the land. Then, there was thunder.

It came from Tahrir Square; an irony of history considering that for most Americans, only oil and Israel are of any relevance in the Middle East. Yet, images and sounds of people's determination to bring down dictatorships against all odds, at whatever cost, rekindled faith in people's power, at least in some activists' quarters. The echo of the Arab revolts was amplified by the news coming from Europe, and particularly from Spain, proposing novel forms of mobilization and organization, based on the practice of direct democracy as a way to further the demand for real democracy. In a world connected live by the Internet, concerned citizens became immediately aware of struggles and projects they could identify with.

[handwritten margin notes: MOBILIZ. + ORGANI. ↓ PRACTICE OF DIRECT DEMOCRACY ↓ DEMAND FOR REAL DEMOCRACY ↓ INTERNET]

The Obama campaign had left an imprint on thousands who had believed in the possibility of real change, and had enacted a new form of political mobilization in which the Internet networks became crucial, as far as they connected people meeting face-to-face in neighborhoods and living rooms, to form an insurgent political movement. I documented the power of this truly new form of politics, inspired by hope and powered by the Internet, in my book *Communication Power* (2009).[1]

Many former Obamists, together with thousands of people who have been at the forefront of struggles against social injustice for quite some time, including the public sector unions that mobilized in and around the Wisconsin campaign for bargaining rights, were receptive of the buzz surrounding the #spanishrevolution and of the Greek demonstrations against the crisis. Some of them traveled to Europe. They saw the camps, participated in the General Assemblies and experienced a new form of deliberation and decision-making, actually connecting with a historical tradition of assembly-led movements on both sides of the Atlantic. They participated in meetings in which the call for a global demonstration on October 15, 2011, under the slogan "United for Global Change," was discussed and decided. In this way, the global networks of hope extended decisively to the United States in the summer of 2011. Then came the spark.

On July 13, 2011, Adbusters, a Vancouver-based journal of cultural critique, posted the following call on its blog:

> #occupywallstreet
> Are you ready for a Tahrir moment? On September 17th, flood into lower Manhattan, set up tents, kitchens, peaceful barricades and occupy Wall Street.

And they went on to elaborate:

> A worldwide shift in revolutionary tactics is underway right now that bodes well for the future. [There is a] spirit of this fresh tactic, a fusion of Tahrir with the acampadas of Spain.
>
> The beauty of this new formula ... is its pragmatic simplicity: we talk to each other in various physical gatherings and virtual people's assemblies. We zero in on what our one demand will be, a demand that awakens the imagination and, if achieved, would propel us toward the radical democracy of the future ... and then we go out and seize a square of singular symbolic significance and put our asses on the line to make it happen. The time has come to deploy this emerging stratagem against the greatest corrupter of our democracy: Wall Street, the financial Gomorrah of America.
>
> On September 17, we want to see 20,000 people flood

into lower Manhattan, set up tents, kitchens, peaceful barricades and occupy Wall Street for a few months. Once there,
we shall incessantly repeat one simple demand in a plural-
ity of voices ... Following this model, what is our equally
uncomplicated demand? ... [It is the one] that gets at the
core of why the American political establishment is currently unworthy of being called a democracy: we demand
that Barack Obama ordain a Presidential Commission
tasked with ending the influence money has over our representatives in Washington. It's time for DEMOCRACY
NOT CORPORATOCRACY, we're doomed without it.

This demand seems to capture the current national
mood because cleaning up corruption in Washington is
something all Americans, right and left, yearn for and can
stand behind ... This could be the beginning of a whole
new social dynamic in America, a step beyond the Tea
Party movement, where, instead of being caught helpless
by the current power structure, we the people start get-
ting what we want whether it be the dismantling of half the
1,000 military bases America has around the world to the
reinstatement of the Glass-Steagall Act or a three strikes
and you're out law for corporate criminals. Beginning from
one simple demand – a presidential commission to separate money from politics – we start setting the agenda for
a new America. Post a comment and help each other zero
in on what our one demand will be. And then let's screw up
our courage, pack our tents and head to Wall Street with a
vengeance September 17. **For the wild, Culture Jammers
HQ.**

The date selected was symbolic: September 17 is the anniversary of the signing of the American Constitution, although
few people are aware of it. And so, the initial call to occupy
was aimed at restoring democracy by making the political

system independent from the power of money. To be sure, there were other networks and groups involved in the origins of the Occupy movement, and some in the movement have resented the attribution of the first call to Adbusters. For instance, AmpedStatus, a network of activists organized around a website, had been posting for quite a while analysis and information on the financial destruction of the US economy. On February 15, 2010, David DeGraw posted the first of a six-part series on the financial crisis in America whose first sentence read "It's time for 99% of Americans to mobilize and aggressively move on common sense political reforms."[2] The AmpedStatus website came under repeated cyber attacks by mysterious aggressors. Anonymous came to the rescue and the website, and the network behind it, survived and started to build a 99% movement, planning for an "Empire State Rebellion" and calling for the occupation of Wall Street. A subgroup within Anonymous joined forces with AmpedStatus and they created an A99 platform presented in AmpedStatus's social network. On March 23, 2011, Anonymous called for a Day of Rage, in the wake of similar calls in the Arab world. The A99 coalition also called, unsuccessfully, to occupy on June 14 Liberty Park (later named Zuccotti Park), two blocks from Wall Street. They came together with a group of New York activists protesting against budget cuts who had set up a camp known as Bloombergville. These activists' networks evolved to form the New York City General Assembly, building the protest on grassroots mobilization and community-based organizing. It is in this context of rampant activism in New York that Adbusters issued its call to occupy on September 17. All of the pre-existing networks did not see any problem in joining the call and preparing jointly the occupation. A paternity test would have been contradictory to the spirit of a collaborative, decentralized movement, and so everybody called for people to "rebel against the system of economic tyranny in a non-violent manner," and to come to Wall Street on September 17. About 1,000 people came, demonstrated in Wall Street and occupied Zuccotti Park. The spark had lit a fire.

## THE PRAIRIE ON FIRE

The September 17 demonstration on Wall Street, with the subsequent occupation of Zuccotti Park, was followed by several demonstrations in New York, in spite of the police making hundreds of arrests under several pretexts. The more the police resorted to repression, the more the images posted on YouTube of these actions mobilized protesters. Solidarity with the occupiers came from many quarters. Anonymous revealed the name of an NYPD police officer who maced, without any reason, young women marching in a demonstration. On September 27, 2,000 people gathered in the General Assembly at the occupied camp, with New York Councilman Charles Barron, intellectuals such as Cornel West and others addressing the assembly, as Michael Moore had done two days earlier. The New York Local of the Transport Workers Union of America voted to support the movement and to join in the demonstrations. The AFL-CIO also declared its support and called upon its membership to demonstrate. On October 1, 5,000 people took over the Brooklyn Bridge and the police set up a trap on the bridge and proceeded to arrest over 700. In response, on October 5, following a call from Occupy Wall Street together with the labor unions, 15,000 people demonstrated from Foley Square, in Lower Manhattan, to Zuccotti Park. The occupation was consolidated. With images and news spreading over the Internet, occupations started spontaneously in many other cities during the first few days of October: Chicago, Boston, Washington DC, San Francisco, Oakland,

Los Angeles, Atlanta, Fort Lauderdale, Tampa, Houston, Austin, Philadelphia, New Orleans, Cleveland, Las Vegas, Jersey City, Hartford, Salt Lake City, Cincinnati, Seattle, and even outside the White House, as well as countless neighborhoods and small towns around the country. Maps 1 and 2 show the *speed* and the *spread* of the Occupy movement. Moreover, the data represented in the maps are incomplete, as there is no reliable, unified database on the occupation, although the activists who are building the directory section of the website occupy.net are making good progress toward this goal. However, it is safe to estimate that the number of demonstrations throughout the United States was over 600. For instance, according to a study conducted by a team directed by Christopher Chase-Dunn at the University of California Riverside, out of 482 towns in California, 143 had Occupy groups on Facebook, usually indicating the existence of an occupied space.[3] Not all occupy camps were permanent; many of them were daily gatherings in assemblies and working groups. Thus, Occupy Youngstown, Ohio would hold regular weekly meetings to discuss issues, post on their Facebook page, and then go home for the night. In other words, there was considerable diversity in the forms of protest and in the shape of the occupations. But what is clear is the fast spread of the movement throughout the entire geography of the country: Mosier, Oregon, population 430, may have been the smallest town to have an occupation, and every state had at least one occupied site – even North Dakota, the last one to start a camp.

The rapid propagation of the Occupy fire across the American prairie is full of meaning. It shows the depth and spontaneity of the protest, rooted in the outrage felt by the majority of the population across the country and in society at large. It also shows the seizing of the opportunity by many to voice their concerns and to discuss alternatives

COUNTERMAP

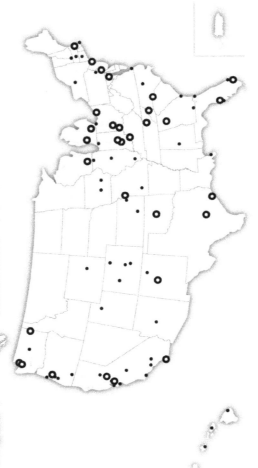

## Spread of Occupations in the United States, September 17–October 9, 2011

This map depicts the location of occupations that began by October 9, 2011. It demonstrates the rapid spread of the movement after the initial spark in New York City on September 17, 2011. Larger circles represent particularly active locations, as indicated by large occupations, demonstrations, arrests, and/or online activity. Although it is impossible to be as totally comprehensive, the map is intended to be as inclusive and as accurate as possible based on

existing information. It was compiled by cross-referencing data pulled from the Facebook API, news coverage, and lists produced by Chase-Dunn and Curran-Strange (2011). collectivedisorder.com, firedoglake.com, occupylist.org, occupywallstreetevents.com, and especially directory. occupy.net, which includes the most extensive list of cities. Collected and elaborated by Lana Swartz.

*Map 1: Spread of occupations in the United States, September 17–October 9, 2011*

COUNTERMAP

## Geography of the Occupy Movement in the United States

This map depicts the location of Occupy-related activity in over 1000 American cities and towns in all 50 states and Puerto Rico. It demonstrates the deep penetration of the movement throughout the country. Larger circles represent particularly active locations, as indicated by large occupations, demonstrations, arrests, and/or online activity. Although it is impossible to be totally comprehensive, the map is intended to be as inclusive and as accurate as

possible based on existing information. It was compiled by cross-referencing data pulled from the Facebook API, news coverage, and lists produced by Chase-Dunn and Curran-Strange (2011), collectivedisorder.com, firedoglake.com, occupylist.org, occupywallstreetevents.com, and especially directory.occupy.net, which includes the most extensive list of cities. Collected and elaborated by Lana Swartz.

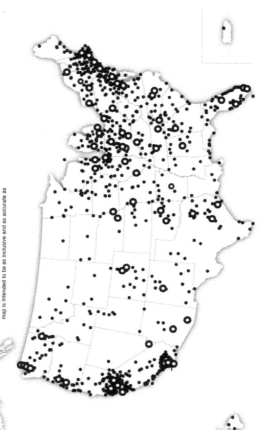

*Map 2: Geography of the Occupy movement in the United States*

in the midst of a generalized crisis of trust in the economy and in the polity. This was not a campus revolt or a cosmopolitan counter-culture. It was spoken with as many voices and accents as there are present in a highly diverse and multicultural society.

Who, then, were these occupiers? There was in fact a great deal of social and political diversity among those participating in the movement. There was also a wide variation depending on the level of involvement in the movement, from full-time presence in the camps to participating in the assemblies or engaging in demonstrations or actions of protest. At the time of this writing, the various data-gathering efforts in process are still not available. Yet, I have been able to use some preliminary results from what appears to be a reliable data source: the online survey coordinated by MIT's Sasha Costanza-Chock and the Occupy Research Network[4] of Occupy activists in the country. I have also compared his data with the findings of Baruch College's Hector Cordero-Guzman's non-representative sample of visitors to OccupyWallSt.org.[5] On the basis of these surveys, and personal observation from participants in the movement, it appears that the majority of those fully engaged in most camps were young professionals and students in the 20–40 age group, with a slightly higher percentage of women than men. About one half of them had a full-time job, with a significant number being unemployed, underemployed, temporarily employed or employed part-time. The income level of the majority seemed to be around the median income level of Americans. They were an educated group, with half of them holding a college degree, and many more having finished some college. Thus, as in similar movements in other countries, the Occupy participants appear to be relatively young, educated people whose professional expectations are limited in the current economy. They are white/Caucasian in their large majority, although there is a presence of minorities, particularly African Americans, who often organized their own caucuses within the movement. However, only about one fifth of the occupiers actually slept in the camps. The large majority participated in daily activities, and about three-quarters in street demonstrations. Thus, to apprehend the diversity of the movement, we must include many other stakeholders who were present in its activities, particularly middle-aged union members, as well as working-class people in their fifties, some unemployed and bearing the brunt of the recession on their lives. Numerous veterans were in the camps and at the forefront of the demonstrations. And, as the occupations lengthened, most sites became havens for homeless people who could find food, shelter, and protection. Yet, their proportion among the occupiers was limited, in spite of their high social visibility. There was often tension among occupiers about how to handle their presence, yet it was ideologically impossible to reproduce the same kind of prejudice toward the homeless that permeates the mainstream society.

The diversity within the occupiers was even greater in terms of their ideological and political preferences: anarchists were the most vocal, but Libertarians (some of them Republican) were present, as were some disappointed former Tea Party activists, and a few fringe leftists. But by and large the movement was made up of a large majority of democratic voters, as well as of politically independent-minded people who were in search of new forms of changing the world and/ or fending off the threat of the crisis on their lives.

Perhaps the most significant characteristic of the occupiers is that this movement did not come out of the blue, even if it was spontaneous and leaderless. Preliminary findings from the Occupy Research Network survey indicate that the vast majority of the active persons in the movement had participated in various social movements, and had been involved in non-governmental organizations and political campaigns. They had also been present in networks of activism on the Internet, posting videos and participating in animated political forums. By converging on Occupy Wall Street from multiple streams of resistance and alternative politics, they formed a wide river of protest and projects that flooded the plains, climbed the mountains and nested in the towns of the entire country.

The rapid geographical spread of the movement reflected its viral diffusion on the Internet. The movement was born on the Internet, diffused by the Internet, and maintained its presence on the Internet, as most occupations set up their own websites, as well as their specific groups and other social networks.

Yet, at the same time, the movement's material form of existence was the *occupation of public space*. A space where the protesters could come together and form a community beyond their differences. A space of conviviality. A space of debate, to move from contesting an unjust system to reconstructing society from the bottom up. In sum, a space of autonomy. Because only by being autonomous could they overcome multiple forms of ideological and political control and find, individually and collectively, new ways of life.

Thus, the Occupy movement built *a new form of space*, a mixture of space of places, in a given territory, and space of flows, on the Internet. One could not function without the other; it is this hybrid space that characterized the movement. Places made possible face-to-face interaction, sharing the experience, the danger and the difficulties as well as facing together the police and enduring together rain, cold, and the loss of comfort in their daily lives. But social networks on the Internet allowed the experience to be communicated and amplified, bringing the entire world into the movement, and creating a permanent forum of solidarity, debate, and strategic planning.

Occupied spaces also created *a new form of time*, which some in the camps characterized as a feeling of "forever." The routine of their daily lives was interrupted; a parenthesis was open with an undefined time horizon. Many thought that the occupation would last as long as the institutions remained unresponsive to their critiques and requests. Given the uncertainty of when and if the eviction would come, the occupations lived on a day-by-day basis, without deadlines, thus freeing themselves from time constraints, while rooting the occupation in everyday life experience. This made the timeless time of the occupation an experience that was exhausting and exhilarating at the same time because, as one occupier in Washington DC put it:

> We are tired, and get wet and cold. Sharing Porta-Potties, walking 13 blocks to the showers the CWA lets us use and brushing our teeth and spitting into a soggy paper coffee cup takes its toll ... But we show up [for General Assembly] and listen to everyone who has an opinion or proposal and eventually we do reach consensus ... As I sat there, watching the fully engaged occupiers, one more time I marveled. This is the way it is supposed to be. We've got a long way to go, but every so often I get to feel the chill running up and down my spine telling me that this is what hope looks like.[6]

This hope was born from the material verification that another life is possible in the makeshift community rising from the protest.

In the large occupations, such as New York, Los Angeles, or Oakland, daily life was organized with great care. Tents were set up, then toilets, kitchens, daycare centers, children's play spaces, a community garden, a people's library, an

Occupy University where lecturers were invited to address the occupiers, and media centers, sometimes powered by bicycles. Medical assistance provided by volunteer medical personnel was organized, legal teams were on hand, Wi-Fi networks were constructed, a website was developed, security of the camp was taken care of, conflicts were mediated, and even a hosting team would offer tours of the occupation to visitors who were curious about the movement, and perhaps also interested in joining. There was also the thorny issue of managing donations. Money was necessary to buy supplies for hundreds of people, but also to bail out those who were arrested, and to support the activities of the movement. In fact, the Occupy movement received hundreds of thousands of dollars in donations. The question then became how to manage them, since there was no legal entity able to set up a bank account. In some cases those in charge of the donations committee just put it in their own personal accounts. But of course this raised issues of paying personal taxes as well as potential embezzlement of the funds. It is striking that there are few known cases of undue appropriation. However, in many cases there was an incorporation of the camp as a legal entity to set up financial accountability. The issue then was the need to pay taxes for the money deposited in these accounts, something that the libertarian branch of the movement would oppose. Yet, all these decisions to be made are what constituted the process of experimentation that was at the heart of the movement.

As important as the material organization of the occupation was, it was the process of communication that enabled the movement to find internal cohesion and external support. Communication networks were the blood vessels of the Occupy movement.

## A NETWORKED MOVEMENT

Occupy Wall Street was born digital. The cry of outrage and the call to occupy came from various blogs (Adbusters, AmpedStatus and Anonymous, among others), and was posted on Facebook and spread by Twitter. Adbusters registered the hashtag #occupywallstreet on June 9, 2011 and included it in its first call to demonstrate on its blog, which was linked to its Facebook group on July 13. Groups and networks of activists around the Internet heard and distributed the call, and commented in support of the initiative. A good share of the first wave of tweets in July came from Spain, where the *indignants* movement found new hope in the direct confrontation planned against the core of financial capitalism. As the movement expanded, Twitter became an essential tool for internal communication in the camps, as well as for linking to other occupations and for planning specific actions. An unpublished study by Kevin Driscoll and François Bar at the University of Southern California Annenberg Innovation Lab collected Occupy tweets continuously beginning on October 12, 2011 by comparing them against an evolving set of approximately 289 related keywords and phrases. During the month of November, they observed approximately 120,000 Occupy-related tweets on a typical day with a peak of over 500,000 during the raid of Zuccotti Park on November 15. The analysis by Gilad Lotan on Twitter traffic related to the movement shows that the peaks are associated with crucial moments in the movement, such as the first attempt to evict the occupation of Zuccotti Park on October 13.[7] In most instances of threatened police action against occupations, Twitter networks alerted thousands, and their instant mobilization in solidarity played a role in protecting the occupiers. Using Twitter from their cell phones, the protesters were able to constantly distribute information, photos, videos and comments to build a real-time network of communication overlaid on the occupied space.

The 99% theme was popularized, in large part, by the "We are the 99%" Tumblr page, started in mid-August, in advance of the September 17 protests, by Chris (who chose not to give his last name) and Priscilla Grim, who both work professionally in media in New York, and were involved in social activism. At first, both chose to remain anonymous, writing "Brought to you by the people who will Occupy Wall Street." Tumblr, a social network started in 2007, has been characterized by *The Atlantic*'s Rebecca Rosen as a "collaborative confessional" that can, in the case of social movements, be used to create "self-service history" and demonstrates that "the power of personal narrative, whether on the radio, in a book, on YouTube, or on a Tumblr, can cut through the noise and cynicism of punditry and give shape and texture to our national story" (Rosen 2011). Posts on Tumblr can consist of a quote, a picture, a video or a link, instead of a long text as in a traditional blog post. Many Tumblr blogs consist of pictures and other media expressions around a particular theme. Topics are often humorous and playful. Users "follow" other Tumblr blogs and can see from their account an aggregation of all followed Tumblr blog posts together. Tumblr allows users to be part of collaboratively produced group blogs. They can "reblog" others' posts to post them onto their Tumblr blog and share the post with their own followers. And it is easy to implement a form that allows users to submit anonymous messages. This was crucial for the spread of the "We are the 99%" group because Tumblr provided a platform for personal storytelling in anonymity, with most people hiding their faces in the video, yet narrating their personal drama in coping with an unjust society. In October 2011, the group site was receiving about 100 submissions a day. As of February 2012 there were 225 pages of posts. Emphasizing the role of Tumblr as a distinctive feature of the Occupy Wall Street movement, Graham-Felsen (2011) wrote:

> Why has Tumblr become the go-to platform of this moment? As we saw in Iran, Twitter can be a powerful broadcast tool for delivering minute-by-minute accounts of breaking news and amplifying concrete messages ("Down with Ahmedinejad"). And in Egypt, Facebook was pivotal for recruiting protesters and scheduling rallies in Tahrir Square. But Tumblr has served neither of these purposes for Occupy Wall Street, a diffuse and leaderless movement with a deliberately undefined goal. Instead, Tumblr has humanized the movement. Tumblr is a powerful storytelling medium, and this movement is about stories – about how the nation's economic policies have priced us out of school, swallowed us in debt, permanently postponed retirements, and torn apart families. "We Are the 99 Percent" is the closest thing we've had to the work of Farm Security Administration – which paid photojournalists to document the plight of farmers during the Great Depression – and it may well go down as the definitive social history of this recession.
>
> In a telling comment, Ezra Klein wrote in *The Washington Post*: "It's not the arrests that convinced me that 'Occupy Wall Street' was worth covering seriously. Nor was it their press strategy, which largely consisted of tweeting journalists to cover a small protest that couldn't say what, exactly, it hoped to achieve. It was as Tumblr called, 'We Are The 99 Percent'" (2011).

Internet social networks mobilized enough support for people to come together and occupy public space, territorializing their protest. Once the camps were organized, they established their presence as specific occupations on the Internet. Most camps created their own website, set up a group on Facebook, or both. Members of the web committee created hot spots in the camp, and people tethered their phones to computers to go online. The diversity of the Occupy movement could be detected in its existence on the web, sometimes with very rich web pages in terms of content and graphics. Most large or particularly active occupations had their own website. These served as sites to organize the movement, but also to create a public presence for it. Most had the following sections: contact (to get in touch with members of the Press Relations committees, etc.), how to get involved (a list of committees, times and locations of General Assemblies), supplies requested for donation, resources (a set of documents explaining how to occupy, the protocols of the General Assembly, how to deal with the police), calendar of events and announcements, and message boards (some open, some password-protected). Also, most of these websites had a forum on which a visitor could create an account. Some message boards could be viewed by any visitor, but others were password-protected and open only to registered users. Minutes, proposals, and ratified documents (including lists of demands) were posted on the web, usually with a comment thread beneath. This was an essential practice to ensure transparency within the movement.

Most occupations also had a Facebook group. These were used to complement the websites of larger occupations, and served as primary sites of organizing for smaller or less tech-savvy occupations. They also served as directories to help members stay in touch with each other, send private messages, or post on each other's walls. The groups were also used for organizing: to make announcements, post calendar items, and send messages to all members of the group. Despite its utility, Facebook has been criticized within the movement for being a proprietary platform and thus at odds with the openness valued within the movement. Also, new Facebook facial recognition software can automatically tag people in photographs, and this was resented, given the lack of trust in that Facebook will not protect privacy if subpoenaed by authorities. Therefore, some skilled occupiers were trying to use alternatives to Facebook, such as N-1, Ning or Diaspora. Others engaged in working on an "Occupy Facebook" called Global Square, widely publicized by WikiLeaks. A functional prototype was supposed to be available sometime in 2012. In the words of the developers:

> The aim of the platform should not be to replace the physical assemblies but rather to empower them by providing the online tools for local and (trans)national organization and collaboration. The ideal would be both to foster individual participation and to structure collective action. The Global Square will be our own public space where different groups can come together to organize their local squares and assemblies.[8]

However, overall, the movement relied mainly on commercially available platforms that were ready to be used. So doing, activists became vulnerable to subpoenas trying to obtain information on tweets, violating the privacy of the users with potentially serious consequences.[9]

Livestreams, a collection of tools that allows users to broadcast real-time video content over the Internet, was also an important technology for the movement. Livestreams are ephemeral, but they are essential during moments of police repression. During raids, there was often a blackout on mainstream media, which did not apply to livestreamers. For instance, in the early hours of October 11, Occupy

Boston faced a wave of police violence and arrests. Over 8,000 people were reported to be watching the livestream at 3am. When the livestream of an occupation stopped broadcasting, it became a symbol that the demonstration had been effectively shut down, which can be a mobilizing experience for those watching at home. However, livestreaming is in fact controversial within the movement. Because livestreamers show the occupation from their own point of view, narrating the events as they see them, many have achieved some degree of celebrity within the movement and have been identified as spokespeople by those outside of it. This has lead to criticism that some are exploiting the movement for personal gain, including sponsorship from livestreaming service companies. Most of the time, the occupations were very boring, with repression, violence and other "action" relatively infrequent. Livestreamers have been criticized for gravitating toward sensationalism and misrepresenting the actual experience of most present at the occupations. They also were blamed for being, as one livestreamer put it, "dry snitches," that is, people who unintentionally provide evidence to the police of people engaged in the occupation.[10]

Thus, the occupy sites were nodes of communication networks toward the world at large and within the occupation. These networks were a hybrid of communication forms, both digital and face-to-face, based on community building, interpersonal interaction, social networking and posting on the Internet. Thus, SMS was important, particularly for coordinating actions and staying in touch, as were email listservs to diffuse information. Conference calls, using Mumble and other VOIP technologies, allowed deliberation between distant sites. But print publications were also a significant medium with journals such as *Occupied WJS*, *Occupy! N+1* or *Tidal*, as well as a multitude of local print bulletins. People's deliberation and decision-making in the camp were based on direct human interaction, such as hand signals in the General Assemblies and the widespread use of People's Mic, in which someone says something to an audience who repeats each sentence loudly so that everybody can hear without amplification equipment. Besides its practical uses, People's Mic symbolizes belonging and community experience, reproducing forms of communication used in past movements of civil disobedience.

After the occupied sites were vacated under pressure from police and winter, the movement did not disappear: it went on in the diverse forms of the Internet networks, always buzzing with proclamations and ideas, and always ready to land again with a vengeance from the space of flows into the space of places. Indeed, the Occupy Wall Street movement is a hybrid networked movement that links cyberspace and urban space in multiple forms of communication.

Furthermore, to be autonomous vis-à-vis the mainstream media without accepting isolation from the 99%, the movement is self-mediated, both over the Internet and within its autonomous public space, mixing in its messages both grievances and hope. Indeed, the hand signals used in the General Assemblies are shaped to facilitate their viral diffusion on the Internet. The entire activity of the camp and in the demonstrations is largely staged for their expression in social media, connecting in this way to society at large. There is a constant practice of storytelling in the movement, with everybody taking pictures and making videos, and uploading them to YouTube and to multiple social networking sites. This is the first kind of movement that tells every day its own story in its multiple voices in a way that transcends both time and space, projecting itself in history and reaching out to the global visions and voices of our world.

In deeper terms, the movement set out to occupy Wall Street, the key node of the global networks of financial domination of the world, by occupying surrounding territories and making free communities. The occupiers used the autonomous space of flows of Internet networks to seize symbolic spaces of places, from where they could challenge, by their presence and their messages, the financial space of flows from where global powers dominate human life.

## DIRECT DEMOCRACY IN PRACTICE

From its onset, the Occupy movement experimented with new forms of organization, deliberation and decision-making as a way of learning, by doing, what real democracy is. This is a fundamental feature of the movement. Instrumentality was not paramount. Authenticity was. The occupiers did not want to reproduce in their practice the kind of formal democracy and personalized leadership they were opposing. They invented, incrementally, a new organizational model that, with variations, was present in most of the occupations. It originally came from experiences in Egypt and Spain, and then it co-evolved between the many occupied sites through cross-fertilization, mutual consultation and feedback. Since most occupations created their own website, all the guidelines for organization and the experiences in collaborative decision-making were posted and communicated throughout the network of occupations. This is how a largely common organizational pattern emerged.

Its most important characteristic was the deliberate absence of formal leadership. There were no leaders in the movement, not locally, not nationally, and not globally. This was a fundamental principle that was enforced by the multitude of occupiers with utmost determination at any instance when someone tried to assume a prominent role. This was truly an experiment in social movement organization. It belied deep-seated assumptions that no socio-political process could work without some sort of strategic guidance and vertical authority. In the Occupy movement, there was no traditional leadership, no rational leadership and no charismatic leadership. And certainly no personalized leadership. There were leadership functions, but these were exercised locally by the General Assembly meeting regularly in the occupied space. There were also coordinating functions that would help to shape collective decisions, and these were assumed by networks of iterative consultation over the Internet.

However, to ensure some form of effective initiative in a compatible way with the principle of sovereign assemblies with no delegation, more complex organizational forms emerged. Since this was one of the fundamental social innovations of the movement, it is worthwhile to analyze it in some detail. It goes without saying that the diversity of organizational experiences cannot be reduced to one single pattern. Yet, in what follows I will try to convey the key features that were often repeated in the largest occupations, so that we can consider that there is an implicit model of direct democracy emerging from the practice of the movement. To construct this ideal type of Occupy organization with my team, we have relied on the websites of the occupations that often post guides explaining how to participate and how to organize. The description here relies on direct quotes from these guides. This is because since these documents have circulated freely within the movement and between the occupations, many of them include similar wording and images. This is another example of the importance of the Internet in the practice of the movement.

The decision-making power for a given occupied site is exclusively in the hands of the General Assembly (GA). It is a "horizontal, leaderless, consensus-based open meeting" (this description is used on almost every Occupation website and GA guide). Everyone present at the GA has the ability to participate in the GA. Anyone can make a proposal or address a proposal. Everyone, except for those who choose to stand aside or observe, is expected to participate in the decision-making process through hand signals. Although there is no leader in the GA, it is facilitated or moderated by individuals from the Facilitation Committee and usually rotates each time.

Most occupations follow the same general rules, although some may have slightly different norms: "There is no single leader or governing body of the GA – everyone's voice is equal. Anyone is free to propose an idea or express an opinion as part of the GA." Ideally, only decisions that affect the entire group are brought to the GA. Smaller actions that happen outside the occupation can be planned in smaller groups without the GA's approval. Affinity groups and working groups can make decisions within themselves but must bring matters that affect the entire occupation to the GA for approval. Each proposal follows the same basic format: an individual describes the proposal and explains why it is being proposed and how it can be carried out. Other members of the GA express their support, ask questions, or react to the proposal. After sufficient discussion, and when it seems that the group may be near consensus, the facilitator will call for the entire GA to express, through a series of hand gestures, their opinion of each proposal (see figure 2). If there is positive consensus for a proposal, it is accepted and direct action begins. If there is not consensus, the individual making the proposal is asked to revise and resubmit it to the GA until a consensus is achieved. Some GAs required full consensus, but others adopted modified or partial consensus, such as 90 percent. This has been a controversial issue at many occupations. Because reaching consensus is so difficult, the members of the GA express different kinds of disagreement: Stand-aside – for reasons including non-support, reservations,

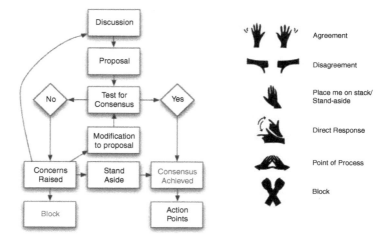

*Figure 2: Consensus flow and hand signals in Occupy Movement*

and personal conflict – and Blocking. Blocking consensus is something that should, in theory, only be done in extreme situations. In practice, it was used quite frequently.

To implement decisions of the General Assembly, organize the camp, and engage in a practice, committees are formed. Most occupations include some combination of the following committees, although some may use different names or have slightly different categories: Facilitation, Media, Outreach, Food, Direct Action, Peace Keeping/ Security, Sanitation/Sustainability, Finance/Resources, Legal, Medical, Social Media, Programming, People of Color, Press Relations, etc. In order to be officially recognized, committees must be agreed upon by the GA, but less formal groups, called Affinity Groups, need not be. The role of the committees is to figure out specifics and formulate proposals to present to the GA for general consensus and to identify and communicate information that everyone needs to take into consideration. Membership and leadership within the working groups is open to anyone, but actually formed by those who show up regularly and take on responsibility and deliver on promises. Eventually these roles become associated with particular individuals who become the point persons for the committee.

To be more operative without betraying the principle of leaderlessness, many occupations adopted the Spokes Council model in an attempt to ensure better communication among working groups and committees, create more accountability and limit the power of visitors to derail the consensus process. Spokes are individuals designated by committees and affinity groups to represent their views.[11] The main tasks for the Spokes Council are described as: effectively coordinating between Operations Groups and Caucuses; making budgetary decisions; and enabling the GA to engage in broader movement discussions, rather than being "bogged down" with time-consuming decisions on implementing its general orientations.

The Spokes Council has been considered controversial among many in the movement, and some do not recognize it. As one occupier told *The Village Voice*, "I think through the Spokes Council process, working groups become organizations and they become parties. What's the reason for us to marginalize ourselves?"[12] However, no occupation can adopt a Spokes Council without the approval of the GA. The Spokes Council was designed to facilitate productive, expeditious decision-making among those who are actively working on behalf of the movement. It is open to all to witness, but to participate one must be an active participant in a Working Group or Caucus. However, measures have been taken to ensure that these decisions are open-access and transparent: all decisions made in the Spokes Council take place in a well-publicized indoor location with amplified sound so all can hear, and are broadcast over the Livestream: furthermore, all decisions, meeting minutes and budget details must be completely transparent and posted on the website.

There are different kinds of groups that participate in the Spokes Council:

(a) Working Groups, which engage logistical work on behalf of the occupation. Some Occupations split these into Operations Groups, which work on the material and financial organization of the movement on a daily basis, and Movement Groups, which work on the actions and campaigns of the movement, often on a project basis.

(b) Caucuses, self-determined groups based on the common experience of being marginalized in society on bases including, but not limited to, race, gender identity, sexuality, physical ability, or homelessness status. Caucus Clusters have the same powers as Working Group Clusters. In addition, they have the ability to halt proposals that may have disproportionately adverse consequences for their constituency.

(c) In addition, a Spoke is allotted to represent those who are camping full-time but not involved in any Working Group or Caucus.

In terms of process, before each Spokes Council, each Working Group and Caucus decides on a Cluster to align with. Prior to meeting in the Spokes Council, each Cluster meets to discuss and craft proposals. Each Cluster chooses a person to serve as a "Spoke." The Spokes sit in a circle in the middle of the meeting space, with the rest of the Cluster sitting directly behind them. Individuals in multiple Working Groups and Caucuses are free to sit with any Cluster they are a part of. The Spoke rotates every meeting. Spokes are the only individuals to speak at the Spokes Council, but they must confer with and accurately reflect the members of their

Cluster before speaking for them. Cluster can recall their Spoke at any time if they are failing to accurately reflect the will of the Cluster. Spokes present proposals crafted by the Clusters to the Spokes Council. Clusters discuss the proposal among themselves, and the Spoke presents those discussions to the entire group. After sufficient discussion, the Spokes call for modified consensus on the proposal. The Spokes Council model makes it more difficult for individuals to Hard Block a proposal without consensus from their Cluster.

The complexity of this organizational model expresses the tension between the principle of integral democracy, based on the non-delegation of power in decision-making, and the instrumental need to reach consensus leading to action. While many of the observed practices deviated from the interactive, multilayered flows of decision presented in this synthetic view of an assembly-led and committee-implemented movement, it conveys the depth of the search for new political forms within the movement that could pre-figure new forms of democracy in society at large. So doing, the Occupy movement is challenging the current practice of political institutions in the US, while reaching back to the founding principles of community-based democracy as one of the sources of the American Revolution.

## A NON-DEMAND MOVEMENT: "THE PROCESS IS THE MESSAGE"[13]

The movement surged as a largely spontaneous expression of outrage. It was infused with hope for a better world, which began to materialize in the daily life of the camps, in the dialogue and cooperation of social networks, and in the courageous street demonstrations where the bonding was enacted. But for what? For most observers, the diffi-culty of assessing the Occupy Wall Street movement came from the absence of precise demands that could be won or negotiated. There was a concrete demand in the initial call to demonstrate: the appointment of a presidential commission to enact the independence of government in regard to Wall Street. Indeed, former Wall Street executives have been at the key posts of the cabinets of all recent presidents, including Obama. An IMF study found a significant statistical association between the money spent by financial industry lobbyists in 2000–6 and Congressional votes in favor of the financial industry on 51 important bills.[14] If the outrage was directed at Wall Street, it appeared logical that the demand to separate money and politics would be the unifying goal of the movement. It was not. The movement demanded everything and nothing at the same time. In fact, given the widespread character of the movement, each occupation had its local and regional specificity: everybody brought in her own grievances and defined her own targets. There were multiple proposals of various natures, voted on in the General Assemblies, but little effort to translate them into a policy campaign going beyond combating the effects of mortgage foreclosures or financial abuses on borrowers and consumers. The list of most frequently mentioned demands debated in various occupations hints at the extraordinary diversity of the movement's targets: controlling financial speculation, particularly high frequency trading; auditing the Federal Reserve; addressing the housing crisis; regulating overdraft fees; controlling currency manipulation; opposing the outsourcing of jobs; defending collective bargaining and union rights; reducing income inequality; reforming tax law; reforming political campaign finance; reversing the Supreme Court's decision allowing unlimited campaign contributions from corporations; banning bailouts of companies; controlling the military-industrial complex; improving the care of veterans; limiting terms for elected politicians; defending

freedom on the Internet; assuring privacy on the Internet
and in the media; combating economic exploitation; reforming the prison system; reforming health care; combating
racism, sexism, and xenophobia; improving student loans;
opposing the Keystone pipeline and other environmentally
predatory projects; enacting policies against global warming;
fining and controlling BP and similar oil spillers; enforcing
animal rights; supporting alternative energy sources; cri-
tiquing personal leadership and vertical authority, beginning
with a new democratic culture in the camps; and watching
out for co-optation in the political system (as happened with
the Tea Party). As Sydney Tarrow wrote: "That is hardly a
policy platform. But policy platforms are not the point of
this new kind of movement" (2011: 1).

   Some occupations, such as Fort Lauderdale and New York,
approved elaborate documents providing the rationale for a
long list of demands. The Declaration of the Occupation of
New York City was the most widely distributed document
from the movement, approved by the New York City General
Assembly on September 29, 2011, and translated into 26
languages. But it presented more grievances than demands.
And the demands included in the document were of generic
character. Other documents, such as the "99% Declaration"
from New York, or draft statements from Chicago,
Washington DC, and many others, did not reach consensus
and could not represent the views of the movement as such.
Indeed, the movement was popular and attractive to many
precisely because it remained open to all kinds of proposals,
and did not present specific policy positions that would have
elicited support but also opposition within the movement, as
shown in the divisiveness that emerged in most occupations
each time a committee put forward specific programs for
reform. For many people in the movement, and for almost
all external observers, particularly those intellectuals on the

left always looking for the politics of their dreams, the lack of specific demands by the movement was a fundamental flaw. In a dire economic and social situation, there is an urgent need for a change of course, and this can only be achieved by channeling the energy liberated by the movement into some achievable, short-term goals that, in return, would empower the movement.

The problem, though, is that "the movement" is not a single entity, but multiple streams that converge into a diverse challenge to the existing order. Furthermore, a very strong sentiment in the movement is that any pragmatic approach to achieving demands would be required to go through the mediation of the political system, and this would contradict the generalized distrust of the representativeness of political institutions as they presently exist in America. I think that a statement retrieved from the discussions in the Demands Committee of the New York General Assembly expresses a widespread feeling in the movement:

> I wanted to introduce a different way of thinking about this. The movement doesn't need to make demands, because this movement is an assertive process. This movement has the power to affect change. It does not need to ask for it. The OWS does not make demands. We will simply assert our own power to achieve what we desire. The more of us gather to the cause, the more power we have. Make no demands for others to solve these problems. Assert yourself.[15]

While this position is controversial, and considered suicidal outside the movement by the old political left, it does correspond to two fundamental trends: (a) most people simply do not trust the political process as it is currently framed, so they only count on themselves; (b) the movement is wide and strong because it unites outrage and dreams while skipping politics as usual. This is its strength and its weakness. But this is what this movement is, not a surrogate for an old left always looking to find fresh support for its unreconstructed view of the world. No demands, and every demand; not a piece of this society, but the whole of a different society.

## VIOLENCE AGAINST A NON-VIOLENT MOVEMENT

The Occupy movement was overwhelmingly non-violent, both in philosophy and in its practice. But it was confrontational, because its tactics of occupying space to build autonomy, and of demonstrating in the streets against functional nodes of the system, were bound to be met with police action. This was anticipated by the participants in the movement. Challenging the system outside the institutionalized channels of dissent meant taking risks of police repression. But there is always a gray zone of legality and political calculation that the movement tried to use to its advantage. For instance, the occupation of Zuccotti Park was paradoxically protected for a while because it is private property and the owning company took some time to proceed with the cost/benefit analysis of calling for an eviction.

In city after city, the local authorities in control of the territory had to evaluate the potential backlash for their political futures in terms of the different options they would take relating to the movement. For instance, in Los Angeles, Mayor Villaraigosa, nurturing political ambitions for higher office, issued a statement, with the majority of the City Council, supporting the goals of the movement but falling short of supporting a long-term occupation of the lawn in front of City Hall (it is often used as a stand-in for Washington DC in Hollywood movies, so the city would lose revenue if it

allowed it to be used too long just for the purpose of exercising democracy). Los Angeles was the last major occupation
to be evicted, which was done with a Hollywood-style display
of force (hundreds of policemen in full riot gear emerging
by surprise from the building), but without any major incident. On the other hand, the City of Oakland unleashed its
ferocious attack police, well known in the city and around
the country for numerous incidents of unjustified killings,
detentions, and violent charges on demonstrators. Oakland
witnessed several major, violent confrontations in repeated
attempts to dislodge the occupied square, with dozens of
injured, hundreds of arrests, and two veterans seriously
injured and hospitalized. This police action radicalized the
movement in Oakland, to the point that on November
3 demonstrators succeeded in shutting down the Port of
Oakland, the second largest on the US Pacific Coast, at the
price of pitched street battles with the police. New York
oscillated between its initial tolerance of the occupation and
several instances of harsh repression. Many university campuses, including some of the elite universities such as Yale,
Berkeley, and Harvard, were occupied. At one point, campus
security only allowed those with Harvard identification cards
to enter the occupied Harvard Yard. Response from the academic authorities varied. In one instance at the University of
California at Davis, the campus police pepper sprayed, without justification, peacefully seated demonstrations, inducing
outrage around the world and a disciplinary suspension of
the provocative officers.

In general terms, the movement was calm but determined,
and local police forces everywhere were ready to club and
arrest at the slightest legal possibility of doing so, although
some policemen privately expressed their agreement with
the goals of the movement. The violence that often ensued
had two different effects: on the one hand, it increased sol-

idarity with those occupiers subject to violence, prompting wider mobilization beyond the localities where the repression took place. On the other hand, any broadcast of violence on television drew a wedge between the movement and the 99% they aspired to represent. A critical element in protecting the movement from violence is the massive practice of video reporting by hundreds of people branding their cell phones in every demonstration. The mainstream media only reported what their editors wanted, but the movement self-reported everything, posting on the Internet all the actions that took place in every confrontation. In some cases, the vision of police brutality re-energized the demonstrators and induced popular sympathy countering the prejudice against the movement, which was portrayed as violent in some media. There were some radical, organized groups (particularly the Black Bloc) as well as "autonomous actors" participating in demonstrations who attacked the police, public buildings, banks, and stores. They were only effective in creating violence in situations where the police had provoked a violent atmosphere. This was particularly the case in Oakland, where demonstrators invaded City Hall and burned an American flag on January 28, 2012. However, the General Assemblies often debated the issue of violence and were systematically opposed to it, devising several strategies to diffuse police violence as well as provocations of the radical fringe of the movement, including provocateurs external to the movement itself. By and large, they succeeded. Yet, police presence was constantly felt around the occupied sites and street marches, increasing both the radicalism of the movement and the separation between the movement's actions and the perception of a majority of people whose life is dominated by fear.

In mid-November 2011, 18 mayors of cities with active occupations reportedly took part in conference calls to discuss how they were handling the movement. In what seemed to many like a coordinated action, many sites all over the US were evicted in the weeks following. The pretext used for the forced eviction was the same everywhere: concern for public hygiene, in spite of the cleaning and sanitation efforts that had been made daily in most occupied sites. In a few weeks local police forces succeeded in dislodging the occupiers from their camps, usually with limited violence, since in most cases the remaining people had decided to hibernate elsewhere, regroup and strategize for a spring offensive under new forms. To be continued.

## WHAT DID THE MOVEMENT ACHIEVE?

Since the movement did not mobilize in support of specific policies, no major policy changes resulted directly from the movement's action. However, there were multiple campaigns everywhere that obtained partial corrections in a number of unfair practices. This was particularly the case of the housing campaigns, a major issue in the Occupy movement. Occupy groups "occupied" foreclosed homes in many areas of the country on the December 6 Day of Action, with the goal of pressuring lenders to offer loan modifications with substantial reductions. They succeeded in some cases, even reinstating mortgages that had previously been canceled. They showcased especially poignant foreclosures of aged persons or invalid veterans as a way to denounce the unfairness of the system in the public light.

There were also widespread attempts to put pressure on the major banks using customers' power with the "Bank Transfer Day" initiative. It drew on pre-existing campaigns that encouraged individuals and institutions to divest from the nation's largest Wall Street banks and move to local financial institutions and non-profit credit unions. Among these were Arianna Huffington's "Move Your Money" in 2009, and the 2010 Valentine's Day movement to "Break up with your Bank." Then in September 2011, after Bank of America announced that it would impose a $5 monthly fee on debit card and checking accounts, there was a wave of protests, with many customers canceling their accounts. After the backlash, Bank of America rescinded the increased fees, but other fees are quietly coming back. As of October 15, 2011, a Facebook page devoted to the effort had drawn more than 54,900 "likes." November 5, 2011 was declared "Bank Transfer Day," calling people to switch their accounts from commercial banks to not-for-profit credit unions. According to the Credit Union National Association (CUNA), the association's website aimed at informing customers about credit union services saw traffic double in this period. CUNA estimated that nearly 650,000 consumers had opened new accounts at credit unions between late September and the November 5 target date.[16] In other instances of starting up new financial institutions, some Occupy movements, such as Occupy Orange County in Southern California, created their own credit unions. Similar efforts of new, community-based credit unions were reported in San Francisco, Boston, and Washington State.

Yet, while these actions were exemplary in character, they were mere drops in the ocean of injustice confronted by the movement. The hope was that these initiatives would give people the courage to resist, and would alert the public at large on a socially unbearable situation. In this sense, George Lakoff's characterization of Occupy Wall Street as a moral movement aiming to impact the public discourse seems to be supported by observation (2011). Indeed, in spite of its limitations, public opinion surveys seem to indicate a significant cultural change in America as a result of the movement's actions and proclamations. According to a *New York Times* poll of a national sample in November 9, 2011, almost 50 percent of the public thought that the sentiments at the root of the movement generally reflected the view of most Americans.[17]

A Pew Institute Survey on the attitudes toward Occupy Wall Street among a national sample of 1,521 adults, released on December 15, 2011,[18] showed that 44 percent supported the movement, while 39 percent opposed it. Moreover, 48 percent agreed with the concerns expressed by OWS while 30 percent disagreed. However, when it came to tactics (meaning occupations, demonstrations), 49 percent disagreed, while only 29 percent agreed. It seems that crossing the line toward non-institutional action is still a barrier for most citizens, even when they agree with the causes of the protest. The attitudes about the movement vary of course depending on income level, education, age, and political ideology: older, conservative, more affluent, and less-educated citizens opposed the movement, while the movement received widespread support from other demographic groups. However, the most salient point is that a movement that clearly places itself outside institutional politics and challenges up front the heart of global capitalism – namely Wall Street – has received significant support in mainstream America.

However, what is truly decisive in assessing the political effect of a social movement is its impact on people's consciousness, as I have argued throughout this book, and more thoroughly in previous works (Castells 2003, 2009). As a result of the movement, and of the debates it has generated on the Internet and in the mainstream media, the issue of social inequality, epitomized by the opposition between the 99% and the 1%, has come to the forefront of public discourse. Politicians (including President Obama), media commentators, and comedians have embraced the term, claiming they represent the 99%.

Regardless of the cynicism of such a statement in a political class usually defending the interests of the financial and corporate elites as a prerequisite for their political future, the simple fact of accepting this dichotomy has deep consequences in terms of trust in the fairness of the system. Indeed, the old American dream about equality of opportunities on the basis of personal effort has been shattered, if we are to believe the results of a Pew Institute Survey taken in December 2011, as shown in figure 3 and tables 3 and 4. Furthermore, 61 percent think that the country's economic system "unfairly favors the wealthy," and 77 percent agree with the statement that "there is too much power in the hands of a few rich people and large corporations," including 53 percent of Republicans.

Yet, what is relatively new and meaningful is that there are indications that Occupy Wall Street has shaped the awareness of Americans on the reality of what I would dare to call class struggle. Thus, according to a Pew Institute survey on a national representative sample of adults in the age group 18 to 34, released on January 11, 2012, 66 percent believe there are "very strong" or "strong" conflicts between the rich and the poor: *an increase of 19 percentage points since 2009.* Not only have perceptions of class conflict grown more prevalent; so, too, has the belief that these disputes are acute: 30 percent say there are "very strong conflicts" between poor people and rich people, double the proportion that offered a similar view in July 2009 and *the largest percentage expressing this opinion since the question was first asked in 1987.* Conflicts between rich and poor now rank ahead of three other potential sources of group tension: between immigrants and the native born, between blacks and whites, and between young and old. All major demographic groups now perceive significantly more class conflict than two years ago. However, the survey found that younger adults, women, Democrats, and African Americans are somewhat more likely than older

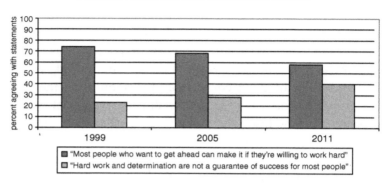

*Figure 3: Decreased attitude that "hard work leads to success"*

**Table 3: Perception of social conflicts in society**

*Percent who say there are "very strong" or "strong" conflicts between . . .*

|                             | 2009 | 2011 |
|-----------------------------|------|------|
| Rich and poor               | 47   | 66   |
| Immigrants and native born  | 55   | 62   |
| Black and whites            | 39   | 38   |
| Young and old               | 25   | 34   |

people, men, Republicans, whites, or Hispanics to say that there are strong disagreements between the rich and the poor. The biggest increase in perceptions of class conflicts occurred among political liberals and Americans who say they are not affiliated with either major party. In each group, the proportion who said there are major disagreements between rich and poor Americans *increased by 19 percentage points since 2009*. To quote the report:

These changes in attitudes over a relatively short period of time may reflect the income and wealth inequality message conveyed by Occupy Wall Street protesters across the

**Table 4: Support and opposition to Occupy Wall Street, concerns raised by protests, and way protests are conducted**

|  | Republicans | Democrats | Independents | Total |
|---|---|---|---|---|
| *OWS overall* | % | % | % | % |
| Support | 21 | 60 | 46 | 44 |
| Oppose | 59 | 21 | 34 | 35 |
| Neither | 5 | 4 | 7 | 6 |
| Don't know | 15 | 15 | 14 | 16 |
| *Concerns raised by OWS protests* | | | | |
| Agree | 31 | 62 | 50 | 48 |
| Disagree | 47 | 19 | 27 | 30 |
| Don't know | 22 | 19 | 23 | 22 |
| *Way OWS protests are conducted* | | | | |
| Approve | 14 | 43 | 29 | 29 |
| Disapprove | 67 | 37 | 49 | 49 |
| Don't know | 19 | 20 | 22 | 23 |

country in late 2011 that led to a spike in media attention to the topic. But the changes may also reflect a growing public awareness of underlying shifts in the distribution of wealth in American society.[19]

However, it is to be noticed that perceptions of capitalism and socialism have changed little since 2010. Indeed, the majority of supporters of the Occupy movement are not openly critical of capitalism: there are as many positive as negative opinions about capitalism among its ranks. The criticism is focused on financial capitalism and on its influence on government, not on capitalism as such. The movement does not embrace ideologies of the past. Its quest aims at eradicating evil in the present, while reinventing community for the future. Its fundamental achievement has been to rekindle hope that another life is possible.

## THE SALT OF THE EARTH[20]

How can people enact fundamental change when they do not trust their political institutions and refuse to engage in the violent overthrowing of said institutions? When the mechanisms of representation do not function properly, when unaccountable powers, such as financial institutions and corporate media, define the terms and outcomes of deliberation and decision-making within a framed field of options, and when major deviations of behavior from the biased rules of the game are subjected to intimidation by the security forces and a politically appointed judiciary? This was the dilemma confronting those who did not submit to resignation and passivity, those who took risks and dared to explore new avenues of political resistance and social change when forced to assume the hardship of a financial crisis unfairly imposed upon them. After deliberation on the Internet networks, with the help of occasional meetings face-to-face to connect with one another and exercise togetherness, they resorted to the oldest tactic of power when people do not yield to the temptation of becoming like the enemy in order to overcome the enemy: they engaged in civil disobedience. They targeted the most essential commodity shaping their lives, and everybody's life: virtual money. The value that does not exist materially and yet permeates everything. The value that has escaped into the computer networks of the global financial markets, but still lives out of territorial nodes that manage and control the space of financial flows from the places they inhabit. By challenging the inviolability of absolute financial power on the shores of the ocean of global capital, they materialized resistance, giving a face to the source of oppression that was asphyxiating people's lives and establishing its rule over the rulers. They set up a convivial community in the sites where before there were only headquarters of power and greed. They created experience out of defiance. They self-mediated their connection to the world and the connections among themselves. They opposed the threat of violence with peaceful assertiveness. They believed in their right to believe. They connected to each other and reached out to the others. They found meaning in being together. They did not collect money, nor did they pay their debts. They harvested themselves. They harvested the salt of the earth. And they became free.

## NOTES

1 In concluding my analysis of the Obama campaign, after he won the election, I wrote:

> How much [Obama] will have to deviate from his original ideas when confronted with the harsh economic and geopolitical realities of our world is a matter for future appraisal and further study. Yet, as I write this and you read it in another time/space warp, the fundamental analytical lesson to retain is how the insurgent politics of hope came to the forefront in the world's political scene at a critical moment when despair descended upon us. We will always have Berlin. Or for that matter Grant Park (2009: 412).

Thus, there was despair, then came hope, at least for enough people to elect president an African-American against the Clinton machine, and against the Republican machine. Then, rather quickly, there was widespread despair again in the country and among his most enthusiastic supporters. Yet, the seeds of hope planted in the hearts of the multitudes that cheered Obama in Berlin and Grant Park, were not washed away by the crisis of crisis management. They yielded new hope, under different

forms, when the time came again to move beyond outrage. Indeed there are some indications that there was
a transfer of energy from disappointment with Obama
to the Occupy movement. According to the Fordham
University Poll by Political Science professor Costas
Panagopoulos from October 2011, 60 percent of occupiers voted for Obama in 2008 but 73 percent of occupiers
now disapprove of the way Barack Obama is handling his
job as president. A sign in Occupy Wall Street in NYC
read, "The Barack Obama we elected would be out here
with us." Another read, "Standing Up For The Change
We Voted For," referring to Obama's 2008 campaign
slogan. "The very people who supported Obama in '08
are the Occupy organizers. That same energy has shifted
from the electoral arena to the streets," David Goodner, a
volunteer with Occupy Des Moines, told the *LA Times* in
December 2011. Shepherd Fairey, who made the famous
and influential Obama Hope poster in 2008, made a new
poster in the same style with the image of Guy Fawkes
(representing Anonymous) that read, "Mr. President
we HOPE you're on our side" and a small emblem
that reads, "We are the 99%." The artist wrote on his
website:

> I still see Obama as the closest thing to "a man on the
> inside" that we have presently. Obviously, just voting is
> not enough. We need to use all of our tools to help us
> achieve our goals and ideals. However, I think idealism
> and realism need to exist hand in hand. Change is not
> about one election, one rally, one leader, it is about a
> constant dedication to progress and a constant push in
> the right direction.

It must be noticed, nonetheless, that according to some
polls on occupiers, the overwhelming majority were

planning to vote in the 2012 presidential election, and about half of them were inclined to vote Democrat, with a very small number supporting a Republican candidate. But almost 40 percent were undecided about their potential vote. There are some cases of active members of the movement running for office in order to support the demands of the movement. For instance, Nate Kleinman, 29-year-old active member of the Occupy Philadelphia movement, is a candidate for congress in Pennsylvania's 13th district against Democratic incumbent Allyson Schwartz. However, the movement as such did not support his candidacy. In other words, most occupiers are political, and most of them are progressive. They simply do not trust that their goals can be fulfilled by elections without a previous transformation of the public mind among people at large.

2 DeGraw, D. (2010) The economic elite have engineered an extraordinary coup, threatening the very existence of the middle class. AmpedStatus/Alternet. Available at: <http://www.alternet.org/economy/145667/?page=entire>.

3 Chase-Dunn, C. and Curran-Strange, M. (2011) Diffusion of the Occupy Movement in California. IROWS Working Paper # 74. Available at: <http://irows.ucr.edu/papers/irows74/irows74.h>.

4 Occupy Research Network. (2012) *General Demographic and Political Participation Survey*. Available at: <http://occupyresearch.net>.

5 Cordero-Guzman, H. (2011) *Main Stream Support for a Mainstream Movement: The 99% Movement Comes From and Looks Like the 99%*. Profile of web traffic taken from occupywallst.org. Available at: <http://occupywallst.org/media/pdf/OWS-profile1-10-18-11-sent-v2-HRCG.pdf>.

6 Zevon, C. (2011) We're Still Here: This is what a holiday looks like at Occupy Washington DC. *OpenMike*.

Available    at:    <http://www.michaelmoore.com/words/
mike-friends-blog/were-still-here>.

7  Lotan, G. (2011) *#OccupyWallStreet Analyses*. Available at:
<http://giladlotan.com/2012/02/occupywallstreet-analy
ses>.

8  The Global Square. (2011) *The Global Square: A project to
perpetuate the creative and cooperative spirit of the occupations
and transform them into lasting forms of social organization.*
Available at: <http://theglobalsquare.org>.

9  On 14 December, Twitter received a subpoena from
the Boston-area district attorney's office requesting
all available information for accounts associated with
two hashtags, two accounts, and one name, seemingly
connected with Occupy Boston and members of
Anonymous who had released online logins, physical
addresses, and payroll information for 40 senior officers
of Boston Police Department. It was very confusingly
worded, as if the DA does not really understand how
Twitter works, as there is no specific account association
with hashtags, and if they wanted user information for
all users who used those hashtags, they would number
in the hundreds of thousands. In addition, one account
named @occupyboston, is fallow and not associated with
the movement. It is Twitter's policy to send subpoenas
to users in order to give that user a chance to fight it
unless the company is specifically placed under a gag
order. It seems that one targeted user received a copy
from Twitter and posted it online. The ACLU filed to
dismiss the subpoena but was rejected by Judge Carol
Ball, who also issued an Impoundment Order, an extraordinary measure preventing either side from talking about
arguments that is generally granted only in cases involv-
ing sensitive security issues, investigative issues, witness
intimidation, or the possibility of the suspect running. In

another instance, in January 2012, the Criminal Court of the City of New York requested "any and all user information" from September 15 to December 31, 2011 for the account @destructuremal, which belongs to Malcolm Harris, an Occupy protester who was arrested, along with 700 others, on the Brooklyn Bridge on October 5, 2011.

10 Dupay, T. (2012) The rise of the livestream: telling the truth about Occupy in real time. *AlterNet*. Available at: <http://www.alternet.org/occupywallst/154272/rise_of _the_livestreamer_telling_the_truth_about_occupy_in_ real_time?page=1>.

11 The name "Spokes Council" refers both to the "spokespeople," who speak for their cluster and, more metaphorically, to "spokes" of a wheel, as the group sits in a circle and spokes are rotated each meeting.

12 Gray, R. (2011) "Occupy Wall Street debuts the new Spokes Council." *The Village Voice*. Available at: <http:// blogs.villagevoice.com/runninscared/2011/11/occupy_ wall_str_25.php>.

13 Occupier Meghann Sheridan wrote "The process is the message" on Occupy Boston's Facebook page, quoted by Hoffman, M. (2011) Protesters debate what demands, if any, to make. *The New York Times*. Available at: <http:// www.nytimes.com/2011/10/17/nyregion/occupy-wall-street-trying-to-settle-on-demands.html>.

14 Cited by Lawson-Remer, T. (2011) #OccupyDemocracy. *Possible Futures: A Project of the Social Science Research Council.* Available at: <http://www.possible-futures. org/2011/12/08/occupydemocracy>.

15 Comment on "Demands Working Group." Available at: <http://occupywallst.org/article/so-called-demands-working-group/#comment-175161>.

16 Rapport, M. (2011) Bank Transfer Day: CUNA Says

650,000 have so far. *Credit Union Times.* Available at: <http://www.cutimes.com/2011/11/03/bank-transfer-day-cuna-says-650000-have-so-far>.

17 *The New York Times* (2011) Public opinion and the Occupy Movement. Available at: <http://www.nytimes. com/interactive/2011/11/09/us/ows-grid.html>.

18 The Pew Research Center for the People and the Press. (2011) Frustration with congress could hurt Republican incumbents. Available at: <http://www.people-press. org/2011/12/15/frustration-with-congress-could-hurt-republican-incumbents/>.

19 The Pew Research Center for the People and the Press. (2011) A Political Rhetoric Test: little change in public's response to "Capitalism," "Socialism." Available at: <http://www.people-press.org/files/legacy-pdf/12-28-11%20Words%20release.pdf>.

20 "Ye are the salt of the earth: but if the salt have lost its savor, wherewith shall it be salted? It is thenceforth good for nothing but to be cast out and trodden under the foot of men" (Matthew 5:3–16).

"Salt of the earth: A person or group of people regarded as the finest of their kind" (Collins English Dictionary).

The obvious historical analogy is Gandhi's march to the ocean to collect salt, challenging the British colonial prohibition, and so starting the process to bring down the empire. I acknowledge Terra Lawson-Remer for suggesting the comparison.

## REFERENCES

Castells, M. (2003) *The Power of Identity*, 2nd edn. Blackwell, Oxford.

Castells, M. (2009) *Communication Power*. Oxford University Press, Oxford.

Costanza-Chock, S. (2012) Preliminary Findings: Occupy Research Demographic and Political Participation Survey 2012. *Occupy Research.* <http://www.occupyresearch.net/2012/03/23/preliminary-findings-occupy-research-demographic-and-political-participation-survey/>.

Graham-Felsen, S. (2011) Is Occupy Wall Street the Tumblr Revolution? *GOOD: Technology.* Available at: <http://www.good.is/post/is-occupy-wall-street-the-tumblr-revolution>.

Klein, E. (2011) Who are the 99 percent? *Wonkblog, The Washington Post.* Available at: <http://www.washingtonpost.com/blogs/ezra-klein/post/who-are-the-99-percent/2011/08/25/gIQAt87jKL_blog.html>.

Lakoff, G. (2011) How Occupy Wall Street's moral vision can beat the disastrous conservative world view. *AlterNet.* Available at: <http://www.alternet.org/teaparty/152800/lakoff%3A_how_occupy_wall_street%27s_moral_vision_can_beat_the_disastrous_conservative_worldview>.

Lawson-Remer, T. (2011) #OccupyDemocracy. *Possible Futures: A Project of the Social Science Research Council.* Available at: <http://www.possible-futures.org/2011/12/08/occupydemocracy>.

Rosen, R. (2011) The 99 Percent Tumblr: self-service history. *The Atlantic.* Available at: <http://www.theatlantic.com/technology/archive/2011/10/the-99-percent-tumblr-self-service-history/246385/>.

Tarrow, S. (2011) Why Occupy Wall Street is not the Tea Party of the Left. *Foreign Affairs, Snapshot.* Available at: <http://www.foreignaffairs.com/articles/136401/sidney-tarrow/why-occupy-wall-street-is-not-the-tea-party-of-the-left>.

SELECTED OTHER SOURCES USED
IN THIS CHAPTER

## On the origins and development of the Occupy Wall Street movement

Beeston, L. (2011) The ballerina and the bull. *The Link*. Available at: <http://thelinknewspaper.ca/article/1951>.

Chafkin, M. (2012) Revolution Number 99: An oral history of Occupy Wall Street. *Vanity Fair*. Available at: <http://www.vanityfair.com/politics/2012/02/occupy-wall-street-201202>.

Eifling, S. (2011) AdBusters' Kalle Lasn talks about Occupy Wall Street. *The Tyee*. Available at: <http://thetyee.ca/News/2011/10/07/Kalle-Lasn-Occupy-Wall-Street/>.

Elliott, J. (2011) The origins of Occupy Wall Street explained. *Salon*. Available at: <http://www.salon.com/2011/10/04/adbusters_occupy_wall_st/>.

Kaste, M. (2011) Exploring Occupy Wall Street's "AdBuster" origin. *NPR Morning Edition*. Available at: <http://www.npr.org/2011/10/20/141526467/exploring-occupy-wall-streets-adbuster-origins>.

Kennedy, M. (2011) Global solidarity and the Occupy Movement. *Possible Futures*. Available at: <http://www.possible-futures.org/2011/12/05/global-solidarity-occupy-movement/>.

Kroll, A. (2011) How Occupy Wall Street really got started. *Mother Jones*. Available at: <http://motherjones.com/politics/2011/10/occupy-wall-street-international-origins>.

Schwartz. M. (2011) Pre-occupied: the origins and future of Occupy Wall Street. *The New Yorker*. Available at: <http://www.newyorker.com/reporting/2011/11/28/111128fa_fact_schwartz>.

Sledge, M. (2011) Reawakening the radical imagination: the

origins of Occupy Wall Street. *The Huffington Post.* Available at: <http://www.huffingtonpost.com/2011/11/10/occupy-wall-street-origins_n_1083977.html>.

Weigel, D. and Hepler, L. (2011) A timeline of the movement, from February to today. *Slate.* Available at: <http://www.slate.com/articles/news_and_politics/politics/features/2011/occupy_wall_street/what_is_ows_a_complete_timeline.html>.

## On daily life of camps

Ashraf, N. (2011) Brown Power at #OccupyWallStreet. *Killing New York.* Available at: <http://killingnewyork.tumblr.com/post/10839600460/brownpower>.

Carney, J. (2011) Occupy Wall Street: What life is like for protesters. *NetNet, CNBC.* Available at: <http://www.cnbc.com/id/44874685/Occupy_Wall_Street_What_Life_Is_Like_for_Protesters>.

Donovan, J. (2011) Who are the people in your neighborhood, #OccupyLA? *Occupy the Social.* Available at: <http://www.occupythesocial.com/post/12316820038/who-are-the-people-in-your-neighborhood-occupyla>.

Kleinfield, N. and Buckley, C. (2011) Wall Street occupiers, protesting till whenever. *New York Times.* Available at: <http://www.nytimes.com/2011/10/01/nyregion/wall-street-occupiers-protesting-till-whenever.html?pagewanted=all>.

Packer, G. (2011) All the angry people. *New Yorker.* Available at: <http://www.newyorker.com/reporting/2011/12/05/111205fa_fact_packer>.

Scradie, J. (2011) Why tents (still) matter for the Occupy Movement. *Common Dreams.* Available at: <http://www.commondreams.org/view/2011/11/24-1>.

Stoller, M. (2011) #OccupyWallStreet is a church of dissent, not a protest. *Naked Capitalism.* Available at: <http://

www.nakedcapitalism.com/2011/09/matt-stoller-occupy
wallstreet-is-a-church-of-dissent-not-a-protest.html>.

"The State of the Occupation." (2012) *Fire Dog Lake*. Available
at: <http://firedoglake.com/state-of-the-occupation>.

Tool. (2011) A day in the life of Occupy Wall Street.
*Daily Kos*. Available at: <http://www.dailykos.com/
story/2011/10/23/1029380/-A-Day-In-A-Life-At-Occupy-
Wallstreet>.

## On communication networks in the movement

Captain, S. (2011) Inside Occupy Wall Street's (kinda) secret
media HQ. *Threat Level, Wired*. Available at: <http://
www.wired.com/threatlevel/2011/11/inside-ows-media-
hq/?pid=195&pageid=32957>.

Donovan, J. (2012) Conference calling across the Occupy
rhizome. *The Occupied Wall Street Journal*. Available at:
<http://occupiedmedia.us/2012/02/conference-calling-
across-the-occupy-rhizome/>.

Gladstone, B. (2011) Occupy Wall Street after Zuccotti
Park. *On the Media*. Available at: <http://www.onthemedia.
org/2011/nov/18/ows-communications/>.

*Global Revolution*. (2012) Available at: <http://www.livestream.
com/globalrevolution>.

Kessler, S. (2011) How Occupy Wall Street is building its
own Internet. *Mashable*. Available at: <http://mashable.
com/2011/11/14/how-occupy-wall-street-is-building-its-
own-internet-video/>.

Martin, A. (2011) Occupy Wall Street is building its own
social network. *Atlantic Wire*. Available at: <http://www.
theatlanticwire.com/national/2011/10/occupy-wall-street-
building-its-own-social-network/43637/>.

Occupy Streams. (2012) Available at <http://occupystreams.
com>.

Polletta, F. (2011) Maybe you're better off not holding hands and singing We Shall Overcome. *Mobilizing Ideas.* Available at: <http://mobilizingideas.wordpress.com/2011/11/21/maybe-youre-better-off-not-holding-hands-and-singing-we-shall-overcome/>.

Porzucki, N. (2011) The informal media team behind Occupy Wall Street. *All Things Considered.* Available at: <http://www.npr.org/2011/10/19/141510541/the-informal-media-team-behind-occupy-wall-street>.

Santo, A. (2011) Occupy Wall Street's media team. *Columbia Journalism Review.* Available at: <http://www.cjr.org/the_news_frontier/occupy_wall_streets_media_team.php>.

Shlinkert, S. (2011) The technology propelling Occupy Wall Street. *Daily Beast.* Available at: <http://www.thedailybeast.com/articles/2011/10/06/occupy-wall-street-protests-tech-gurus-televise-the-demonstrations.html>.

Stetler, B. (2011) Occupy Wall Street puts protests in the spotlight. *New York Times.* Available at: <http://www.nytimes.com/2011/11/21/business/media/occupy-wall-street-puts-the-coverage-in-the-spotlight.html>.

Trope, A. and Swartz, L. (2011) A visual primer of the occupation, month one and counting. *Civic* Paths. Available at: <http://civicpaths.uscannenberg.org/2011/10/the-visual-culture-of-the-occupation-month-one-and-counting/>.

Ungerleider, N. (2011) How virtual private networks keep Occupy Wall Street networks up and protesting. Available at: <http://www.fastcompany.com/1792974/why-occupy-wall-street-uses-vpns>.

Wagstaff, K. (2012) Occupy the Internet: Protests give rise to DIY data networks. *Techland, Time.* Available at: <http://techland.time.com/2012/03/28/occupy-the-internet-protests-give-rise-to-diy-networks/>.

Weinstein, A. (2011) "We are the 99%" creators revealed.

*Mother Jones.* Available at: <http://motherjones.com/
politics/2011/10/we-are-the-99-percent-creators>.

## On organization and decision-making in the camps

Graeber, D. (2011a) Enacting the impossible (on consensus
decision making). *Occupy Wall Street.* Available at: <http://
occupywallst.org/article/enacting-the-impossible/>.

Graeber, D. (2011b) Occupy Wall Street's anarchist roots. *Al
Jazeera.* Available at: <http://www.aljazeera.com/indepth/
opinion/2011/11/2011112872835904508.html>.

Grusin, R. (2011) Premediation and the virtual occupation of
Wall Street. *Theory and Event,* 114 (4).

Hepler, L. and Weigel, D. (2011) Twinkling, "mic check,"
and Zuccotti Park: a guide to protest terminology. *Slate.*
Available at: <http://www.slate.com/articles/news_and_poli
tics/politics/features/2011/occupy_wall_street/what_is_
ows_a_glossary_of_the_protest_movement_.html>.

Kim, R. (2011) We are all human microphones now.
*The Nation.* Available at: <http://www.thenation.com/
blog/163767/we-are-all-human-microphones-now>.

Klein, A. (2011) Jazz hands and waggling fingers: How
Occupy Wall Street makes decisions. *New York Magazine.*
Available at: <http://nymag.com/daily/intel/2011/10/occu
py_wall_street_hand_gestur.html>.

Loofbourow, L. (2011) The livestream ended: How I got
off my computer and into the streets at Occupy Oakland.
*The Awl.* Available at: <http://www.theawl.com/2011/10/
the-livestream-ended-how-i-got-off-my-computer-and-
into-the-streets-at-occupy-oakland>.

Schneider, N. (2011) Wall Street occupiers inch toward a
demand – by living it. *Waging Nonviolence.* Available at:
<http://wagingnonviolence.org/2011/09/wall-street-occu
piers-inch-toward-a-demandby-living-it/>.

Vargas-Cooper, N. (2011) The night Occupy LA tore itself in two. *The Awl*. Available at: <http://www.theawl. com/2011/10/the-night-occupy-los-angeles-tore-itself-in-two>.

Wood, D. and Goodale, G. (2011) Does "Occupy Wall Street" have leaders? Does it need any? *Christian Science Monitor*. Available at: <http://www.csmonitor.com/USA/Politics/2011/1010/Does-Occupy-Wall-Street-have-lea ders-Does-it-need-any>.

W.W. (2011) Leaderless, consensus-based participatory democracy and its discontents. *Economist*. Available at: <http://www.economist.com/blogs/democracyinamerica/2011/10/occupy-wall-street-3>.

Zick, T. (2012) Occupy Wall Street and democratic protest. *Al Jazeera*. Available at: <http://www.aljazeera.com/indepth/opinion/2012/03/20123185220379942.html>.

## On violence and non-violence

Calhoun, C. (2011) Evicting the public. *Possible Futures*. Available at: <http://www.ssrc.org/calhoun/2011/11/18/evicting-the-public-why-has-occupying-public-spaces-brought-such-heavy-handed-repression>.

Elliott, J. (2011) Occupy Wall Street's struggle for non-violence. *Salon*. Available at: <http://www.salon. com/2011/10/17/occupy_wall_streets_struggle_for_non_violence>.

Goodale, G. (2012) Occupy Wall Street non-violence: Is Oakland the exception or the future? *The Christian Science Monitor*. Available at: <http://www.csmonitor.com/USA/Politics/2012/0131/Occupy-Wall-St.-nonviolence-Is-Oak land-the-exception-or-the-future-video>.

Gordillo, G. (2011) The human chain as a non-violent weapon. *Space and Politics*. Available at: <http://spaceandpolitics.

blogspot.com/2011/11/weapon-of-occupy-movement_23. html>.

Graeber, D. (2012) Concerning the Violent Peace-Police: an open letter to Chris Hedges. *n+1*. Available at: <http:// nplusonemag.com/concerning-the-violent-peace-police>.

Haberman, C. (2011) *A new generation of dissenters*. City Room, *New York Times*. Available at: <http://cityroom.nytimes. com/2011/10/10/a-new-generation-of-dissenters>.

Hedges, C. (2012) The cancer in Occupy. *Truth Dig*. Available at: <http://www.truthdig.com/report/item/the_cancer_of_ occupy_20120206/>.

"Occupy LA protesters are evicted – in pictures." (2011) *The Guardian*.    <http://www.guardian.co.uk/world/gallery/20 11/nov/30/occupy-la-protesters-are-evicted-in-pictures>.

Schneider, N. (2011) What "diversity of tactics" really means for Occupy Wall Street. *Waging Nonviolence*. Available at: <http://wagingnonviolence.org/2011/10/what-diversity- of-tactics-really-means-for-occupy-wall-street/>.

## On campaigns and actions in the movement

Doll, J. (2011) Kristen Christian, who created "Bank Transfer Day," the November 5 bank boycott, tells us why. *The Village Voice*. Available at: <http://blogs.villagevoice.com/ runninscared/2011/10/kristen_christian_bank_boycott_ba nk_transfer_day_occupy_wall_street.php>.

Gabbat, A. (2011) Occupy aims to shut down West Coast ports – as it happened. *The Guardian*. Available at: <http://www. guardian.co.uk/world/blog/2011/dec/12/occupy-west -coast-ports-shut-down>.

Goodale, G. (2011) Bank Transfer Day: How much impact did it have? *Christian Science Monitor*. Available at: <http:// www.csmonitor.com/USA/Politics/2011/1107/Bank-Tran sfer-Day-How-much-impact-did-it-have>.

Hamilton, W., Reckard, S., and Willon, P. (2011) Occupy Movement moves into neighborhoods. *Los Angeles Times.* Available at: <http://articles.latimes.com/2011/dec/06/business/la-fi-occupy-home-20111206>.

"Occupy Wall Street goes home." (2011) *Occupy Wall Street.* Available at: <http://occupywallst.org/article/occupy-wall-street-goes-home/>.

Riquier, A., Gopal, P., and Brandt, N. (2011) Occupy Movement targets home evictions in US Day of Action. *Bloomberg.* Available at: <http://www.bloomberg.com/news/2011-12-06/occupy-protest-movement-targets-home-evictions-in-u-s-day-of-action-.html>.

Swartz, L. (2010) Ghoulish ATMs, It's a Wonderful Bank, and Bloody Valentines: Personal finance as civic communication. *Civic Paths.* Available at: <http://civicpaths.uscannenberg.org/2010/11/ghoulish-atms-its-a-wonderful-bank-and-bloody-valentines-personal-finance-as-civic-communication/>.

## On relationships between the movement and politics

Bowers, C. (2011) Politicians start to take sides on Occupy Wall Street. *Daily Kos.* Available at: <http://www.dailykos.com/story/2011/10/05/1023087/-Politicians-start-to-take-sides-on-Occupy-Wall-Street>.

Dovi, C. (2011) Can Occupy and the Tea Party team up? *Salon.* Available at: <http://www.salon.com/2011/12/07/can_occupy_and_the_tea_party_team_up/>.

Francis, D. (2011) The politics and economics of Occupy Wall Street. *US News.* Available at: <http://money.usnews.com/money/business-economy/articles/2011/12/12/the-economics-of-occupy-wall-street>.

Gautney, H. (2011) Why Occupy Wall Street wants nothing to do with our politicians. *Washington Post.* Available at:

<http://www.washingtonpost.com/national/on-leadership/
why-occupy-wall-street-wants-nothing-to-do-with-our-
politicians/2011/10/21/gIQAc2wT3L_story.html>.

Klein, R. (2011) Democrats seek to own "Occupy Wall
Street." *ABC News*. Available at: <http://abcnews.go.com/
Politics/democrats-seek-occupy-wall-street-movement/
story?id=14701337>.

Lawler, K. (2011) Fear of a slacker revolution. *Possible
Futures*. Available at: <http://www.possible-futures.org/
2011/12/01/fear-slacker-revolution-occupy-wall-street-
cultural-politics-class-struggle/>.

Lessig, L. (2011) #OccupyWallSt, then #OccupyKSt, then
#OccupyMainSt. *Huffington Post*. Available at: <http://
www.huffingtonpost.com/lawrence-lessig/occupywallst-
then-occupyk_b_995547.html>.

Marcuse, P. (2011) Perspective on Occupy: occupiers, sympathizers, and antagonists. *Peter Marcuse's Blog*. Available
at: <http://pmarcuse.wordpress.com/2011/12/31/perspec
tive-on-occuppy-occupiers-sympathizers-and-antagonis
ts/>.

Neal, M. (2012) Politicians react to the Occupy Wall Street
Movement. *Huffington Post*. Available at: <http://www.
huffingtonpost.com/2011/10/17/occupy-wall-street-politi
cian-reactions_n_1014273.html>.

"Occupy Wall Street protesters fed up with both parties."
(2011) *AP/Huffington Post*. Available at: <http://www.
huffingtonpost.com/2011/10/06/occupy-wall-street-pro
testers_n_999289.html>.

Pierce, C. (2011) We must give Occupy a politics worthy
of its courage. *Politics Blog, Esquire*. Available at:
<http://www.esquire.com/blogs/politics/occupy-class-
warfare-6592653>.

Wolf, N. (2011) How to Occupy the moral and political high
ground. *The Guardian*. Available at: <http://www.guardian.

co.uk/commentisfree/2011/nov/06/naomi-wolf-occupy-movement>.

## On public opinion and the movement

Bartels, L. (2012) Occupy's impact beyond the beltway. *Bill Moyers*. Available at: <http://billmoyers.com/2012/01/18/has-the-occupy-movement-altered-public-opinion/>.

"Bay Areas news group poll finds 94% support for Occupy Oakland." (2012) *Occupy Oakland*. Available at: <http://occupyoakland.org/2012/02/bay-area-news-group-poll-finds-94-support-occupy/>.

Montopoli, B. (2011) Occupy Wall Street: More popular than you think. *CBS News*. Available at: <http://www.cbsnews.com/8301-503544_162-20120052-503544.html?tag=mncol;lst;1>.

Reich, R. (2011) Occupy Wall Street has transformed public opinion. *Salon*. Available at: <http://www.salon.com/2011/10/31/how_ows_has_transformed_public_opinion/>.

Sargeant, G. (2011) Will Occupy Wall Street alienate the middle of the country? It hasn't yet. *Washington Post*. Available at: <http://www.washingtonpost.com/blogs/plum-line/post/will-occupy-wall-street-alienate-the-middle-of-the-country-it-hasn't yet/2011/10/24/gIQAZ1zJDM_blog.html>.

## General sources

Blodget, H. (2011) CHARTS: Here's what the Occupy Wall Street protesters are so angry about. *Business Insider*. Available at: <http://www.businessinsider.com/what-wall-street-protesters-are-so-angry-about-2011-10?op=1>.

"By the Numbers." (2011) *Demos*. Available at: <http://archive.demos.org/inequality/numbers.cfm>.

Gilson, D. (2011) Charts: Who are the 1%? *Mother Jones*. Available at: <http://motherjones.com/mojo/2011/10/one-percent-income-inequality-OWS>.

Gosztola, K. (2011-2012) The dissenter. *Fire Dog Lake*. Available at: <http://dissenter.firedoglake.com/>.

*InterOccupy: Connecting Occupations*. Available at: <http://interoccupy.org/>.

Kilkenny, A. (2011) Occupy Wall Street: Searching for hope in America. *The Nation*. Available at: <http://www.thenation.com/blog/163462/occupywallstreet-searching-hope-america>.

Mitchell, G. (2011-2012) The Occupy USA blog. *The Nation*. Available at: <http://www.thenation.com/blogs/greg-mitchell>.

*New York City General Assembly*. Available at: <http://www.nycga.net/>.

*Occupied Wall Street Journal*. Available at: <http://occupiedmedia.us/>.

*Occupy! N+1*. Available at: <http://nplusonemag.com/occupy/>.

*Occupy Together*. Available at: <http://www.occupytogether.org/>.

Rushkoff, D. (2011) Think Occupy Wall Street is a phase? You don't get it. *CNN*. Available at: <http://www.cnn.com/2011/10/05/opinion/rushkoff-occupy-wall-street/index.html>.

Samuelson, T. (2011) Meet the occupants. *New York Magazine*. Available at: <http://nymag.com/news/intelligencer/topic/occupy-wall-street-2011-10/>.

Sassen, S. (2011) The global street comes to Wall Street. *Possible Futures*. Available at: <http://www.possible-futures.org/2011/11/22/the-global-street-comes-to-wall-street/>.

Schneider, N. (2011) Occupy Wall Street: FAQs. *The Nation*.

Available at: <http://www.thenation.com/article/163719/occupy-wall-street-faq>.

Sifry, M. (2011) #OccupyWallstreet: There's something happening here, Mr. Jones. *Tech President*. Available at: <http://techpresident.com/blog-entry/occupywallstreet-theres-something-happening-here-mr-jones>.

*Tidal: Occupy Theory, Occupy Strategy*. Available at <http://www.occupytheory.org>.

*Waging Nonviolence*. Available at: <http://wagingnonviolence.org>.

Weigel, D. (2011) A complete guide to the anti-corporate protests taking place around the nation. *Slate*. Available at: <http://www.slate.com/articles/news_and_politics/politics/features/2011/occupy_wall_street/what_is_ows_a_guide_to_the_anti_corporate_protests.html>.

Wolff, R. (2011) Occupy Wall Street ends capitalism's alibi. *The Guardian*. Available at: <http://www.guardian.co.uk/commentisfree/cifamerica/2011/oct/04/occupy-wall-street-new-york>.

# NETWORKED SOCIAL MOVEMENTS:

## A GLOBAL TREND?

Time leap in this chapter. We are now in December 2014. With the hindsight of four years after new social movements exploded around the world, how can we assess their potential as agents of social change in the global network society?

## OVERVIEW

In 2012–14 there have been major social movements with similar characteristics to those analyzed in this book in a variety of contexts. Some of the most salient of them are the Turkish movement around the defense of Gezi Park in June 2013, and the relentless demonstrations in Brazil in 2013–14 asserting people's dignity and claiming their right to change the model of development and the priorities in public spending while fighting political corruption. Furthermore, there were a number of other major social movements such as: the student movement in Chile, initiated in May 2011 and extended to 2014; the Mexican movement #YoSoy132,

formed in May 2012, seeking the regeneration of politics; the Mexican mass protests in September–November
2014 against the assassination and kidnapping of students
in Iguala, Guerrero, by the agents of the narco-state in
September 2014; the Moscow demonstrations in defense of
democratic rights against Putin authoritarianism in 2011–12;
the nationalist Ukrainian movement in Kiev in 2013, occupying Maidan square; Hong Kong's Umbrella Revolution
of September/October 2014; and the continuing mobilizations in Spain, Greece, and Portugal. All these events, and
others that may happen between the time of this writing and
the time of your reading, express the vitality and continuity of the new forms of social movements in spite of their
diversity and differential outcomes. Furthermore, there have
been multiple local mobilizations nurtured in cyberspace and
enacted in urban space in a number of countries, including
China (e.g. the Southern Weekly incident in Guangzhou in
January 2013, or the Wukan village revolt against land grab
in Guandong Province in 2011–12). The detailed analysis of
these movements is beyond the scope of this book and of the
capacity of this author. Fortunately, there is a growing interest among social researchers, some of them action research
oriented, about this fundamental theme of inquiry, so that
we now have a body of reliable observation and analysis that
is bound to produce an understanding of the social movements characteristic of the network society.[1] Therefore, I will
not pursue here the strategy of detailed case studies that I
present in the other chapters of this volume. Instead, I will
simply reflect on the main features of some of these movements to broaden the empirical basis of the analysis to be
presented in the following chapter.

Before focusing on some of the most significant movements that took place in the 2012–14 period, it is important
to emphasize that networked social movements have

occurred in extremely different contexts; not only in different cultures, institutional settings, and levels of development, but in vastly divergent economic and political conditions. Thus, while in the Arab countries the revolts were aimed at bringing down longstanding, bloody dictatorships, and in Europe and the United States the financial crisis was the trigger for the protest, Brazil, Turkey, and Chile are democracies that have enjoyed substantial economic growth in the last decade. Brazil has a progressive government under the Partido dos Trebalhadores (PT) led by Presidents Lula and Dilma Rousseff, and has experienced significant alleviation of poverty and improvement of the overall living standards of the population in relationship to previous times, in spite of an economic recession in 2014. The economic and social conditions for most people have improved significantly in Turkey and Chile in spite of the persistence of pockets of poverty. Thus, it is important to emphasize that social movements are not the direct consequence of economic crises, poverty, or authoritarian regimes. It is so in some cases but not in others. And yet, most of these movements display similar features that I will summarize in the next chapter. They also share two major contextual factors that appear to be decisive. The first is a fundamental crisis of legitimacy of the political system, regardless of the form of political regime, be it authoritarian or based on democratic elections. Political parties are despised in most countries, government corruption is a recurrent theme, and professional politicians as a collective have become "La Casta" in the minds of most citizens around the world, deemed to take care of their own interests rather than to represent the people who elect and pay them.[2] This is essential because, whatever the grievances people have, they do not find channels of expression and adequate representation in the political institutions. Thus, they resort to alternative forms of direct manifestations of their needs and desires, and aim at reinventing democracy. Therefore, the interaction between social movements and political institutions becomes a fundamental question that may yield the actual potential of these social movements as agents of social change. I will deal with this matter in some detail in the last chapter of this volume.

The second major feature common to the context in which all these movements were formed is their autonomous communicative capacity; being able to connect among the participants and with society as a whole via the new social media, mediated by smart phones and the whole galaxy of communication networks (Cardoso and De Fatim, forthcoming). This new communication system is not just the Internet, but the digital social networks based on the Internet and wireless communication that have exploded in the last decade. Friendster, the first relevant social networking site, was created in 2002, Facebook in 2004, and Twitter in 2007. Many others dot the planet now, with differential presence depending on the institutional environment. In 2013, there were 3 billion users on these social networks, as documented in figure 4.

This communicative potential is disproportionately in the hands of the younger groups of the population (aged 16–34 mainly), those who are technically savvy in digital communication, and those more prone to rebellion against what they perceive as an unbearable social order. However, this is not to say that social networks are the cause of social movements, as the prime minister of Turkey, Recep Tayyip Erdogan (elected president in 2014), put it ("Twitter is the enemy of the people"). They are the tools at the disposal of any individual or self-created network of individuals who want to have their views aired and who call upon those who share their indignation to join them in protest in the urban space. It is this connection between the public cyber-space, bypassing the

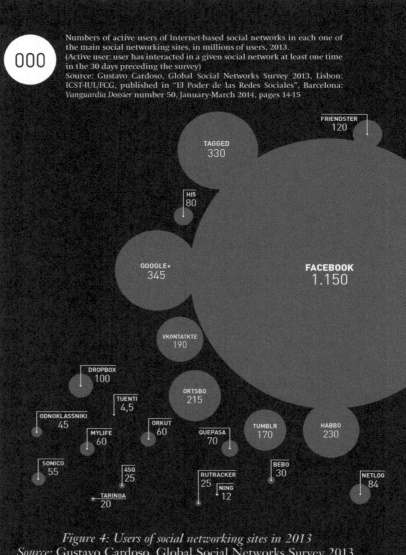

*Figure 4: Users of social networking sites in 2013*
*Source:* Gustavo Cardoso, Global Social Networks Survey 2013,
Lisbon: ICST-IUL/FCG, published in "El Poder de las Redes
Sociales," *Vanguardia Dossier*, 50, January–March 2014, pp. 14–15.

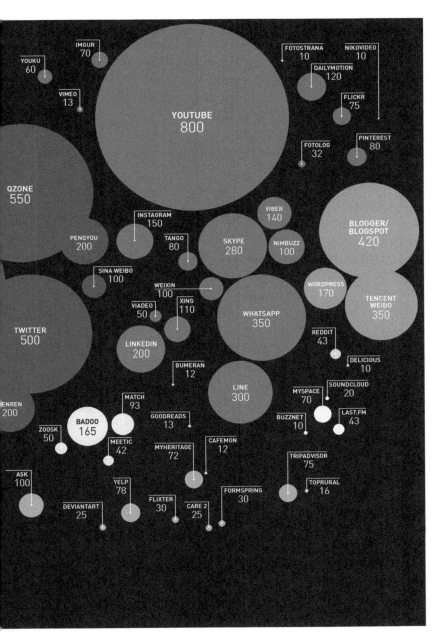

controlled mainstream media, and the public urban space, whose occupation challenges institutional authority, that is at the core of the new social movements. Indeed, the diffusion of Internet-based social networks is a necessary condition for the existence of these new social movements in our time. But it is not a sufficient condition. The global survey conducted by Gustavo Cardoso on the uses of social networks shows that less than 18 percent of internauts have used social networks for social or political campaigns (Cardoso 2014). Presence on social networks is simply a way of life for the majority of the young population of the planet for all kinds of purposes in the diverse range of human activity. And so, when they protest, they also do it on the social networks that they inhabit. But they do not necessarily protest. In fact, in most countries the protests, even using social media, have not scaled up to a threshold of political significance. So, I believe it can be safely said that given enough social unrest and rebellious potential in a given society, the widespread use of social media allows individual rebellions to become social protests and ultimately social movements (Cardoso and De Fatima, forthcoming). However, in some situations, history, culture, and institutions may channel these protests toward different forms of political expression, away from autonomous social movements and closer to populist reactions within the political system. This is the case, for instance, for right-wing political movements in Europe, be it the French Front National, UKIP in Britain, Golden Dawn in Greece, the True Finns in Finland, or the Republican-associated Tea Party in the United States. All these political factions also use social networks, of course – everybody does these days – but rather than social movements, they are straightforward political actors who are not nurtured in the autonomous expression of social revolts originated on the Internet and translated in spatial and institutional occupations. In other words, proto-social movements could become social movements in an environment of communicative autonomy. But social revolts are not present in every society and some of these social revolts may become channeled in the populist tradition of demagogic politics.

Some of the elements of this analysis may be clarified by a summary reference to some of the meaningful social movements that took place in the 2012–14 period. In my account, I will not dwell on the narrative of the events, referring only to those features that are significant for their understanding.

## THE CLASH BETWEEN OLD AND NEW TURKEY: GEZI PARK, JUNE 2013

The defense of Gezi Park in Istanbul in June 2013 became a major source of social protest when the AKP government of Erdogan decided to destroy the last park remaining in the historic center of Istanbul, adjacent to Taksim Square. The park was to be destroyed in order to build a shopping center that would also be a theme park for tourists around a historic Artillery building. However, the administrative procedure legally required to change the land use was disregarded. Gezi Park had become a symbol for ecologists and conservationist architects as well as a meeting place for gays and lesbians. It was in the vicinity of Taksim Square, and of Istiklal Avenue, the hangout place for music, art, and informal meetings for the youth of Istanbul. Thus, when the park was threatened with destruction, defenders of a free way of life decided to save the park and to camp in Taksim to avert the park's destruction. Following direct orders from the prime minister, the riot police attacked the protesters with extreme violence. The images of police brutality immediately distributed over YouTube and other social networks induced widespread outrage. Twitter was intensely used to mobilize thousands of demonstrators who came to join the protest in Gezi Park, and many thousands more did so in other areas of Istanbul (such as Besiktas), as well as in other Turkish cities, particularly in Ankara.[3] The confrontations lasted for weeks and generated a national debate in which Erdogan actively participated using derogatory terms against his critics and threatening harsh repressive measures. Overall, seven people died (one of them a policeman), hundreds were injured, and thousands were arrested. In the end, the conciliatory attitude of the governor of Istanbul and of the president of Turkey at the time, the support of some members of the political opposition, and the empathy of many young people around the country forced the government to suspend indefinitely the demolition of the park. However, the challenge to the plans of urban development was extended to a broader criticism of the policies of the AKP. Yet, both the municipal elections and the parliamentary elections held in 2014 in Turkey resulted in a resounding victory for the AKP that appeared to vindicate Erdogan's dismissal of the social protest. The apparent contradiction between the intensity of the movement and the political opinion of the majority of the population may be explained by two factors (Cinmen 2014; Gokmenoglu 2013a, 2013b, 2014). On the one hand, the mainstream media aligned themselves with the government, did not report on the movement at first and then manipulated information by focusing on the violent incidents that followed the intervention of the police. On the other hand, the Gezi movement revealed the sharp cultural and social divide in Turkish society. The reaction of Erdogan and his law and order government against the expression of the youth culture in Taksim was part of a broader policy to gradually induce strict Muslim conservative values into people's personal lives, particularly for women. The stringent limits imposed on alcohol sales clashed directly with the personal freedom that the new generation of Turks had come to appreciate in a highly modernized society. The values of environmentalism, of democracy, and of tolerance were at odds with the traditional, deeply religious culture prevalent in the rural areas and in the less educated segments of the urban population. In fact, the impact of the movement deepened the split in the coalition that had brought the AKP to power, shaking the imposed secularist rule favored by the politically interventionist armed forces. AKP voters represented an alliance between the conservative religious majority of the country and the liberal urban middle class opposed to military rule and supportive of European standards of democracy. Wrapped in the legitimacy of the ballot box, Erdogan was able to counter the authoritarian secularism of the heirs of Kemal Ataturk to engage in a gradual move toward a moderate re-Islamization of Turkey that came in direct contradiction with the aspirations of the highly educated urban middle class to be fully European. Moreover, while being culturally integrist, Erdogan embraced economic globalization and neoliberal policies with considerable economic success. And he presented himself on the world scene as the political bridge between the Muslim world and the West.

This is why Gezi Park became much more than a conflict between environmentalism and speculative redevelopment. It was a fight over urban space that represented the contradiction between the citizens' right to their city as a public space and the conservative policy aimed at restricting cultural life and submitting it to the pattern of traditional family life, with women being asked to have at least three children, abortion sharply limited, the wearing of the veil coming back into daily life, and the uses of public space regulated and curfewed. This cultural conflict started to grow on the social networks a long time before it would explode in the open confrontation at Gezi. It emerged from a spontaneous debate initiated by youth groups, political activists, artists, musicians, ecologists, women's groups, gay and lesbian rights groups, and anti-capitalist movements who were debating and coordinating their action against the increasingly repressive, culturally conservative orthodoxy of the Islamist party. As in other contexts, the debate on the social networks shifted to the urban space; Gezi Park becoming a symbolic site of autonomous urban life. A most fundamental conflict of the new Turkish society was played out in terms of contemporary social movements: autonomous social networks constructing an autonomous urban space to confront the old repressive forces of state and God, cemented now by their integration in global capitalism.

## CHALLENGING THE DEVELOPMENT MODEL, DENOUNCING POLITICAL CORRUPTION: BRAZIL 2013–14

Brazil has been at the forefront of networked social movements in 2013 and, to a lesser extent, in 2014 (Branco 2014a, 2014b). The impact of these movements, which started as localized, sectoral protests in January 2013, has transformed the public debate and the political landscape in one of the most important and dynamic countries in the world. In this case, the original anchoring point of the protest was urban transportation. As in all industrializing countries, the Brazilian landscape has been transformed by a gigantic wave of metropolitanization; 82 percent of the population is now urban, and the nerve centers of the country are in very large metropolitan regions, of which São Paulo, with 18 million people, is the largest and most problematic in terms of quality of life. Brazil has engaged on a path of economic growth in the last two decades in spite of an economic downturn in 2014. It has also achieved a substantial reduction of poverty and a significant betterment of health and education. Yet, the living conditions in these metropolises have actually worsened in terms of environmental degradation, housing, urban amenities, and transportation. Corrupt local governments, based on political patronage and informal connections to real estate and urban infrastructure industries, have surrendered to a pattern of speculative land development that follows the interests of the builders and transportation companies at the expense of the quality of life of urban dwellers. An average daily commuting time of 3–4 hours is the norm. This is time to live that is wasted for the benefit of speculators and the complacency of an unaccountable bureaucracy. The only response public transportation companies had to growing costs derived from their inefficiency was to raise tariffs for the users who are defenseless in a captive market. So, when in late 2012 it was found that there was fraud in the calculation of new tariffs for public transportation companies, hundreds demonstrated against the rise in fares on January 1, 2013 in Porto Alegre. Porto Alegre is a symbolic city in contemporary social change. It elected a progressive mayor, Olivio Dutra, who implemented audacious measures of citizen participation, including a consultative process to decide the budget. The mayor was later elected governor of Rio Grande do Sul in 1999–2003. Dutra was succeeded both as mayor and as governor by Tarso Genro, who extended the participatory scheme (using the Internet) to the state government. The city was also the convener of the first three World Social Forums, a global gathering that was organized as an alternative to the corporate World Economic Forum meeting at Davos. So naturally, in 2013, a new Block of Struggles for Public Transportation was formed there. The movement soon shifted to other regions, particularly Amazon, Rio Grande do Norte, Bahia, etc. Between February and May 2013, following calls posted on the social networks, thousands of people demonstrated in several cities opposing the increase in transportation fares. In São Paulo, the main economic and knowledge center of South America, massive protests started on June 3, 2013. The campaign on transportation was taken up by the Movement for Free Pass (Movimento de Passe Livre – MPL in Portuguese), created precisely in the meeting of the World Social Forum in Porto Alegre in 2005, and that extended its presence to São Paulo. After a judge canceled the rise dictated by local authorities, on June 6, a coordinated protest, organized over the Internet by MPL, Anonymous, and Ninja (independent media), took place nationally. In São Paulo, 20,000 protesters blocked the main avenue, this time asking for free public transportation. There was a violent repression from the local and state police. Some demonstrators responded in kind. The demonstrations continued for several days before reaching a dramatic confrontation on June 13 with barricades being erected in the center of São Paulo. In this context, a new theme came to the forefront of the protest: the corruption and wasteful spending associated with the construction of soccer stadiums in preparation for the World Cup of 2014. A pivotal day was June 15 in Brasilia during the inauguration of a new stadium in the presence of President Dilma Rousseff. New violent clashes followed, the Congress was partially occupied and the landmark building of Planalto, site of the Ministry of Foreign Affairs, was ransacked. The media then turned their attention to the movement, dismissing its demands and focusing on the acts of violence. However, the attention of the media made aware the public opinion at large of the reasons for the protests, and while condemning the violence, the majority of public opinion expressed support for the criticism concerning the huge spending on stadiums and infrastructure without accountability, and for the benefit of corrupt public corporations and construction companies. Given the public image of soccer-loving Brazilians, it would have been unthinkable that there be a protest against the organization of the World Cup in their country. And yet, the slogan "We would trade one hospital for ten stadiums" became a motto of the protest. Expanding the reach of its demands, the movement, that in late June extended to over 100 cities, with Rio de Janeiro now taking the lead in the action, called for greater public investment in transportation, health, and education, and appealed to the federal government to curtail the corruption of local politicians and their crony companies. Given the intensity and growing popularity of the protests, several local governments canceled the rise in transportation fares. Yet, the movement did not stop. In fact, when activists were blamed for inducing such turmoil for an increase of just 20 cents, their answer was: "It is not about the 20 cents, it is about our rights." It was, in fact, a cry to be respected, to assert their dignity as they put it. On June 20, in the one and a half million strong demonstration in São Paulo, the main target of the protest was political corruption – exposing the practices of government and the political class at large. In a stunning turn of events, President Dilma Rousseff sided with the demonstrators (while, of course, condemning violence), promised a revision of the tariffs for public services, requested the cancelation of the rise in tariffs, and announced a substantial increase in public spending in transportation, urban services, health, and education. Furthermore, she acknowledged – at that time and later in her speech in the UN General Assembly in September – the flaws in the political system, the nepotism and unaccountability of political parties, and the need for a new Constitution to be submitted to popular referendum, bypassing the control of the Congress by the political class. In July, the pressure of the movement led to the repeal of the law known as PEC 37 that exonerated the prosecution of illegal deals in the Congress from the supervision of judicial control. Yet, mass demonstrations took place again in Brazil in the following months. On September 7, 2013, the day of Brazilian independence, hundreds of thousands took to the streets in Brasilia, São Paulo, Rio de Janeiro, Porto Alegre, Belo Horizonte, and many other cities. The main target this time was the corruption of politicians. It was prompted by a vote in Congress maintaining the salary of their fellow representative, Natan Donadon, who was in prison, convicted of embezzling public funds, yet he requested to keep his pay while in prison. Demonstrators in every city added their own list of local corrupt people, including São Paulo's Governor Alminck, suspected of illegal deals in the construction of the Metro system. In Rio, hundreds of mothers living in the favelas (shanty towns) demonstrated against the elite police forces accused of disappearing their sons during their raids. Public opinion, the media, and politicians were shocked and surprised by the intensity and popularity of the protests, with the majority of public opinion supporting the criticisms voiced by the movement in the streets and on the social networks (about 89 percent of public support according to some polls). In spite of President Rousseff's understanding of rightfulness of the movements, all political parties, including many cadres in the governing party, the PT, condemned the demonstrations, with two important exceptions: President Lula joined President Rousseff in calling for a positive response to the "voice of the streets," and ecologist and activist Marina Silva and her "Sustainability Network," who had led the Green Party in the presidential campaign of 2010, sided with the movement in a move that would have full political meaning in 2014. However, as the protests challenged the PT government in office, the September 2013 demonstrations saw a sizable presence of conservative and extreme right groups, more on the social networks than in the streets. For instance, the group most present on the social networks, calling for "the greatest protest in Brazilian history on Independence Day," was the "Movement Against Corruption," led by right-wing Senator Demostenes Torres, who made his reputation in the media denouncing corruption and was ultimately indicted for accepting bribes in a video-recorded police sting. Anonymous supported the demonstrations but there are seven competing Anonymous groups in Brazil, some of them undercover operations from the extreme right, financed by business groups. Yet, other groups that were genuine expressions of social protest saw the demonstrations as a platform to voice their demands for social change. This was particularly the case with "Grito da Terra," a progressive Catholic movement mobilizing for agrarian reform and defense of family farms.

In sum, as Brazilian social networks and Brazilian streets became the sites of protest by the hundreds of thousands, all forms of social demands, ideological groupings, and political projects converged toward this multifaceted movement, making it less spontaneous and more ambiguous in their criticism of the political order. The right-wing opposition to the most progressive government in Brazilian history mixed with the stand taken by social movements against political corruption and for new forms of participatory democracy.

The contradictory character of social protests was even more evident in yet another round of protests that took place in the weeks preceding the opening of the World Cup in June 2014. Some of these protests focused on the rights of urban dwellers displaced to clear the land for stadium construction in several areas, particularly again in São Paulo. Their demands were accepted, and the federal government set up a compensation system for all those affected by the public works related to the World Cup. On the other hand, the challenge to the World Cup, betting on the failure of its organization, was led by radical anarchists and conservative groups, converging in their opposition to the left-wing government. However, this time the protests were not massive and it was mainly activists that took part. They were also frequently overtaken by the violent faction of the Black Block, a mixture of radical anarchists, gang members, and provocateurs. Many of the games were played in the shadow of violent clashes with the police, something despised by public opinion. A large segment of the population still wanted the World Cup to succeed, and in fact the logistics of the event actually worked; it was a success in spite of the poor performance of the national team. Thus, although social protests still showed the deep dissatisfaction of most Brazilians with the political and economic system governing their lives, the protesters lost their chance to become the voice of the Brazilian people at large. With presidential elections looming on the horizon on October 5, 2014, much of the energy of the movement was channeled toward the public debate on the issues that the presidential candidates would have to tackle. Such a debate was decisively framed by the demands and proposals that the movement had put forward for over a year of relentless campaigns on the social networks and demonstrations in the streets. The unity of the two forms of expression of the protest was made unequivocally clear by the huge banner presiding over one of the largest street demonstrations in Rio de Janeiro: "We are the social networks"; as social networks are made up of people and people were both debating on Internet networking sites and marching in the streets of Brazilian cities.

In terms of the goals of the Brazilian movement, two themes appeared as the most significant. First, the critique of politicians, of political corruption, and of the actual functioning of democracy while still defending representative democracy. Second, the challenge to the model of development that the political and economic elites of Brazil – of all ideologies – have embraced in the last two decades. It is, in fact, a traditional model of growth at all costs to generate resources to lift millions out of poverty and to improve the well-being of the population at the expense of the deterioration of the quality of urban life. That most demands focused spontaneously on urban transportation, housing, and public services (primarily education and health) shows that most people's perception is that jobs and income are not enough for a decent life. Moreover, the criticism from the movement was expressed outside the traditional labor unions and was directed against all political parties, including the left-wing party in government (PT) in spite of the popularity of its historic leader, President Lula. In fact, the entire political class, with the exception of Presidents Lula and Rousseff, was violently critical of the movement, denouncing it as a threat to democracy. Thus, the Brazilian demonstrations of 2013 and 2014 appear to be a challenge to the development model based on unfettered economic growth and a rebuttal to the political agents that hold the power of the Brazilian state. While the movement did not have a precise program, let alone an organized leadership, its stands clearly indicated a collective desire to create a different kind of society and state based on the search for a multidimensional quality of life and experimentation with participatory democracy.

## BEYOND NEOLIBERALISM:
## STUDENT MOVEMENT IN CHILE, 2011–13

A similar interpretation can be proposed about the significant Chilean student movement that periodically occupied the streets of Santiago and other cities, always rooted in Internet social networks, in 2011–13. While Chile is still considered the most successful example of economic growth in the framework of globalization and liberalization in the whole of Latin America, during the administration of Conservative President Piñera, elected in 2010 after decades of center-left governments, the majority of Chileans became highly critical of their economic model and requested greater attention from the government toward education, health, pensions, environmental quality, and social redistribution (Calderon and Castells 2014). The student movement, while originally mobilized for reducing the cost of the public universities, obtaining financial aid, and requesting tighter government control on mediocre private universities, extended their demands to ask for free college education, for an improvement of health, housing, and education in general, and for the defense of women's rights and the rights of the Indian Mapuche minority. They also asked for new forms of participatory democracy and for tighter control of political corruption. Indeed, they questioned the legitimacy of traditional democracy based on the monopoly of power by political parties. Because of the broad range of its demands, the student movement obtained the consistent support of over 80 percent of citizens and became the harbinger of social change in democratic Chile.

The Chilean student movement presents the special feature of being a mix of autonomous social movement and political left-wing activism. The charismatic leader of the movement, student Camila Vallejo, was a member of the Communist Party, yet she respected the decisions of the democratic assemblies. Thus, Communists coexisted with Anarchists, Socialists, and independent students in the same movement, all being careful to keep the movement away from partisan politics. In 2014, the candidate of the center-left, Michelle Bachelet, a lifelong Socialist, was elected president of Chile by an overwhelming majority

after running a campaign in which she explicitly adopted
most of the demands of the student movement, including
to move toward free public college education by the end of
her presidency. She acted quickly to implement her promises. Furthermore, several of the student leaders, including
Vallejo, were elected to Congress under various political
labels. Thus, the Chilean student movement shows the possibility of a direct connection with the political system in spite
of its frontal critique of traditional political parties and of
professional politicians. This may have been made possible
because of the leadership of President Michelle Bachelet,
known for her independence vis-à-vis the party machines,
including her own Socialist Party. The symbiotic connection
between an autonomous social movement and a charismatic
political leader offers a model of social change that could
reform the institutions of democracy from the inside. Yet,
the construction of the autonomy of the movement took
place, originally, in the free space of social networks, and was
expressed in street demonstrations and general assemblies in
occupied university locales in which the pre-figurative forms
of democracy were experimented with.

## UNDOING THE MEDIA-STATE COMPLEX: MEXICO'S #YOSOY132

The Mexican Movement, #YoSoy132, is one of the most
interesting experiences of networked social movements
because it directly addresses the connection between mainstream mass media and institutional politics as the template
where political power is controlled in most societies. Mexico
is precisely characterized by a television duopoly (Televisa
and Television Azteca) both directly connected to dominant
business interests and political elites. On the other hand, the
Mexican state has largely been controlled (by legal or illegal

procedures) by two parties: the Revolutionary Institutional Party (PRI) that dominated Mexican politics for 70 years, and the Conservative Partido de Acción Nacional (PAN), coming to the presidency of the country in recent years. The left-wing PRD (Partido Revolucionario Democrático) holds some local and state governments, particularly Mexico City, but has been kept out of national power sometimes by blatant electoral fraud. Thus, the party duopoly and the TV duopoly and their connection constitute the heart of Mexico's political power system. This is what, by an accidental circumstance, the spontaneous #YoSoy132 movement came to expose and challenge.

A succinct description of this movement may help to understand its significance (Monterde and Aragon 2014). On May 11, 2012, in the midst of the campaign for presidential elections in Mexico, the PRI candidate, Enrique Peña Nieto, participated in a panel organized by the students at the School of Communication of the Universidad Iberoamericana, a leading Jesuit university in Mexico City. Some students blamed him for the murderous violence of the police against the population in Atenco during his tenure as governor of the state of Mexico. After Peña Nieto defended his policies, most students in the audience started shouting at him. He took refuge in the toilets and then left the campus escorted by a security detail while hundreds of young people continued to voice their rejection of the corrupt PRI policies. Students recorded the episode in a video that was immediately uploaded onto social networks and had viral distribution. Television networks and the PRI leaders dismissed the protest as a political plot and argued that the protesters were not in fact students of the university and that there were just a handful of them. Responding to this statement, 131 students of Iberoamericana made a new video, diffused on YouTube, giving their names and showing their student ID cards and stated their independence from any political affiliation. Within a few hours, 20,000 YouTube users had forwarded the video. Spontaneously, a movement of support for the students was started on the social networks under the hashtag #YoSoy132, everybody adding herself to the 131 who initiated the protest. As in other movements, the protest shifted from the social networks into the streets, this time of Mexico City. On May 19, 2012, 30,000 people marched in the Zocalo (main square of the city) against Peña Nieto. On May 30, #YoSoy132 organized its first General Assembly at the Universidad Nacional Autónoma de México, the main university in the country. Fifteen panels discussed and proposed new policies, from education to transgenic food, and strategized about how to counter neoliberalism. Yet, the main demand of the movement was to reclaim freedom of expression, rejecting the manipulation of national television networks.

The movement then decided to intervene in the electoral campaign and organized a debate among all the main presidential candidates. They were all invited, and all came, with the notorious exception of Peña Nieto. The movement positioned itself as the platform of independent youth asking for participation and voice beyond partisan lines. In July, the movement published two videos exposing some of the irregularities they detected in the campaign and in the election itself. Ultimately, Peña Nieto was elected president of Mexico: the coalition of interests constructed around PRI was too powerful for a newborn movement to reverse the media blitz and patronage networks built around the country. Yet something changed in the minds of young Mexicans: it became possible to oppose the corrupt elites that had governed the country forever. Moreover, the monopoly of information was broken. Television was no longer the only source of reports and images on the Mexican reality. The movement built communicative autonomy and influenced those sectors of the political system, particularly the left-wing PRD, looking for ways to construct an alternative to the entrenched populist machine of PRI. In 2014, around the entire geography of Mexico, there were groups that emerged from the #YoSoy132 and continued to defend just causes in every domain of their local experience. The seeds of change are planted in the minds of thousands of people and continue to inspire debates on social networks. These seeds grow every day following the rhizomatic logic which character-izes networked social movements. After a group of students from a rural education school in the state of Guerrero were assassinated or kidnapped by local police working for nar-co-traffickers in September 2014, hundreds of thousands of Mexicans took to the streets in October and November, denouncing the complicity between the criminal cartels and the authorities of the state at all levels. As a result of these social movements a significant change has occurred in the public mind (78 percent of Mexicans did not trust political parties or the government in November 2014), as large sec-tors of Mexican society are rejecting the legitimacy of the Mexican state. Once again, networked social movements are agents of consciousness building, thus creating conditions for social and political change.

## NETWORKED SOCIAL MOVEMENTS AND SOCIAL PROTESTS

Similar reports could be provided from the frontlines of multiple social movements around the world, some of them unknown outside their locality because of the deliberate opacity of mass media vis-à-vis the new forms of social pro-test. Yet, for my analytical purpose what is relevant is to show the rise of a common pattern of social mobilization in a wide variety of contexts and within a broad range of motivations. It is this common pattern, both as a process and as a new socio-political project, which I will try to identify in the next chapter. However, it is essential to keep in mind that not all contemporary social protests are expressions of this new form of social movement. Indeed, most are not. Even if they do use social networks and ultimately disrupt social order by demonstrating in the streets. Thus, traditional politics or revolts of all kinds are also present on social networks. But this does not make then a networked social movement. A case in point is China. Against the Western image of a country under tight control, in 2010, there were over 100,000 disorderly protests, many of them violent, up from less than 10,000 one decade earlier, according to data of the Chinese government (Hsing 2014). Other sources put this number at 180,000. Yet, there are very few instances in which an autonomous social movement has been formed through this dynamic, with the exception of a few mobilizations limited in space and time. This is in contrast to Hong Kong's Umbrella Revolution of September/October 2014, a truly autonomous, networked social movement claiming the right to representative democracy and challenging Beijing's control (Fang 2014). Thus, if social mobilizations and political campaigns are distinct from networked social movements, even if they widely use social networks, which are the specific components of these social movements that make them agents of social change in the network society? I now turn to this analysis.

## NOTES

1 An excellent source of analysis and information about the most important networked social movements in 2011–13 is the series of original articles and reports from observers

and researchers from different countries published in *Vanguardia Dossier*, 50 (2014). See also Gustavo Cardoso and Branco De Fatima (forthcoming).

2  The term "La Casta" (The Cast) originated in Italy, from the book *La Casta* (Rome: Saggi Italiani, 2007) authored by two journalists, Sergio Rizzo and Gian Antonio Stella, referring to the privileges of an unaccountable professional political class. It now has become popularized around the world, particularly under the influence of social movements, as a pejorative term to refer to the arrogance and cynicism of professional politicians. The worldwide crisis of political legitimacy is at the source of many contemporary social movements as those institutions are no longer considered to be democratic. This view is echoed by a majority of public opinion in most countries.

3  Journalist Isil Cinmen writes that "the Turkish revolution won't be televised, but it will be tweeted") (Cinmen 2014).

## REFERENCES

Branco, M. (2014a) Brasil 2013. La calle y la presidenta. *Vanguardia Dossier*, 50: 83–93.

Branco, M. (2014b) Personal communication.

Calderon, F. and Castells, M. (2014) Development, democracy and social change in Chile. In Castells, M. and Himanen, P. (eds.) Reconceptualizing Development in the Global Information Age. Oxford University Press, Oxford, pp. 175–204.

Cardoso, G. (2014) Movilizacion social y medios sociales. *Vanguardia Dossier*, 50: 17–28.

Cardoso, G. and De Fatima, B. (forthcoming) "People are the message: Social Mobilization and Social Media in Brazil."

Cinmen, I. (2014) Turquia: La Rebelion de Junio. *Vanguardia Dossier*, 50: 72–80.

Fang, K. (2014) New media technology in Hong Kong's Umbrella Revolution. Philadelphia: Annenberg School of Communication, University of Pennsylvania, Center for Global Communication Studies, Research Paper (published online).

Gokmenoglu, B. (2013a) The Gezi Movement: A comparative perspective. Los Angeles: University of Southern California, Department of Sociology, Research Paper.

Gokmenoglu, B. (2013b) The Gezi Movement: A personal account. Los Angeles, University of Southern California, Department of Sociology, Research Paper.

Gokmenoglu, B. (2014) The 2014 local elections in Turkey: A research note. Los Angeles, University of Southern California, Department of Sociology.

Hsing, Y.-T. (2014) Development as culture: Human development and information development in China. In Castells, M. and Himanen, P. (eds.) Reconceptualizing Development in the Global Information Age. Oxford University Press, Oxford, pp. 116–39.

Monterde, A. and Aragon, P. (2014) #YoSoy132: Un movimiento en red. Autocomunicacion, redes policentricas y comunicaciones globales. Barcelona: Internet Interdisciplinary Institute, Universitat Oberta de Catalunya, Research Report.

*Vanguardia Dossier*, Number 50 (January–March 2014) "El Poder de las Redes Sociales." Barcelona: Ediciones La Vanguardia.

# CHANGING THE WORLD IN
# THE NETWORK SOCIETY

*We have brought down the wall of fear*
*U brought down the wall of our house*
*We'll rebuild our homes*
*But u will never build that wall of fear*
> Tweet from @souriastrong (Rawia Alhoussaini)

Throughout history, social movements have been, and continue to be, the levers of social change.[1] They usually stem from a crisis of living conditions that makes everyday life unbearable for most people. They are prompted by a deep distrust of the political institutions managing society. The combination of a degradation of the material conditions of life and of a crisis of legitimacy of the rulers in charge with the conduct of public affairs induces people to take matters into their own hands, engaging in collective action outside the prescribed institutional channels, to defend their demands and, eventually, to change the rulers, and even the rules shaping their lives. Yet, this is risky behavior, because the maintenance of social order and the stability of politi-cal institutions express power relationships that are enforced, if necessary, by intimidation and, in the last resort, by the use of force. Thus, in the historical experience, and in the observation of the movements analyzed in this book, social movements are most often triggered by emotions derived from some meaningful event that help the protesters to overcome fear and challenge the powers that be in spite of the danger inherent to their action. Indeed, social change involves an action, individual and/or collective that, at its root, is motivated emotionally, as is all human behavior, according to recent research in social neuroscience (Damasio 2009). In the context of the six basic emotions that have been identified by neuro-psychologists (fear, disgust, surprise, sad-ness, happiness, anger; Ekman 1973), the theory of affective intelligence in political communication (Neuman et al. 2007) argues that the trigger is anger, and the repressor is fear. Anger increases with the perception of an unjust action and with the identification of the agent responsible for the action. Fear triggers anxiety, which is associated with avoidance of danger. Fear is overcome by sharing and identifying with others in a process of communicative action. Then anger takes over: it leads to risk-taking behavior. When the pro-cess of communicative action induces collective action and change is enacted, the most potent positive emotion prevails: enthusiasm, which powers purposive social mobilization. Enthusiastic networked individuals, having overcome fear, are transformed into a conscious, collective actor. Thus social change results from communicative action that involves con-nection between networks of neural networks from human brains stimulated by signals from a communication environ-ment through communication networks. The technology and morphology of these communication networks shape the process of mobilization, and thus of social change, both

*[handwritten margin notes: FEEL STRONGLY ABOUT ONE THING; STRENGTH IN NUMBERS]*

as a process and as an outcome (Toret, coordinator, 2014). In recent years, large-scale communication has experienced a deep technological and organizational transformation, with the rise of what I have called mass self-communication, based on horizontal networks of interactive, multidirectional communication on the Internet and, even more so, in wireless communication networks, the now prevalent platform of communication everywhere (Castells 2009; Castells et al. 2006; Hussain and Howard 2012; Shirky 2008; Nahon and Hemsley 2013). This is the new context, at the core of the network society as a new social structure, in which the social movements of the twenty-first century are being formed.

The movements studied in this book, and similar social movements that have sprung up around the world, did originate from a structural economic crisis and from a deepening crisis of legitimacy (see Appendix). The financial crisis that shook up the foundations of global informational capitalism from 2008 onwards called into question prosperity in Europe and in the United States; threatened governments, countries and major corporations with financial collapse; and led to a substantial shrinking of the welfare state on which social stability had been predicated for decades (Castells et al. 2012; Engelen et al. 2011). The global food crisis impacted the livelihood of most people in the Arab countries as the price of basic staples, and particularly of bread, reached unaffordable levels for a population that spends most of its meager income on food. Rampant social inequality everywhere became intolerable in the eyes of many suffering the crisis without hope and without trust. The cauldron of social and political indignation reached boiling point. Yet, social movements do not arise just from poverty or political despair. They require an emotional mobilization triggered by outrage against blatant injustice, and by hope of a possible change as a result of examples of successful uprisings in other parts of the world, each revolt inspiring the next one by networking images and messages in the Internet. Moreover, in spite of the sharp differences between the contexts in which these movements arose, there are certain common features that constitute a common pattern: the shape of the social movements of the Internet Age.

## NETWORKED SOCIAL MOVEMENTS: AN EMERGING PATTERN

The social movements studied in this book, as well as others taking place around the world in recent years,[2] present a number of common characteristics.

*They are networked in multiple forms*. The use of Internet and mobile communication networks is essential, but the networking form is multimodal. It includes social networks online and offline, as well as pre-existing social networks, and networks formed during the actions of the movement. Networks are within the movement, with other movements around the world, with the Internet blogosphere, with the media and with society at large. Networking technologies are meaningful because they provide the platform for this continuing, expansive networking practice that evolves with the changing shape of the movement. Although movements are usually rooted in urban space through occupations and street demonstrations, their ongoing existence takes place in the free space of the Internet. Because they are a network of networks, they can afford not to have an identifiable center, and yet ensure coordination functions, as well as deliberation, by interaction between multiple nodes. Thus, they do not need a formal leadership, command and control center, or a vertical organization to distribute information or instructions. This decentered structure maximizes chances of participation in the movement, given that these are open-ended networks without defined boundaries, always reconfiguring themselves according to the level of involvement of the population at large. It also reduces the vulnerability of the movement to the threat of repression, since there are few specific targets to repress, except for the occupied sites, and the network can reform itself as long as there are enough participants in the movement, loosely connected by their common goals and shared values. Networking as the movement's way of life protects the movement both against its adversaries and against its own internal dangers of bureaucratization and manipulation.

While these movements usually start on the Internet social networks, *they become a movement by occupying the urban space,* be it the standing occupation of public squares or the persistence of street demonstrations. The space of the movement is always made of an interaction between the space of flows on the Internet and wireless communication networks, and the space of places of the occupied sites and of symbolic buildings targeted by protest actions. This hybrid of cyberspace and urban space constitutes a third space that I call the space of autonomy (Castells 2014). This is because autonomy can only be insured by the capacity to organize in the free space of communication networks, but at the same time can only be exercised as a transformative force by challenging the disciplinary institutional order by reclaiming the space of the city for its citizens. Autonomy without defiance becomes withdrawal. Defiance without a permanent basis for autonomy in the space of flows is tantamount to discontinuous activism. *The space of autonomy is the new spatial form of networked social movements.*

*Movements are local and global at the same time.* They start in specific contexts, for their own reasons, build their own networks, and construct their public space by occupying urban space and connecting to the Internet networks. But

*[margin handwritten notes: MOVEMENTS ARE GLOBAL + LOCAL — LEARN FROM OTHER EXPERIENCES]*

*[bottom handwritten note: PHYSICALLY OCCUPYING URBAN SPACE + THEN CONNECTING TO INTERNET NETWORKS]*

they are also global, because they are connected through-out the world, they learn from other experiences, and in fact they are often inspired by these experiences to engage in their own mobilization. Furthermore, they keep an ongo-ing, global debate on the Internet, and sometimes they call for joint, global demonstrations in a network of local spaces in simultaneous time. They express an acute consciousness of the intertwining of issues and problems for humanity at large, and they clearly display a cosmopolitan culture, while being rooted in their specific identity. They prefigure to some extent the supersession of the current split between local communal identity and global individual networking.

CONTAINING PEOPLE → FROM MANY DIFFERENT COUNTRIES

Like many other social movements in history, they have generated their own form of time: *timeless time*, a trans-historical form of time, by combining two different types of experience. On the one hand, in the occupied settlements, they live day by day, not knowing when the eviction will come, organizing their living as if this could be the alterna-tive society of their dreams, limitless in their time horizon, and free of the chronological constraints of their previous, disciplined daily lives. On the other hand, in their debates and in their projects they refer to an unlimited horizon of possibilities of new forms of life and community emerging from the practice of the movement. They live in the moment in terms of their experience, and they project their time in the future of history-making in terms of their anticipation. In between these two temporal practices, they refuse the subservient clock time imposed by the chronometers of their existence. Since human time only exists in human practice, this dual timeless time is no less real than the measured time of the assembly line worker or the around the clock time of the financial executive. It is an emerging, alternative time, made of a hybrid between the now and the long now.

In terms of their genesis, these movements are largely

*spontaneous in their origin, usually triggered by a spark of indig-nation* either related to a specific event or to a peak of disgust with the actions of the rulers. In all cases they are originated by a call to action from the space of flows that aims to create an instant community of insurgent practice in the space of places. The source of the call is less relevant than the impact of the message on the multiple, unspecified receivers, whose emotions connect with the content and form of the message. The power of images is paramount. YouTube has been prob-ably one of the most potent mobilizing tools in the early stages of the movement. Particularly meaningful are images of violent repression by police or thugs.

*Movements are viral*, following the logic of the Internet net-works (Nahon and Hemsley 2013). This is not only because of the viral character of the diffusion of messages themselves, particularly of mobilizing images, but because of the demon-stration effect of movements springing up everywhere. We have observed virality from one country to another, from one city to another, from one institution to another (Toret, coordinator, 2014). Seeing and listening to protests some-where else, even in distant contexts and different cultures, inspires mobilization because it triggers *hope* of the possibil-ity of change.

*The transition from outrage to hope is accomplished by delibera-tion in the space of autonomy*. Decision-making usually happens in assemblies and committees designated in the assemblies. Indeed, these are usually, although not always, *leaderless movements*. Not because of the lack of would-be leaders, but because of the deep, spontaneous distrust of most partici-pants in the movement toward any form of power delegation. This essential feature of the observed movements results directly from one of the causes of the movements: rejection of political representatives by the represented, after feeling betrayed and manipulated in their experience of politics as usual. There are multiple instances in which some of the participants are more active or more influential than others, just by committing themselves full-time to the movement. But these activists are only accepted in their role as long as they do not make major decisions by themselves. Thus, in spite of obvious tensions in the daily practice of the movement, the widely accepted, implicit rule is the self-government of the movement by the people in the movement. This is at the same time an organizational procedure and a political goal: it is setting the foundations of a future real democracy by practicing it in the movement.

*MOVEMENTS PRACTICE DEMOCRACY*

Horizontal, multimodal networks, both on the Internet and in the urban space, create *togetherness*. This is a key issue for the movement because it is through togetherness that people overcome fear and discover hope. Togetherness is not community because community implies a set of common values, and this is a work in progress in the movement, since most people come to the movement with their own motivations and goals, setting out to discover potential commonality in the practice of the movement. Thus, community is a goal to achieve, but togetherness is a starting point and the source of empowerment: *"Juntas podemos"* ("Together we can"). *The horizontality of networks supports cooperation and solidarity while undermining the need for formal leadership*. Thus, what appears to be an ineffective form of deliberation and decision-making is in fact the foundation needed to generate trust, without which no common action could be undertaken against the backdrop of a political culture characterized by competition and cynicism. The movement builds its own antidotes against the pervasiveness of the social values that they wish to counter. This is the constant principle emerging from the debates in all movements: not only does the goal not justify the means; the means, in fact, embody the goals of transformation.

*AUTONOMY*

*MOVEMENT GOAL IS TO CREATE COMMUNITY*

These are *highly self-reflective movements*. They constantly interrogate themselves as movements, and as individuals, about who they are, what they want, what they want to achieve, which kind of democracy and society they wish for, and how to avoid the traps and pitfalls of so many movements that have failed by reproducing in themselves the mechanisms of the system they want to change, particularly in terms of political delegation of autonomy and sovereignty. This self-reflexivity is manifested in the process of assembly deliberations, but also in multiple forums on the Internet, in a myriad of blogs and group discussions on the social networks. One of the key themes in debate is the question of violence, which the movements, everywhere, encounter in their practice. In principle, *they are non-violent movements*, usually engaging, at their origin, in peaceful, civil disobedience. But they are bound to engage in occupation of public space and in disruptive tactics to put pressure on political authorities and business organizations, since they do not recognize the feasibility of fair participation in the institutional channels. Thus, repression, at different levels of violence depending on the institutional context and the intensity of the challenge by the movement, is a recurrent experience throughout the process of collective action. Since the goal of all movements is to speak out on behalf of society at large, it is critical to sustain their legitimacy by juxtaposing their peaceful character with the violence of the system. Indeed, in every instance, images of police violence have increased the sympathy for the movement among citizens, and have reactivated the movement itself. On the other hand, it is difficult, individually and collectively, to refrain from the basic instinct of self-defence. This was particularly important in the case of the Arab uprisings when, faced with repeated massacres by using utmost military violence, some democratic movements ultimately became contenders in bloody civil wars. By so doing, social movements disappeared, replaced by violent factions fighting for state power. The situation is obviously different in liberal democracies, but the arbitrariness and impunity of police violence in many cases opens the way for the action of small, determined groups ready to confront the system with violence in order to expose its violent character. Violence provides spectacular, selective footage for the media, and plays into the hands of those politicians and opinion leaders whose aim is to suppress as swiftly as possible the criticism embodied in the movement. The thorny question of violence is not just a matter of tactics. It is the defining question in the life and death of the movements, since they only stand a chance of enacting social change if their practice and discourse generates consensus in society at large (the 99%) (Lawrence and Karim 2007).

*These movements are rarely programmatic movements*, except when they focus on a clear, single issue: down with the dictatorial regime. They do have multiple demands: most of the time, all possible demands from citizens avid about deciding the conditions of their own lives. But because demands are multiple and motivations unlimited, they cannot formalize any organization or leadership because their consensus, their togetherness, depends on ad hoc deliberation and protest, not on fulfilling a program built around specific goals: this is both their strength (wide open appeal), and their weakness (how can anything be achieved when the goals to be achieved are undefined?). Accordingly, they cannot focus on one task or project. On the other hand they cannot easily be channeled into a political action that is narrowly instrumental. Therefore, they can hardly be co-opted by political parties (which are universally distrusted), although political parties may profit from the change of mind provoked by the movement in the public opinion. Thus, they are social movements, *aimed at changing the values of society*, and they can also be public opinion movements, with electoral consequences.

They aim to transform the state but not to seize the state. They express feelings and stir debate but do not create parties or support governments, although they may become a target of choice for political marketing. In certain cases, they may induce the formation of a new kind of political party, close to the original inspiration of the movement, yet clearly distinct from the movement. However, in all cases, these social movements *are very political in a fundamental sense*. Particularly, when they propose and practice direct, deliberative democracy based on networked democracy. They project a new utopia of networked democracy based on local communities and virtual communities in interaction. But utopias are not mere fantasy. Most modern political ideologies at the roots of political systems (liberalism, socialism, communism) originated from utopias. Because utopias become material force by incarnating in people's minds, by inspiring their dreams, by guiding their actions and inducing their reactions. What these networked social movements are proposing in their practice is a new utopia at the heart of the culture of the network society: the utopia of the autonomy of the subject vis-à-vis the institutions of society. Indeed, when societies fail in managing their structural crises by the existing institutions, change can only take place out of the system by a transformation of power relations that starts in people's minds and develops in the form of the networks built by the projects of new actors constituting themselves as the subjects of the new history in the making. And the Internet that, like all technologies, embodies material culture, is a privileged platform for the social construction of autonomy.

## INTERNET AND THE CULTURE OF AUTONOMY

The role of the Internet and wireless communication in the current networked social movements is crucial, as documented in this book. But their understanding has been obscured by a meaningless discussion in the media and in the academic circles denying that communication technologies are at the roots of social movements. This is obvious. Neither the Internet, nor any other technology for that matter, can be a source of social causation. Social movements arise from the contradictions and conflicts of specific societies, and they express people's revolts and projects resulting from their multidimensional experience. Yet, at the same time, it is essential to emphasize the critical role of communication in the formation and practice of social movements, now and in history.[3] Because people can only challenge domination by connecting with each other, by sharing outrage, by feeling togetherness, and by constructing alternative projects for themselves and for society at large. Their connectivity depends on interactive networks of communication. And the fundamental form of large-scale, horizontal communication in our society is based on the Internet and wireless networks. Furthermore, it is through these digital communication networks that the movements live and act, certainly in interaction with face-to-face communication and with the occupation of urban space. But digital communication networks are an indispensable component in the practice and organization of these movements as they exist. The networked social movements of our time are largely based on the Internet, a necessary though not sufficient component of their collective action. The digital social networks based on the Internet and on wireless platforms are decisive tools for mobilizing, for organizing, for deliberating, for coordinating and for deciding. Yet, the role of the Internet goes beyond instrumentality: it creates the conditions for a form of shared practice that allows a leaderless movement to survive, deliberate, coordinate and expand. It protects the movement against the repression of their liberated physical spaces by maintaining communication among the people within the movement and with society at large in the long march of social change that is required to overcome institutionalized domination (Juris 2008).

Furthermore, there is a deeper, fundamental connection between the Internet and networked social movements: *they share a specific culture, the culture of autonomy, the fundamental cultural matrix of contemporary societies*. Social movements, while emerging from the suffering of people, are distinct from protest movements. They are essentially cultural movements, movements that connect the demands of today with the projects for tomorrow. And the movements we are observing embody the fundamental project of transforming people into subjects of their own lives by affirming their autonomy vis-à-vis the institutions of society. This is why, while still demanding remedial measures to the current miseries of a large segment of the population, the movements as collective actors do not trust the current institutions, and engage in the uncertain path of creating new forms of conviviality by searching for a new social contract.

In the background of this process of social change is the cultural transformation of our societies. I have tried to document in other writings that the critical features in this cultural transformation refer to the emergence of a new set of values defined as individuation and autonomy, rising from the social movements of the 1970s, and permeating throughout society in the following decades with increasing intensity (Castells 2009: 116–36). Individuation is the cultural trend that emphasizes the projects of the individual as the paramount principle orienting her/his behavior (Giddens 1991; Beck 1992). Individuation is not individualism, because the project of the individual may be geared toward collective action and shared ideals, such as preserving the environment or creating community, while individualism makes the well-being of the individual the ultimate goal of his/her individuated project. The concept of autonomy is broader, as it can refer both to individual or collective actors. Autonomy refers to the capacity of a social actor to become a subject by defining its action around projects constructed independently of the institutions of society, according to the values and interests of the social actor. The transition from individuation to autonomy is operated through networking, which allows individual actors to build their autonomy with likeminded people in the networks of their choice. I contend that the Internet provides the organizational communication platform to translate the culture of freedom into the practice of autonomy. This is because the technology of the Internet embodies the culture of freedom, as shown in the historical record of its development (Castells 2001). It was deliberately designed by scientists and hackers as a decentered, computer communication network able to withstand control from any command center. It emerged from the culture of freedom prevailing in the university campuses in the 1970s (Markoff 2006). It was based on open source protocols from its inception, the TCP/IP protocols developed by Vint Cerf and Robert Kahn. It became user friendly on a large scale thanks to the World Wide Web, another open source program created by Tim Berners-Lee.

In continuity with this emphasis on autonomy building, the deepest social transformation of the Internet came in the first decade of the twenty-first century, from the shift from individual and corporate interaction on the Internet (the use of email, for instance), to the autonomous construction of social networks controlled and guided by their users. It came from improvements in broadband, and in social software and from the rise of a wide range of distribution systems feeding the Internet networks. Furthermore, wireless communication connects devices, data, people, organizations, everything, with the cloud emerging as the repository of widespread social networking, as a web of communication laid over everything and everybody. Thus, the most important activity on the Internet nowadays goes through social networking sites (SNS), and SNS have become platforms for all kinds of activities, not just for personal friendships or chatting but for marketing, e-commerce, education, cultural creativity, media and entertainment distribution, health applications, and, yes, socio-political activism. SNS are living spaces connecting all dimensions of people's lives (Naughton 2012; boyd 2014). This is a significant trend for society at large. It transforms culture by inducing the culture of sharing. SNS users transcend time and space, yet they produce content, set up links and connect practices. There is now a constantly networked world in every dimension of human experience. People in their networks co-evolve in permanent, multiple interactions. But they choose the terms of their co-evolution. SNS are constructed by users themselves building both on specific criteria of grouping and on broader friendship networks, tailored by people, on the basis of platforms provided by the merchants of free communication, with different levels of profiling and privacy. The key to the success of an SNS is not anonymity, but on the contrary, self-presentation of a real person connecting to real persons. People build networks to be with others, and to be with others they want to be with, on the basis of criteria that include those people who they already know or those they would like to know (Castells 2010). So, it is a self-constructed network society based on perpetual connectivity. But this is not a purely virtual society. There is a close connection between virtual networks and networks in life at large. The real world in our time is a hybrid world, not a virtual world or a segregated world that would separate online from offline interaction (Wellman and Rainie 2012). And it is in this world that networked social movements came to life in a natural transition for many individuals, from sharing their sociability to sharing their outrage, their hope, and their struggle.

Thus, the culture of freedom at the societal level, and the culture of individuation and autonomy at the level of social actors, induced at the same time the Internet networks and the networked social movements. Indeed, there is a synergistic effect between these two developments. Let me illustrate this analysis with the results of the survey research I conducted in 2002–7 with Tubella and others on a representative sample of the population of Catalonia (Castells and Tubella et al. 2005, 2007). We defined empirically in the population at large six statistically independent projects of autonomy: personal, professional, entrepreneurial, communicative, bodily and socio-political. We found that the more people were autonomous in each one of the six dimensions of autonomy, the more frequently and intensely they would use the Internet. And, over a span of time, the more they would use the Internet, the more their degree of autonomy would enhance. There is indeed a virtuous circle between the technologies of freedom and the struggle to free the minds from the frames of domination.

These findings are in cognitive coherence with a 2010 study in Britain, conducted by sociologist Michael Willmott on the basis of the global data obtained from the World Values Survey of the University of Michigan. He analyzed 35,000 individual answers between 2005 and 2007. The study showed that Internet use empowers people by increasing their feelings of security, personal freedom, and influence: all feelings that have a positive effect on personal well-being. The effect is particularly positive for people with lower income and less qualifications, for people in the developing world, and for women. Empowerment, autonomy, and enhanced sociability appear closely connected to the practice of frequent networking on the Internet.

Networked social movements, as all social movements in history, bear the mark of their society. They are largely made of individuals living at ease with digital technologies in the hybrid world of real virtuality. Their values, goals, and organizational style directly refer to the culture of autonomy that characterizes the young generations of a young century. They could not exist without the Internet. But their significance is much deeper. They are suited for their role as agents of change in the network society, in sharp contrast with the obsolete political institutions inherited from a historically superseded social structure.

## NETWORKED SOCIAL MOVEMENTS AND REFORM POLITICS: AN IMPOSSIBLE LOVE?

The impact of social movements on society at large, in the view of most observers, requires the processing of their values and demands by the institutions of society, shaped and controlled by political actors. Yet since the fundamental challenge from these movements concerns the denial of legitimacy of the political class, and the denunciation of their subservience to the financial elites, there is little room for a true acceptance of these values by most governments. Indeed, a comprehensive review of empirical studies on the political consequences of social movements, mainly focusing on the United States, shows that, on the one hand, the biggest social movements in the past have been politically influential in several ways, particularly in contributing to set policy agendas. On the other hand, "for a movement to be influential, state actors need to see it as potentially facilitating or disrupting their own goals – augmenting or cementing new electoral coalitions, gaining in public opinion, increasing the support for the missions of governmental bureaus" (Amenta et al. 2010: 298).

In other words, direct influence of social movements on politics and policies is largely dependent upon their potential contribution to the pre-set agendas of political actors. This is squarely at odds with the main critique of the networked social movements I studied, which concerns the lack of representativeness of the political class, as elections are conditioned by the power of money and media, and constrained by biased electoral laws designed by the political class for its own benefit. Yet, the usual answer to the protest movements from political elites is to refer to the will of the people as expressed in the previous election, and to the opportunity of changing politics according to the results of the next election. This is precisely what is objected to by most movements, in agreement with a substantial proportion of citizens everywhere in the world, as shown in the Appendix. Movements do not object to the principle of representative democracy, but denounce the practice of such democracy as it is today, and do not recognize its legitimacy. Under such conditions, there is little chance of a positive direct interaction between movements and the political class to push for political reform, that is a reform of the institutions of governance that would broaden the channels of political participation, and limit the influence of lobbies and pressure groups in the political system, the fundamental claims of most social movements. The most positive influence of the movement on politics may happen indirectly through the assumption by some political parties or leaders of some of the themes and demands of the movement, particularly when they reach popularity among large sectors of citizens. This is for instance the case in the United States, where the reference to the social cleavage between the 99% and the 1% has come to symbolize the extent of inequality. Yet, cautious leaders, such as Obama, while claiming to represent the aspirations expressed in the movement, stopped short of endorsing its activism out of fear of being seen as condoning radical practices. In fact, the second Obama administration signaled a definitive separation between the hopes of the Occupy movement and the pragmatic politics as usual approach of the president who had embodied the ideals of change for a brief period of American history.

Since the road to policy changes goes through political change, and political change is shaped by the interests of the politicians in charge, the influence of the movement on policy is usually limited, at least in the short term, in the absence of a major crisis that requires the overhaul of the entire system, as happened in Iceland. Nevertheless, there is a much deeper connection between social movements and political reform that could activate social change: it takes place in the minds of the people. The actual goal of these movements is to raise awareness among citizens at large, to empower them through their participation in the movement and in a wide deliberation about their lives and their country, and to trust their ability to make their own decisions in relation to the political class. The influence of the movement in the population at large proceeds through the most unsuspected avenues.[4] If the cultural and social influence of the movement expands, particularly in the younger, more active generations, astute politicians will address their values and concerns, seeking electoral gain. They will do so within the limits of their own allegiance to their bankrollers. But the more the movement is able to convey its messages over the communication networks, the more citizen consciousness rises, and the more the public sphere of communication becomes a contested terrain, and the lesser will be the politicians' capacity to integrate demands and claims with mere cosmetic adjustments. The ultimate battle for social change is decided in the minds of the people, and in this sense networked social movements have made major progress at the international level. As shown in the Appendix, in an international poll of 23 countries conducted in November 2011, with the exception of Japan, more people were favorable than unfavorable toward Occupy and similar movements in their context, and the majority of citizens agreed with their criticism of governments, politicians, and financial institutions. This is particularly remarkable when referring to movements that place themselves outside the institutional system and engage in civil disobedience. True, when polled about the movement's tactics in the United States, only a minority supported the movement, but even in this regard the fact that about 25–30 percent approved of the disruptive actions of the movement indicates a groundswell of support to the challengers of the institutions that have lost the trust of citizens. In Spain or Brazil, public support for the critiques of social movements to the system remains at above two-thirds of citizens. The uncertainty of an uncharted process of political change seems to be the main barrier to overcome for movements that have already exposed the illegitimacy of the current powers that be. Nevertheless, love between social activism and political reformism does not appear to be impossible: it is simply hidden from the public view while citizens waver in their minds between desire and resignation. Thus, to explore this hypothesis, I will now turn to the specific analysis of political effects of networked social movements on the basis of the observation of political change in selected countries in the 2012–2014 period.

## NOTES

1 My theoretical perspective on the analysis of social movements builds on Alain Touraine's theory, as presented in Touraine (1978). The most complete formulation of my own analytical perspective was published in Castells (1983),

and applied in Castells (1983, 2003). See also Johnston (2011), Snow et al. (2004), Tilly (2004), Staggenborg (2008), Chesters and Welsh (2000), Diani and McAdam (2003), Hardt and Negri (2004).

2 In 2008–12 there were a number of powerful, networked social movements, beyond the cases presented in this book, that sprung up around the world, with different emphases, origins, and orientations, particularly in Iran, Greece, Portugal, Italy, Israel, Chile, and Russia. Symbolic occupations of public space that never reached the level of a full-fledged social movement took place in most European countries, and in some Latin American countries. See Shirky (2008), Scafuro (2011), Mason (2012), Cardoso and Jacobetti (2012). In 2012–2014, a new wave of networked social movements took place in very different economic, cultural, and institutional contexts, as analyzed in the previous chapter in this volume. The characterization of the pattern of networked social movements presented here takes into consideration both the case studies presented in this book and the movements that have taken place elsewhere.

3 On the role of communication in the development of social movements, both historically and in contemporary societies, see, besides my own work (2003, 2009), Thompson (2000), Downing (2000), Couldry and Curran (2003), Oberschall (1996), Neveu (1996), Curran (2011), Juris (2008), Cardoso and Jacobetti (2012).

4 For instance, according to a post on March 23, 2012, by Kristen Gwynne from AlterNet:

> Sex strike is being utilized as a form of activism against the banks. According to RT News, high-class escorts in Madrid, Spain are protesting the banking sector by refusing to sell bankers their highly sought-after commodity: Sex.

RT reports: The largest trade association for luxury escorts in the Spanish capital has gone on a general and indefinite strike on sexual services for bankers until they go back to providing credits to Spanish families, small- and medium-size enterprises and companies.

It all started with one of the ladies who forced one of her clients to grant a line credit and a loan simply by halting her sexual services until he "fulfills his responsibility to society." The trade association's spokeswoman praised their success by stressing how the government and the Bank of Spain have previously failed to adjust the credit flow.

"We are the only ones with a real ability to pressure the sector," she stated. "We have been on strike for three days now and we don't think they can withstand much more."

The woman quoted above says bankers are desperate for sex services, and have become so pitiful they are unsuccessfully pretending to have other careers, and have even asked the government for help.

The Minister of Economy and Competitiveness Luis de Guindos reportedly told the Mexican website SDPnoticias.com, which broke the story, that the escort industry's lack of regulations makes government intervention difficult.

"In fact, there has not even been a formal communication of the strike – the escorts are making use of their right of admission or denying entry to ... well, you know. So no one can negotiate," he told SDPnoticias. com, making it clear that sex is a valuable tool, and refusing it sends a very strong, direct message.

By Kristen Gwynne, AlterNet, posted on March 23, 2012; printed on March 23, 2012. <http://www.alternet.org/news andviews/866354/sex_strike%21_madrid%5C%27s_

escorts_launch_coordinated_attack_against_banks%2C_
withhold_sex_services_from_desperate_bankers>

## REFERENCES AND SOURCES

Amenta, E., Caren, N., Chiarello, E., and Su, Y. (2010) The political consequences of social movements. *Annual Review of Sociology*, 36: 287–307.

Beck, U. (1992) *The Risk Society*. Polity Press, Cambridge.

BCS (2010) The Information Dividend: Why IT Makes you "Happier." Wilshire, UK: The British Computer Science Institute, Research Report.

boyd, d. (2014) *It's Complicated. The Social Lives of Networked Teens*. Yale University Press, New Haven, CT.

Cardoso, G. and Jacobetti, P. (2012) Surfing the crisis: Alternative cultures and social movements in Portugal. In Castells, M., Caraca, J. and Cardoso, G. (eds.) *Aftermath: The Cultures of the Economic Crisis*. Oxford University Press, Oxford.

Castells, M. (1983) *The City and the Grassroots. A cross-cultural theory of urban social movements*. University of California Press, Berkeley, CA.

Castells, M. (2001) *The Internet Galaxy*. Oxford University Press, Oxford.

Castells, M. (2003) *The Power of Identity*. Blackwell, Oxford.

Castells, M. (2009) *Communication Power*. Oxford University Press, Oxford.

Castells, M. (2010) Social Networks in the Internet: What Research Knows About It. Lecture delivered at the Symposium: Web Science, a New Frontier, on the Occasion of the 350th Anniversary of the Royal Society, London, September 28.

Castells, M. (2014) The Space of Autonomy. Cyberspace and

Urban Space in Networked Social Movements, Lecture delivered at the Symposium on Manuel Castells Urban Theory, Graduate School of Design, Harvard University, February 18.

Castells, M., Caraca, J., and Cardoso, G. (eds.) (2012) *Aftermath: The cultures of the economic crisis.* Oxford University Press, Oxford.

Castells, M., Fernandez-Ardevol, M., Qiu, L., and Sey, A. (2006) *Mobile Communication and Society. A global perspective.* MIT Press, Cambridge, MA.

Castells, M., Tubella, I., et al. (2005) The transformation of the social structure of the network society: Social uses of the Internet in Catalonia. In M. Castells (ed.) *The Network Society: A cross-cultural perspective.* Edward Elgar, Malden, MA.

Castells, M., Tubella, I., et al. (2007) *La transicion a la sociedad red.* Ariel, Barcelona.

Chesters, G. and Welsh, I. (2000) *Complexity and Social Movements: Multitudes at the edge of chaos.* Routledge, London.

Couldry, N. and Curran, J. (eds.) (2003) *Contesting Media Power: Alternative media in a networked world.* Rowman and Littlefield, Lanham, MD.

Curran, J. (2011) *Media and Democracy.* Routledge, London.

Damasio, A. (2009) *Self Comes to Mind.* Pantheon Books, New York.

Diani, M. and McAdam, D. (2003) *Social Movements and Networks.* Oxford University Press, Oxford.

Downing, J. (2000) *Radical Media: Rebellious communication and social movements.* Sage Publications, Thousand Oaks, CA.

Ekman, P. (1973) *Darwin and Facial Expression: A century of research in review.* Academic Press, New York.

Engelen, E., et al. (2011) *After the Great Complacence:*

*Financial crisis and the politics of reform.* Oxford University Press, Oxford.

Giddens, A. (1991) *Modernity and Self-Identity: Self and society in the Late Modern Age.* Polity Press, Cambridge.

Hardt, M. and Negri, A. *(2004) Multitude: War and democracy in the age of Empire.* Penguin, New York.

Howard, P. (2012) Digital technologies in the Arab Revolutions. Paper delivered at the meeting of the International Studies Association, San Diego, April 1.

Hussain, M.M. and Howard, P.N. (2012) Democracy's Fourth Wave? Information Technology and the Fuzzy Causes of the Arab Spring. Unpublished paper presented at the meeting of the International Studies Association, San Diego, April 1.

Johnston, H. (2011) *States and Social Movements.* Polity Press, Cambridge.

Juris, J. (2008) *Networked Futures.* Duke University Press, Durham, NC.

Lawrence, B.B. and Karim, A. (eds.) (2007) *On Violence: A reader.* Duke University Press, Durham, NC.

Markoff, J. (2006) *What the Dormouse Said: How the sixties counterculture shaped the personal computer industry.* Penguin, New York.

Mason, P. (2012) *Why It's Kicking Off Everywhere: The new global revolutions.* Verso, London.

Nahon, K. (2012) Network Theory and Networked Social Movements: Israel, 2011. Paper delivered at the meeting of the Annenberg Network on Networks, Los Angeles, April 27.

Nahon, K. and Hemsley, J. (2013) *Going Viral.* Polity Press, Cambridge.

Naughton, J. (2012) *What You Really Need To Know About The Internet: From Guttenberg to Zuckerberg.* Quercus, London.

Neuman, W. Russell, Marcus, G.E., Crigler, A.N. and

MacKuen, M. (eds.) (2007) *The Affect Effect: Dynamics of emotions in political thinking and behavior*. University of Chicago Press, Chicago, IL.

Neveu, E. (1996) *Sociologie des mouvements sociaux*. La Decouverte, Paris.

Oberschall, A. (1996) *Social Movements: Ideologies, interests, and identities*. Transaction Publishers, Piscataway, NJ.

Scafuro, E. (2011) *Autocomunicazione orizzontale di massa: Il potere della rete*, Genova, Universita degli Studi di Genova, Facolta di Scienze della Formazione, Masters Thesis.

Shirky, C. (2008) *Here Comes Everybody: The power of organizing without organization*. Penguin Press, New York.

Snow, D., Soule, S., and Kriesi, H. (eds.) (2004) *The Blackwell Companion to Social Movements*. Wiley-Blackwell, Oxford.

Staggenborg, S. (2008) *Social Movements*. Oxford University Press, Oxford.

Thompson, J. (2000) *Political Scandal: Power and visibility in the media age*. Polity Press, Cambridge.

Tilly, C. (2004) *Social Movements, 1768–2004*. Paradigm Publishers, Boulder, CO.

Toret, Javier (coordinator) (2014) *Tecnopolitica: la potencia de las multitudes conectadas. El sistema red 15M, un nuevo paradigma de la politica distribuida*. Universitat Oberta de Catalunya (UOC) Press, Barcelona.

Touraine, A. (1978) *La voix et le regard: sociologie des mouvements sociaux*. Seuil, Paris.

Wellman, B. and Rainie, L. (2012) *Networked*. MIT Press, Cambridge, MA.

# NETWORKED SOCIAL MOVEMENTS AND POLITICAL CHANGE

## OVERVIEW

The consensus in terms of *realpolitik* seems to be that, at the end of the day, the dreams of social change will have to be watered down and channeled through political institutions, either by reform or by revolution. Even in the latter case, the revolutionary ideals will be interpreted (betrayed?) by the new powers in place and their new constitutional order. This creates a major dilemma, both analytical and practical, when assessing the political productivity of movements that, in most cases, do not trust existing political institutions and refuse to believe in the feasibility of their participation in the predetermined channels of political representation. However, never say never. The process of social change is full of surprises. Often a time lag is necessary for the effects of the movement to be observed in the political institutions, in political practice, and ultimately in policies inspired by the defense of public interest. For instance, in July 2009 a major social protest, largely organized around mobile communication networks, shook up the political system in Iran in the wake of the possibly fraudulent re-election of fundamentalist President Ahmadinejad. While supported by the liberal faction of the Ayatollahs power structure, it was violently repressed and eventually subdued. In the Western media's perception, the movement was ineffective because it had no leaders and was largely spontaneous, enacted predominantly by youth (personal communication, 2009). Yet, in 2013, Rohani, a reformer allied to former liberal President Khatami, was unexpectedly elected president because of the massive mobilization of urban youth and the middle class in his favor, particularly in Tehran. His election signaled a significant change of orientation in Iranian politics, perhaps paving the way for democratization and peaceful cooperation with the West, in a process that may have important consequences for the world order. The causal relationship between the 2009 revolts and the 2013 election cannot be empirically demonstrated, given the absence of reliable sources of political opinion data. Yet, it is plausible to think that a mental transformation may have taken place in many people as a result of the experience of mobilization, in a country where 70 percent of the population is under 30 years of age, given the high participation of youth in both the demonstrations and the vote for Rohani.

In broader terms, the road to meaningful political change appears to go through the influence of movements on the public mind. In most of the movements studied, and in similar movements around the world, the critical passage from hope to implementation of change depends on the permeability of political institutions to the demands of the movement, and on the willingness of the movement to engage in a process of negotiation. When both conditions are met in positive terms, a number of demands may be satisfied and political reform may happen, with different degrees of change. Thus, what appears to be a dead end in the relationship between social movements and political change has to be confronted with the observation of what actually happened in the 2012–14 period following the surge of networked social movements in different countries. In doing so, I will distinguish between the effects of the crisis of political legitimacy on the political system (a key factor in inducing political change) and the specific effects of the social movements themselves.

## CRISIS OF LEGITIMACY AND POLITICAL CHANGE: A GLOBAL PERSPECTIVE

Most political systems around the world are being shaken by the challenges posed by globalization to the nation-state and by the crisis of legitimacy of the political system, as I have shown in other publications (Castells 2003, 2009). However, the intensity of the challenge to political institutions by social actors and by civil society at large varies widely depending on context.

The authoritarianism, corruption, and clientelism of states in many of the industrializing countries in Asia and Africa have succeeded by and large in subduing, for the time being, the potential challenge of social movements and social protests within the limits of the system, with the major exception of the social movement unfolding in Hong Kong at the time of this writing. While the unaccountability of the state institutions may provoke uncontrollable, violent, popular explosions occasionally (as in China or Thailand), most states appear to be, at least on the surface, in control of their societies, as long as the winds of globalization favor the economic well-being of the elites and of the urban middle class.

In contrast, in the case of Latin America, networked social movements are on the rise and are putting pressure on the political system, generating some embryos of political transformation in Chile, Uruguay, Brazil, and Mexico, as I will analyze below. In most of South America, however, the emergence of autonomous social movements in the 2000s has been preempted by the success of populist politics that countered the neoliberal model of growth implemented in the 1990s to usher in nationalist governments that have won the support of social groups marginalized by the traditional political elites as shown in Bolivia, Ecuador, Venezuela, and Peru (Calderon and Castells, forthcoming). However, in Venezuela the deliberate class cleavage introduced by these policies, and the increasing authoritarianism of the regime has provoked a wave of social protests, enacted by students and supported by the middle class, which may grow into an anti-populist networked social movement. Overall, the more the state is responsive to the demands of the society, the lesser is the intensity of autonomous social movements, as is the case in Ecuador, Bolivia, Uruguay, and to some extent Argentina (although *peronist* Argentina is always a special case). Yet, when social movements do exist and the state institutions are open to change, the transformative potential of social movements may find an institutional expression, as in Chile and Brazil.

In most countries of Europe, the crisis of political legitimacy, deepened by the economic crisis, prompted right-wing populist political reactions, always ultra-nationalist, often xenophobic, that threaten to undo the European Union and are calling into question the duopoly of center-right and center-left blocks in the political system. The European parliamentary elections of May 25, 2014, were a turning point in this regard. The ultra-nationalist, anti-European UKIP became the top vote getter in the UK. The extreme right Front National of Marine Le Pen was the winner of the elections in France, and opinion polls in the Fall of

2014 were predicting the victory of Le Pen in the presidential elections of 2016. The True Finns, a quasi-Nazi party, continued its ascension in Finland and may well be in the government after the next election. A similar strong influence of xenophobic parties is present in Denmark, Norway, the Netherlands, and Greece, where an explicitly neo-Nazi, ultra-nationalist party, Golden Dawn, is winning votes in each election. Even in Germany, where neo-Nazism is forbidden, small nationalist parties opposed to German "generosity" with other European countries are making inroads in the political system, forcing the grand coalition of conservatives and social democrats to retrench themselves in the last bastions of the bipartisan system. In terms of the analytical perspective of this book, what is essential to emphasize is that in all of these countries, with the major exception of Greece, there have been no autonomous social movements similar to those analyzed in this volume. The reasons lie deep in the history and political culture of each country. For instance, in France, in spite of having been the home of the May 1968 movement, a harbinger of social movements in the last half century, the strong presence of the state in every domain of social and cultural life channeled most protests within the electoral process and political maneuvering (with the exception of some very specific mobilizations, such as the defense of regional identity in Brittany or the opposition of Catholic youth to abortion and same-sex marriage). Given the fact that the political system could not assimilate the demands of an increasingly raucous population, as politicians were occupied with their own quarrels about dividing up the state, embezzling public funds, and indulging in bribes as a way of life,[1] a way of protest was open in the political system through the previously neo-fascist, anti-Semitic, and xenophobic Front National. Under Marine Le Pen, daughter of a former, openly fascist paratrooper who was the founding leader of the party, the Front acquired a mantle of legitimate politics, focusing on rejecting immigration and defending French sovereignty against the German dominance in the European Union.

The reasons for the rise of right-wing populism are different in each country (although they are all rooted in xenophobia and the rejection of European solidarity), but what is common is the absence of autonomous social movements that could regenerate the conduct of public life from the grassroots. I would even venture the hypothesis that from the point of view of the relationship between state and society, networked social movements and reactionary populist movements are functionally equivalent (although their values are fundamentally opposed) and the evolution of political practices as the result of their action will be vastly divergent depending on the origins of the challenge to the political establishment.

However, the distinction between autonomous social movements and populist politics, while analytically essential, is sometimes blurred in practice. The most meaningful example of this ambiguity in the process of social change is the Five Stars Movement (M5S) led by Beppe Grillo, that shook up the political system in Italy in 2009–14 (Pellizzetti 2014).

## CHALLENGING THE FAILURE OF ITALIAN PARLIAMENTARY DEMOCRACY FROM THE INSIDE: BEPPE GRILLO AND HIS FIVE STARS MOVEMENT

Although most of the facts concerning this movement have been widely reported in the media (often a distorted version, as this movement is abhorred by the political class throughout Europe), I will synthesize the key elements of what I consider to be a novel political experiment in order to reflect on its socio-political meaning because it is a symptom of the crisis of traditional representative democracy.

The movement, founded in 2009 as a vehicle to support candidates in the European, local, and regional elections in Italy against the traditional political parties, has always been marked by the personality of its undisputed leader, the charismatic television comedian-turned political activist and blogger, Beppe Grillo (Grillo and Casaleggio 2011). A member of the Italian Socialist Party, he was ousted from television in 1987 when he questioned Craxi, the party leader and prime minister, about corruption in the party. Craxi eventually ended up in exile in Tunisia as a fugitive from Italian justice, and the party disappeared, together with other political forces after the major political scandal known as Tangentopoli, which ultimately brought to power in 1994 an even more corrupt figure, Silvio Berlusconi, real estate and media tycoon, and former associate of Craxi. Grillo campaigned on environmental issues and focused on denouncing political corruption in all parties. Although a veteran of television, he renounced his presence in that medium because of the corporate and political control over television, and instead discovered the possibilities offered by the Internet. He started a political blog that became one of the most visited blogs in Europe. He teamed up with Gianroberto Casaleggio (his buddy to this date), an advertising executive who is reputed to be masterful in the uses of the web for influencing public opinion. They chastised politicians while criticizing the biases in the laws governing political institutions in favor of established parties. They supported candidates in different elections, even before the formal incorporation of the movement in 2009. The first major appearance of the movement took place on June 14, 2007 in

Bologna in what Grillo labeled as V Day. V for Vaffanculo Day (Go Fuck Yourself Day) addressed to corrupt politicians. The main demand aired at the meeting was the reform of the electoral law to prevent nominations to the parliament of those who had criminal convictions (a good number of Italian MPs), as well as to limit elections in office to two terms. Following the model of American MeetUp, Grillo organized local groups all around Italy and intensified the debate on a whole range of political issues using Internet platforms, although his personal blog was always the beacon of the movement. The name of the Movement, formally established on October 4, 2009, referred to the five main issues put forward by the movement: environmental policy, sustainable development, sustainable transport, water policy, and the right to connectivity in a free Internet. Major themes in the program of the movement, propagated from Grillo's blog, are also the fight against corruption and the emphasis on direct democracy through local assemblies and wide-spread Internet use. At some point in 2013, the program included dissolving the Italian parliament and replacing it with a system of citizen deliberation and voting over the Internet. Thus, Internet access, in their view, should be unrestricted and free as a fundamental democratic right. The Five Stars Movement (M5S) exemplified the new form of politics by using the Internet as a deliberative medium to elect their candidates to office on the web, each aspiring candidate presenting her case and her qualifications in a video intended for an audience of registered members of the movement. Then the members would vote to select the final candidacies to go into the ballot. Election to office should be considered as temporary service to the country, and no one should serve more than two terms in any office in order to eradicate the figure of the professional politician. At first, M5S's electoral success was beyond any expectation, stunning the Italian political class. In the municipal elections of May 2011, M5S elected councilors in 28 municipalities. In the elections of 2012 the movement performed even better, and one of its members was elected mayor of Parma, a city that became an experimental ground for new participatory politics. Belying the perception that it was just a party of North-Central Italy, in the Sicilian regional elections of 2012, M5S was the most voted-for party and cast a decisive vote in the formation of the regional government that implemented some of its policies. The pinnacle of the movement came in the general parliamentary elections of February 2013, in the midst of a major political crisis that saw the definitive decline of Berlusconi. M5S combined mass rallies in the squares of Italian cities with an active campaign on social networks and blogs. Among M5S's proposals were: exiting the euro currency, renegotiating Italy's membership in the European Union to preserve national sovereignty, reducing salaries and privileges of politicians, approving and implementing severe legislation against political corruption, providing a minimum income to every Italian citizen as a citizen's right, regardless of her/his condition, and modifying the electoral law to correct the many clauses that were favoring established parties. Although Grillo could not be a candidate according to the rules of the movement because of his criminal conviction in an automobile accident, he was the leader of the campaign, sparking enthusiasm and hope in a large segment of the demoralized citizenry. On February 22, 2013, hundreds of thousands gathered in Piazza San Giovanni in Roma to listen to the inflammatory speech of Beppe Grillo. At the ballot box, M5S became the most voted-for party for the Chamber of Deputies, with 25.6 percent of the vote, although the center-left coalition, led by the Democratic Party, and the center-right coalition, led by Berlusconi, obtained more deputies and barred access of M5S to government. The movement became the largest political force in a number of regions, including Liguria (the home of Grillo), Sicily and Sardinia. It also elected 54 senators, second only to the Democratic Party, and played a significant role in enacting or blocking legislation and appointments, such as the appointment of the President of the Republic. The deputies and senators were representing the decisions taken by registered members over the Internet in a number of legislative measures. Trying to set an example of new politics, the movement's MPs returned millions of euros of their salaries to a fund to amortize Italian debt, and to a fund for micro-credit to support entrepreneurial startups, gestures that were dismissed as demagogic by other political parties. The movement also claimed to have rejected funding from the government for its campaigns, relying instead on crowd-funding from multiple sympathizers. However, the success of the movement was soon tarnished by mistakes and conflicts in the management of its decision-making system. A system based on multiple layers of consultation could not be easily implemented; factionalism developed within the parliamentary group, and the ultimate decision came to be in the hands of the charismatic leader who chastised policies and adversarial personalities in his blog and expelled from the movement a number of challengers to his rule. As a result of these controversies, in the municipal elections of 2013, held a few weeks after the parliamentary elections, M5S lost the majority of its votes in several cities, including Rome. However, while media and politicians celebrated what appeared to be the demise of such an uncontrollable movement, in the European parliamentary elections of May 2014, the movement surged back and became the second largest party with 21 percent of the vote, although it was overshadowed by the success of the Democratic Party under the leadership of a new, young politician, Matteo Renzi, who obtained over 40 percent of the vote and claimed the control of Italian politics. Renzi made occasional agreements with the Berlusconi party as a way to contain the threat that the *Grillini* represented for the stability of the political system. The future of this movement-party is uncertain because of its complete dependence on the mercurial personality of its leader. There is also deep ideological ambiguity among its diverse constituency, particularly the general stand on immigration has shown in a number of instances an undercurrent of xenophobia (for instance, using the fear of the Ebola virus contagion to request stronger measures against undocumented immigrants), which brings M5S close to the European xenophobic parties, such as the French Front National. Furthermore, the hatred against politicians and mainstream media has induced extreme behavior, such as burning of the books of an Italian writer critical of the movement, prompting the alarm of some intellectuals about the connection with the Italian fascist tradition. However, Grillo condemned this action and claimed that there was an ill-intended propaganda campaign to destroy the movement's appeal as it was a threat to the corrupt Italian political system. The jury is still out concerning the ideology of the movement and the actuality of participatory democracy in its practice. What is clear, nonetheless, is that M5S is not an autonomous networked social movement like the ones I observed in other countries because it was created and tightly controlled throughout its existence by one leader, Beppe Grillo, with absolute power over the practice of the movement, using the pulpit of his blog. In this sense, it is closer to the tradition of populist movements that ultimately become political actors on the basis of a frontal challenge to a delegitimized political system. Yet, M5S is a most revealing symptom of the crisis of representative democracy in Italy and in Europe, and it also shows the potential of the Internet as an organizing and mobilizing medium with the power to disintermediate traditional forms of political action dependent on party machines and the control of institutions through manipulated electoral systems. It is important to observe that, in Italy, in the midst of the economic and political crises, there were no autonomous social movements similar to those taking place in Spain, Portugal, or Greece. Citizen's outrage was directly channeled into a political strategy, implemented by a movement-party, inspired by a skillful communicator able to capture the attention of the people at large. The younger segments of the population were most prone to receive the provocative message of Grillo. This was partly because of their disgust with Italian politics, dominated for many years by a Mafia-supported crook such as Berlusconi who was ultimately convicted as soon as he lost his political immunity. M5S has to be understood in the peculiar context of Italian politics, one of the most corrupt, self-serving and delegitimized of Europe, in the absence of any challenge taking place in civil society (Rizzo and Stella 2007). The irony is that one of the possible effects of the M5S may be the regeneration of the Italian political institutions and political parties as a result of the wakeup call that politicians had, fearing a new collapse of the system, similar to the 1992 Tangentopoli debacle. This was particularly the case for the less corrupt and best organized party in Italy, the Democratic Party, the social democratic force that evolved from the old Italian Communist Party and the Christian Democrats, and bet on renewing its leadership with the 39-year-old mayor of Florence, Renzi, who tried to steer a middle course between the old-fashioned corrupt party domination of politics and the populist insurgency. His 2014 electoral victory vindicated his project, but it required compromises with some of the most anti-democratic forces, including Berlusconi. This may offer a new chance for Beppe

Grillo if the backroom deals continue to dominate Italian politics. Unless the Mafia takes care of him.

## THE EFFECTS OF NETWORKED SOCIAL MOVEMENTS ON THE POLITICAL SYSTEM

To assess the potential impact of *genuine* autonomous social movements on political systems, I will refer to four countries in which significant networked social movements took place in 2011–14: the US, Turkey, Brazil, and Spain. This is a summary analysis simply aimed at stimulating reflection and debate by grounding the discussion in events that actually took place.

### Occupying minds, not the state: Post-Occupy blues in the US

In the United States, the intensity and relevance of the Occupy Wall Street Movement, documented in this volume, is in sharp contrast with its scant impact on the political system. This is in spite of the presence of the echoes and heritage of the movement in multiple local actions in the entire geography of the country, from the extraordinary solidarity in helping thousands of people affected by hurricane Sandy in 2012 to divestiture of municipal government investments in favor of local credit unions, defense against evictions from foreclosed homes, and the campaign to cancel student debt. Or, in a more significant expression of the latent groundswell of protest left by the Occupy movement, in the massive demonstrations that took place in New York and other American cities in November and December 2014 against the immunity for police brutality. Yet, the political system as such remained largely untouched, anchored in the party bureaucracies, particularly in the case of the Democratic

Party, although many observers credited the sympathy of Bill de Blasio toward Occupy in New York as a positive factor for his success in being elected mayor in 2013. In Seattle, Kshama Sawant was elected to the City Council after conducting an insurgent campaign based on the themes of Occupy. Both de Blasio and Sawant had been arrested by the police in the Occupy demonstrations of 2011. Ironically, the Republican Party was more sensitive to the integration of a conservative grassroots movement, namely the Tea Party, which became a transformative force in the Republican Party, with meaningful results in terms of electoral success.

The reasons for the weak direct impact of Occupy in US institutional politics are too diverse and too complex to be examined here. Let me just say that part of the reason is the burning out of many activists of the Obama campaign, a genuine insurgent campaign, who felt betrayed by the policies of President Obama. In fact, refugees from the Obama campaign were among the most active participants in Occupy as a reaction to their disappointment with Obama as being yet another example of a traditional politician. This disappointment became indignation when, under the Obama administration's watch, the FBI engaged in surveillance and intimidation tactics against some of the key activists of the movement. Local and federal agencies coordinated in a repressive policy without parallel for this kind of movement in the Western world. Thus, the failed experience of the hope for Obama dug a deeper gap of separation between autonomous social movements and party politics. Furthermore, politics in the United States is a profession dominated by money and focused on personal rewards of influence and access to resources with little room for dreams of change that are relegated outside the iron cage of the bipartisan system (Castells 2009). Between the cynicism of professional politicians and the idealism of activists of social change there is little meeting space in America for the time being. Or so it appears to be as per our observation of the post-Occupy interaction between movement and politics.

There has been, however, a cultural transformation in terms of the perception of American citizens of the poor quality of their democracy and of the social injustice that permeates everyday life. How this mental impact of Occupy will affect political behavior and institutional politics depends on a complex set of factors that are largely unpredictable.

## The streets, the Presidenta, and the would-be Presidenta: Popular protests and presidential elections in Brazil

In Brazil, a significant impact of the networked social movements of 2013 may well be observed in the political landscape, although the evidence is inconclusive at the time of this writing. In the wake of the June 2013 demonstrations, as stated above in this volume, the overwhelming majority of the political parties and political leaders rejected the street protests as a threat to democracy. Indeed, since the main challenge of the movement was the corruption and lack of representativeness of the political class, politicians as a group condemned the demonstrations and tried to delegitimize them by focusing on violence, in spite of the fact that violence was almost always initiated by the military police, notorious for its corruption and ruthless brutality. However, there was a major exception: President Dilma Rousseff. On June 21 she declared that the grievances of the protesters were legitimate and that "the voice of the streets should be heard." She reiterated this opinion in a number of venues, including the United Nations General Assembly, in the following months. Furthermore, she received a delegation of the Movimento Passe Livre and other organizations, supported the cancellation of the rise in the transportation fares at the local and state level, and promised to increase public spending on education and health. She also entered the political debate, accepted the criticism of the corruption and unaccountability of many of the politicians, and proposed widespread political reform. She advanced the project of calling for a Constituent Assembly to reform the Constitution, paving the way for legislation that would impose greater accountability on political parties. She also called for more stringent legislation against corruption and for new mechanisms of political participation. The Constitutional Reform would be submitted to a popular referendum, bypassing the Congress. The movement did not believe her in spite of accepting her good intentions, and her popularity plummeted by mid-July 2013. The pessimistic perception of the movement was accurate. The political class mobilized to block the proposal of the president in the Congress. Particularly vocal against what they labeled as the demagogy of the president was the social democratic party (PSDB), at that time the main contender for the 2014 presidential election. Moreover, even if President Lula supported Dilma Rousseff, her own party, the PT, had a lukewarm reaction to her proposal, and in some cases outright hostility. Thus, Candido Vaccarezza, a PT deputy in São Paulo, made an agreement with its powerful ally, the centrist MDB party, to bury the proposal of Rousseff in the commissions of the Congress. Given the relative weakness of social protests against the World Cup, Dilma Rousseff yielded to the opposition of political parties and tabled her political reform proposals. However, in the weeks leading up to the presidential election of October 2014, she revived her reformist project as an element in the program for her re-election. The reason was that, quite unexpectedly, her main challenger became the only political leader who had steadfastly supported the movement and who was also the one who was spared from criticism by the protesters: Marina Silva.

For a brief period between mid-August and mid-September 2014, Marina Silva appeared to have a serious chance to become the new president of Brazil in the second round of the election on October 26. Several polls showed that a key factor in her popularity was the support she enjoyed among those who participated in or supported the 2013 movements and were left orphans of their desire for change. Indeed, this is Silva's own perception. She referred to her support of the movements in 2013 as the main reason for the unexpected groundswell of support she found as soon as she through circumstances became a presidential candidate on August 20, 2014, after the death of Eduardo Campos in a plane crash. Campos had been the presidential candidate of the small Socialist Party of Brazil with whom Silva was sharing the ticket as potential vice president. Silva was convinced that only the pressure from the grassroots could change the obsolete, corrupt Brazilian political system. In an interview to the Associated Press on September 18, 2014, she stated that "it's neither the parties nor the political leaders who will bring about change. It's the movements who are changing us." The convergence between the hope of the social movements and the political project of Marina Silva can be explained by her fascinating, if dramatic, personal story, and her resilience to keep fighting for her beliefs, leaving powerful positions if necessary, to remain loyal to her convictions. A black woman born in a small town of the poor Amazonian state of Acre, she grew up in extreme poverty, in a family of rubber tappers submitted to outright exploitation. As a child she was seriously ill with malaria and a number of other diseases. She survived but her mother did not. As an orphan at the age of 15, she was taken by Catholic nuns to a convent where she learned to read and write. She worked as a domestic maid while studying secondary education in the evening and then graduated from college with a history degree. She was involved in a political theater group, became an activist, and joined the union of rubber tapper workers led by the legendary Chico Mendes, who achieved world renown by bringing together workers' rights and the environmental conservation of the Amazon. Chico was assassinated in 1988 by the landowners who did not tolerate interference in their destructive deforestation business plans. But the impact of his death on the national and international public opinion prompted the Brazilian government to act: new legislation was introduced to protect Amazonia and federal authorities clamped down on corrupt local bureaucrats and the police at the service of landowners. This experience will last forever in the mind of Marina Silva, who became a prominent environmental activist. She joined the left-wing PT, was elected to the Senate, and in 2003, President Lula appointed Silva Minister of the Environment in his first cabinet. Because of her uncompromising views on environmental policies, she clashed with agro-business lobbies and had open confrontations with other ministers of the PT government, particularly with Dilma Rousseff who was Minister of Energy and a strong advocate of the use of Brazil's natural resources as engines of economic growth. In fact, the opposition between Rousseff and Silva was not a matter of personal rivalry. It was the confrontation between a model of economic growth at all costs and a project of sustainable development based on renewable energies, environmental conservation, and a limitation of the power of Petrobras, the giant Brazilian public oil company that led the charge in pushing exploration for oil and gas everywhere, from the rainforest to the bottom of the ocean. The PT, in the most traditional version of left-wing parties, was a believer, like Marx, in the goodness of the development of productive forces as the lever of progress.

Lula and Rousseff wanted to give priority to alleviate and ultimately eradicate poverty in Brazil, a country that, as former President Fernando Henrique Cardoso put it, "is not a poor country, it is an unjust country." Yet, to correct historical injustice, economic resources were needed, and the natural resource economy was a major asset for Brazil to speed up its growth. Silva was also concerned with anti-poverty policies, having had herself the personal experience of poverty. However, following the legacy of Chico Mendes, she was looking for ways to reconcile development and sustainability, not limiting development, but without yielding to the interests of agro-business and of the bureaucracy of public companies. Thus, in 2009, she resigned from her ministerial post, left the PT, and created a movement, "Sustainability Network," to advocate for sustainable development and participatory politics. She ran in the presidential election of 2010 as a candidate of the Green Party, and obtained a respectable vote of 19 percent. She kept building her movement at the grassroots level, but left the Green Party as she was disappointed with internal factionalism. After the movements of 2013, with whom she identified, she decided to run for the 2014 presidential election as a candidate of her own movement. However, maneuvering from the Electoral Commission invalidated a share of the 500,000 signatures she had to collect to be a candidate, barring her from the electoral process. In a new display of her resilience, she immediately joined the Socialist Party of Brazil who had fewer votes than the Green Party in the preceding election. Yet, the PSB was betting on the appeal of a dynamic, pro-business candidate, Eduardo Campos, governor of Pernambuco, to reach the second round of the election. The support of Silva was exactly what the PSB needed, and so they offered her the vice presidency, a long shot for a party without the clout of the major Brazilian parties, all of them heavily financed and supported by powerful industrial groups, including the public companies that were controlled and milked by whoever was in government, in this case the PT. As soon as Silva became the frontrunner on the ticket, she surged in the polls, displacing the social democratic candidate, Aécio Neves, a politically moderate technocrat, to a distant third position. A critical factor in the charisma of Marina Silva, but also in the negative perception she has among some segments of society, is her deep Christian convictions, after she switched from being a Catholic to becoming a Pentecostalist in 1997. On the one hand, 22 percent of Brazilians are now Pentecostalists. On the other hand, because of her convictions, she opposed abortion and same-sex marriage (but not civil unions), prompting criticism from women's groups and gay rights advocates. Furthermore, Silva's opposition to the politicized bureaucracy of public corporations and to the government control of the Central Bank placed her in alliance with the financial industry and with proponents of the liberalization of markets and international trade. Clearly, while Rousseff, like Lula, was squarely placed in the statist tradition of the Marxist Left, Silva could hardly be catalogued as right-wing or left-wing. Her two main themes were environmentalism and the need for a deep reform of the political system. These were precisely the main issues aired by the networked movements of 2013. And so, the convergence between the demands of the movements and Silva's insurgent campaign was not a tactical matter. It was rooted in the substantive critique that both shared of politics as usual and economic growth as the justification for the deterioration of life in the unsustainable Brazilian metropolises. Thus, the social movements of 2013 influenced public opinion and prepared the ground for support behind a political leader who could link up with the demands of the movement without being intimidated by the all-powerful and mostly corrupt political class. In this sense, there was a major effect of social movements on the Brazilian political system, although the effect did not last. Indeed, the fairy tale of Marina Silva as president of Brazil came to an end in the first round of the election on October 5, as she was a distant third with just 21 percent of the vote, behind Dilma Rousseff with 44 percent and social democrat, Aécio Neves, with 37 percent, and so she was eliminated from the decisive second round of the presidential election. There are some simple reasons for the sudden collapse of Silva's candidacy in just two weeks, and they are mainly to be found in the mechanics of electoral politics. As soon as the PT administration perceived the danger of losing control of the state, it launched a ferocious attack on Silva, using the standard tools of aggressive political marketing, directly misrepresenting Silva's positions on some of the most popular issues, such as accusing her of planning to eliminate the Bolsa Familia program, a program to supplement the income of poor families to lift them from poverty. The PT team also developed a brilliant strategy to withhold its attacks against the other candidate, Aécio Neves, whom they considered more vulnerable to defeat in a run-off. A decisive moment was the television debate a few days before the election in which the powerful Dilma obliterated the spiritual Marina Silva who appeared to be emotionally shaken by the psychological violence she had to endure. "Too weak to be President" summoned President Rousseff when questioned by the media. Most Brazilians appeared to agree. Politics should be about sheer power and open confrontation. Donations were also a factor, the Rousseff campaign out-funding Silva's five to one, in spite of the support of some banks for the economic proposals of Silva, as she was opposed to excessive state intervention. Moreover, all of the resources of the state, and the direct governmental influence over most of the

Brazilian media were mobilized to fight off the threat from outside the political establishment. Their demolition tactics were made even more effective by Silva's vulnerable position on abortion and same-sex marriage that alienated sectors of the urban middle class, her core support group.

However, not all the echoes of the movement were lost in the defeat of Silva. By reviving the calls for participatory democracy that the movements had put forward, Marina Silva prompted Dilma Rousseff to renew her promises of political reform so as to please the progressive intellectuals and grassroots organizations that had been a traditional constituency of the PT. Thus, there does appear to be a connection between the social movements that challenged the political establishment and the themes and potential policies resulting from the debates in this most contested presidential campaign.

However, in political terms, perhaps more significant than the defeat of Silva's candidacy was the success of the conservative candidates in the parliamentary elections that were held simultaneously with the presidential election. Major states, such as São Paulo, Rio de Janeiro, Rio Grande do Sul, and Minas Gerais, elected or re-elected center-right or right-wing politicians, including some who had been directly challenged by the movement. Yes, the PT lost ground in the Congress, but it was to the benefit of the centrist PSDB, the rightist and corrupt PMDB, and a number of extreme-right candidates. As a result, the Brazilian Congress resulting from the 2014 election was the most conservative Congress since the end of the military regime. If there was any indirect electoral impact of the social movements on this election, the evidence suggests it was a shift to the right of the political system. And so, the main lesson of the Brazilian experience is the difficulty to assess a direct effect of social movements on the political system in accordance with the values and proposals put forward by the movements. This is because the process to translate the outrage expressed in society into hope of new politics is mediated by political machines that are not prepared, and not willing, to articulate this hope. They tend rather to reproduce their own bureaucratic, economic, and personal interests. This is exactly the critique from the movement toward formal politics. The insulation of the political system, vis-à-vis new goals, values, and procedures emerging from society, seems to validate this critique, which raises the issue of the growing divide between political institutions and political change, a threatening development for social stability.

## The political schizophrenia of Turkish society: Secular movements and Islamist politics

In Turkey, the significant mobilization that took place in June 2013 around the defense of Gezi Park was expected to have a significant impact on the municipal elections of 2014, particularly after the series of political scandals which rocked Erdogan's government as judges accused several ministers of corruption, forcing their resignation. The scandal was inspired by the Islamic conservative Gulen movement, a former ally of the moderate Islamic AKP party that broke with the AKP over the sharing of economic power. Other political forces decided to remain neutral in this battle between two Islamic factions, and ultimately the effects of the scandal were not as significant as was first thought. Indeed, the 2014 municipal elections saw the victory of the AKP in the main cities of Turkey, as well as in the country as a whole. The distribution of the votes showed remarkable stability. In political terms, Turkey in recent years has been divided between four main political parties: AKP, moderate Islamists; CHP, the pro-secular-rule republican party; the nationalists of the MHP party; and the predominantly Kurdish BDP, more progressive than other parties but rooted in the Kurdish minority (about 15 percent of the population, although largely concentrated in the southeast). Besides wining Istanbul and Ankara, the AKP took 43.3 percent of the national vote against 25.6 percent of the secular CHP, 17.7 percent of the nationalists, and the less than 5 percent of the BDP. The campaign of CHP to capitalize on both Gezi and the political scandals to become an alternative to AKP domination failed because of the identification of the CHP party with the traditionally corrupt political class. The nationalists are always suspected of conspiring with the military to undo democracy. And a share of the Kurds, particularly in Istanbul, are weary of the nationalists, and even of CHP, who rejected their demands for autonomy in previous years, in contrast with the more open attitude of AKP. The only change in the election was the presence of a new progressive party, HDP, which is ideologically left-wing, feminist, and pro-minority rights. It benefitted to some extent from the opinion created by the Gezi movement, but it is usually perceived as a platform created by the Kurdish party to attract votes in the west of the country, and so it only obtained 2 percent of the votes at the ballot box as most of the non-Kurdish population would be suspicious of HDP's attachment to Kurdish nationalism.

Confirming the pre-eminence of AKP in Turkish politics, the first presidential election held in 2014 after a constitutional change to establish a more presidential regime was easily won by Erdogan, the leader of AKP and the most direct adversary of the Gezi movement.

A number of reasons have been advanced to explain this cognitive dissonance between the popularity of the Gezi movement in June 2013 and the undisputed electoral success of AKP and Erdogan in 2014. Beyond specific circumstances that would require a complex analytical journey through the intricacies of Turkish politics, the most convincing explanation is the persistence of fundamental cleavages in the Turkish society that are

fixed in rigid political alignments. These include the historically
rooted hostility between secularism and religion (expressed in
the opposition between CHP and AKP); the confrontation
between nationalism (supported by the still Kemalist armed
forces) and the pro-democracy movement that brings together
the democratic aspirations of the middle class and the need of
the Islamists to use democratic institutions as a protective shield
against secularist armed forces; the significant split between the
Turkish population, and particularly Turkish nationalism, and
the Kurdish minority, in search for national autonomy and
ultimately for independence. Because of the complex interaction between these major social and ideological fractures, the
more radical political options have traditionally fragmented in
a multitude of small groups, now present on the Internet, that
were present in the Gezi movement but were opposed to com-
promise with any of the major political forces that are equally
adversarial to their hopes.

The time interval between the Gezi movement and the
2014 elections was maybe too short to bridge these historical
and ideological cleavages, and so, while the waves of protest
were still alive in people's minds and in the social networks,
no responsive political actor could be fielded in the electoral
arena in just a few months.

This is perhaps a major lesson to retain from our observation: that the transit of social movements to their indirect
political expression in the institutional system requires time,
as it has to be negotiated in the hazardous transition between
outrage, hope, and hopeful pragmatism.

## Reinventing politics, upsetting bipartisan hegemony: *Podemos* in Spain

The political experience of the Spanish *Indignadas* movement in the 2012–14 period may yield invaluable lessons for

the theory and practice of socio-political change. I turn now to this analysis, focusing on the rise of *Podemos* as a new kind of political actor, and on the experience of the local electoral coalitions that, under the shared label of *Ganemos*, were being prepared for the 2015 Spanish municipal elections at the time of this writing (Arnau Monterde, personal communication, 2014).

The 15M of 2011 had a major impact in the minds of Spanish citizens who overwhelmingly supported the criticism expressed by the movement regarding the political system, and against the management of the economic crisis by political and financial elites. Eighty-one percent of the population expressed their agreement with the demands of the protesters in June 2011, and the proportion of support remained at 78 percent in 2012 and 2013, and 72 percent of citizens in 2014, even if the majority of people thought that the movement would not be able to make a difference in the critical situation of the country. Indeed, the political class, almost in its totality, rejected the legitimacy of the movement, while expressing, in some cases, a condescending understanding of their indignation, adding immediately that action in the streets and Internet networks was not the way to solve the problems. In the view of politicians, protests should be exclusively channeled through the political parties and the electoral process. This form of restricted politics is exactly what the movement rejected. Therefore, protests continued in 2011–13 with different levels of intensity depending on time and location of the protest. A number of specific demands were achieved. In one particular issue, to fight the eviction of residents whose mortgages were foreclosed by the banks, a nationwide movement was created: the Platform for the People Affected by Mortgages (Plataforma de Afectados por la Hipoteca – PAH), under the strong leadership of Ada Colau, an independent intellectual from Barcelona.

PAH organized autonomous circles around Spain, mounted campaigns, physically opposed many evictions, intervened in the social networks and in the media, collected hundreds of thousands of signatures behind a legislative proposal that the Spanish parliament refused to consider, and ultimately appealed to the European Court of Justice, obtaining a judicial injunction to stop evictions while new legislation was debated. Given the intensity and popularity of the campaign, the conservative government and the banks agreed on a moratorium of evictions. Yet, in most other issues, and particularly on political reform, the movement had to confront a wall of rejection, sending the protesters to the streets, and then sending the riot police to take the movement off the streets. Thus, in early 2013, many activists in the movement started to reflect on the possibility to intervene in the institutional political arena as a way to defend the interests of millions in an increasingly dire situation because of the economic crisis. Moreover, the exposure of corruption in all political parties, right, left, and nationalists, was undermining even further the legitimacy of democratic institutions. The Crown itself was shaken by corruption of some members of the royal family and the personal scandals of the King, who was still refusing to abdicate in favor of his son Felipe who was clean, intelligent, and widely appreciated for his democratic temper. Gradually, a number of initiatives born in the movement evolved toward the formation of political parties with the intention of running in the European parliamentary elections of May 2014, since the definition of one single electoral district by country makes the election more representative than the procedurally biased national elections. *Partido X* was the first one to be formed in January 2013, followed by Valencia-based *European Spring*, the "*Blank Vote Seats*" coalition, Confederacion Pirata, an additional number of minor groups, and finally *Podemos* (*We Can*), organized in

January 2014. They were all based on the principle of giving legal political form to the principles and goals of the movement without becoming trapped in the same kind of politics and organizations they were opposing. They all made extensive use of Internet networks for debate, consultation, and organization; they also relied on grassroots circles meeting physically at the local level. Most of them proposed the following: election of candidates to office in open debate, without constraining the election within partisan structures; accountability and revocability of those elected by the membership at large; willingness to interact and collaborate with other political groupings in the construction of a shared process to act upon the political system; and rejection of specific ideologies, trying simply to be the instrument of the will of the 99 percent, as per the expression of the citizens trusting each one of the groups. Most of these initiatives thought that the transition of the expression of people's interests to a new form of political practice would take a long time. Yet, the European parliamentary elections on May 25, 2014 triggered a political earthquake in Spain, as in much of Europe. But, unlike in other European countries, in Spain, political insurgency against the system came from those parties and coalitions that emerged from the social movement. This was particularly the case with *Podemos*, a party that did not exist six months prior to the election and that took 8 percent of the national vote (1.2 million), becoming the fourth largest political force in the country and electing 5 MPs (out of Spain's 54) to the European Parliament.

The rise of *Podemos* in less than a year of existence was extraordinary. A poll for the prestigious newspaper *El País* in November 2014 gave *Podemos* 27.7 percent of votes in future 2015 Spanish elections, making it the most voted-for party in the country, ahead of the Socialists of PSOE (26.2 percent) and the conservative Partido Popular, the government party, whose support had collapsed from its 44.6 percent vote in the elections of 2011 to 20.7 percent in the November 2014 poll. The left-wing party Izquierda Unida was relegated to a distant fourth position, signaling the difference between the old left and the new politics emerging from the movement. Even if this was only a political opinion poll, it was considered by observers as a major political shift, and as a signal of the end of the bipartisan system that had dominated Spanish democracy for four decades. In December 2014 a study published in Wikipedia collected the results of opinion polls from different sources, between November 2011, date of the last parliamentary election, and December 2014. On the basis of these sources, the study constructed a synthetic index of voting intentions for the November 2015 election, derived from different polls. Figure 5 displays the results of this exercise. For the sake of clarity, I have limited the data presented in the figure to the two main parties, Conservatives and Socialists, and to *Podemos*. It shows how in just 11 months of its existence, *Podemos* overtook both parties in terms of voting intentions. The detailed data and the methodology used to synthesize the data can be found in the Wikipedia study: http://en.wikipedia.org/wiki/Opinion_polling_for_the _Spanish_general_election,_2015. The assignment of seats in the future parliament did not correspond proportionally to the percentage of votes, because of the usual bias in favor of traditional parties resulting from the design of the electoral districts. However, *Podemos* largely overtook the Socialist Party and came very close to the Conservatives: according to polls in December 2014, Conservatives were projected to obtain 115–118 seats, against *Podemos* 101–104 and Socialists 77–80. Although the results of the election in November 2015 may differ from these poll-based projections, I can predict safely they will be close enough to the final results that no party would be able to govern by itself. In just a few

*Figure 5: Results of voting in the November 2012 election and of opinion polls on voting intentions in Spain from different sources, between November 2011 and December 2014*

months *Podemos* ended the bipartisan hegemony, based on the alternation between Conservatives and Socialists, that had characterized Spanish democracy since its establishment in 1977.

Other indicators show the rise of *Podemos* beyond the opinion polls. After its electoral success in May 2014, *Podemos*, which already had a dominant presence in social networks, became the absolute leader among political parties, with 350,000 followers on Twitter (in contrast to 155,000 for PP and 157,000 for PSOE), and 750,000 followers on Facebook in September 2014. In December 2014, 300,000 had affiliated to *Podemos*, which only opened affiliation in June. This compares with the number of about 200,000 affiliated members in the PSOE, the old Socialist Party, a major actor in Spanish politics throughout the twentieth century.

*Podemos* is organized in social networks, particularly with a system of open discussion and decision-making in the virtual space, *Plaza Podemos*, with 25,000 unique users in September 2014 and a cumulative number of over one million votes on various proposals. It also had over 800 circles at the local level throughout Spain (Flesher Flominaya 2014).

At the time of this writing, *Podemos* had completed a constituent period of two months in September–November 2014 to define a basic programmatic platform, an organizational structure, a procedure for election of its leadership, and ultimately an election of its leaders and candidates to office. The assembly was held both physically and virtually in *Plaza Podemos*.

The extraordinary rate of growth of *Podemos* shows that there was a substantial latent demand for a new form of politics that would channel citizens' outrage and hope without having to clash daily with the police. The eruption of *Podemos* and voters' rejection of mainstream political parties created an immediate crisis in the political institutions.

The leadership of the Socialist Party resigned, and a hurried election brought in a new, much younger secretary general with the difficult task of containing the free fall of the party in the polls and in membership. The conservative party, PP, shaken by continuing and significant corruption scandals, scrambled to modify some of its policies, for instance, abandoning its restrictive law on abortion, thus creating a split within the party. It appeared close to changing some of its leadership. The leftists of Izquierda Unida were pushed by their younger constituency to seek alliances with *Podemos*, its direct competitor on the Left, and the King chose that moment to finally abdicate in favor of his son, Felipe, in a last ditch effort to save the sinking monarchy.

What explains the instant success of *Podemos*? What was the process of transition from 15M to the formation of a significant political force in just a few months? What is the connection between the values and practice of 15M and the emergent new political actor? Because there is no doubt that 15M was the matrix of *Podemos*, but it is equally clear that *Podemos* is not and does not pretend to be 15M, making a clear distinction between institutional politics and social movements. This consciousness of the new political actors rooted in the practice of the movement is a remarkable feature that differentiates *Podemos*, and others, from the marketing strategy of established political parties vis-à-vis social movements.

*Podemos* was formed by a group of seasoned left-wing militants, who were part of various social movements in Spain, particularly in the anti-globalization movement, and actively participated in the 15M movement. They included Juan Carlos Monedero, Inigo Errejon Teresa Rodriguez, Miguel Urban, Ana Castano, Jaime Pastor, Santiago Alba, Candido Gonzalez, Bibiana Medialdea, and many others. On January 12, 2014, they issued a manifesto under the very explicit title "Moving on: to convert indignation into political change" (*Mover ficha: convertir indignacion en cambio politico*) that had originally been produced as an internal document by Izquierda Anticapitalista, an organization that had been active in the anti-globalization movement. It argued for the necessity to create a party that would take the demands and projects of 15M to the electoral realm, starting with the European elections of 2014. Yet, they stated that they would only do so if their web-published manifesto received a minimum of 50,000 signatures of support. They exceeded that number in 24 hours. On January 14, the initiators of the manifesto designated Pablo Iglesias, a 35-year-old professor of political science at the Universidad Complutense de Madrid, as the spokesperson of the movement. He soon became the main asset of *Podemos*. His communicative skills led him to anchor talk shows on some minor TV channels, including the web TV La Tuerka, created by him and his companions. Watching his performance, two mainstream TV networks, La Sexta and Cuatro, invited him frequently to debate on their political shows. His forceful presence on television is credited to be part of the success of the emerging party. Indeed, in the first voting ballots of *Podemos*, instead of the usual logo of most parties, the face of Pablo Iglesias was printed; a sort of personality cult that was considered strictly instrumental by the party, wanting to associate an unknown political party to a known face. It worked out. Yet, it would be wrong to consider *Podemos* as a movement exclusively led by a charismatic leader as in the case of Italy's M5S because Pablo Iglesias always submitted himself to the collective decisions of the movement and kept a principled attitude of wanting to create a transparent, democratic decision-making process without ignoring the asset that his popularity meant. Indeed, *Podemos* is a multilayered organization, very much along the lines of 15M. Its campaign combined a strong presence in social networks, where all major decisions were made, with the organization of local circles and assemblies, and with the interventions in the mainstream media, particularly in television. This multilayered communicative structure created a synergistic dynamic that both informed and mobilized hundreds of thousands who were receptive to the message of reasonable rebellion.

*Podemos* kept in its practice many of the principles of the 15M movement, such as proposing open citizen lists for designating candidates to office, without prior control of the party; refusing bank funding, instead relying on crowdfunding; and transparency in the accounting of the organization. Indeed, for the European elections, *Podemos'* funding was about €100,000 in contrast with €5 million each for the major political parties. In terms of the program, while the long-term program is still debated, some elements of *Podemos'* ideas can be directly traced to the proposal from the social movement such as: the notion that every person in Spain should have the right to a minimum income; that article 128 of the Constitution should be fully implemented: "All wealth of the country in all its forms and no matter who owns it, is subordinated to the people's interest"; that Spain should keep its sovereignty vis-à-vis the European Union and particularly vis-à-vis Germany; that banks saved by public funds should be controlled by the government; that taxing corporations should be used to avoid cuts in social services; that all foreign military bases in Spain should be removed; that Spain should be active in enforcing world peace and solidarity; that the rights for self-determination of the people in the Spanish state should be respected, including the Catalans' right to decide their future state; and, most importantly, that democratic institutions should be reformed with a new electoral law and stronger controls over the corruption of political parties and government officials. Yet, all these demands were discussed and decided in a hurry in preparation for the European elections. The true programmatic goals of *Podemos* were being discussed at the time of this writing, and they were in flux as the process of deliberation was open ended, with tens of thousands of participants in Plaza Podemos, and without real control of the participants. However, *Podemos* is also a technologically sophisticated organization in which participation procedures are organized with the help of a number of web applications that are much more advanced than anything done in Spain before to ensure both security and activity of the participation process. *Podemos* is truly a party of the digital age (Frediani 2014).

However, *Podemos* combined a large participation of its members over the Internet and in local circles with a centralized structure of decision-making. Once the leaders were elected, they exercised their leadership in a forceful manner. In this sense they clearly departed from the practices of the social movement. They justified this centralized structure in the name of efficiency, including to prevent factionalism and internal struggles that would weaken a party that was under attack from the established political system. Contradictions started to appear in the practices of *Podemos* between its vision of participatory democracy and the reality of election of candidates to office, particularly during the process of designation of candidates for municipal elections over the Internet in December 2014. The leadership blamed failures of the computer system managing the internal electoral procedures as the cause of the glitches denounced by many members of *Podemos*. Yet, politicians and media seized the occasion to blame *Podemos* as a manipulative organization. The confrontation between old and new politics came to the forefront of the public debate.

Indeed, the fundamental novelty of *Podemos* is its willingness to confront what they label "La Casta," which is the entire political class, calling for a re-foundation of democracy and trying to find new forms of deliberation and representation in the process of learning by doing. In this sense, *Podemos* is in clear continuity with the fundamental demand of the 15M for real democracy. Because of its success and its denunciation of the corruption of democracy in practice, it was submitted to an all-out critique from politicians, intellectuals, and established opinion makers, as they even compared Pablo Iglesias with Adolf Hitler.

In the wake of *Podemos'* success, multiple groupings at the local level decided toward the end of 2014 to form a series of movement-induced coalitions to run for the municipal elections of May 2015. The first one was formed in Barcelona around the mayoral candidacy of Ada Colau, the leader of the Platform for the People Affected by Mortgages, a most popular movement throughout Spain. Because of the charisma and independence of Ada Colau, a number of parties and groups, including the left-wing *Iniciativa por Catalunya/Izquierda Unida*, *Partido X*, Proces Constituent, and others, came together in a strong coalition that was expected to challenge both the Catalan Nationalists and the Socialists, the current municipal majority parties. The coalition in Barcelona adopted the name (*Barcelona En Comú* – "Barcelona in Common" in Catalan), and inspired at least two dozen similar coalitions in Spain with strong chances of a good performance in Madrid and other important cities. *Podemos* was participating in these coalitions, while planning to focus on the regional elections of May 2015 and on the national parliamentary elections in the Fall of 2015.

If the current projections of voting are proven correct, the major political transformation of Spain could start at the local and regional level where citizens are more aware of who is who, and where the corruption of established parties has been widely exposed.

At the time of writing in December 2014, it is still too early to assess the potential of the *Podemos* and *other* coalitions as major agents of political change in Spain. However, what we can already say about *Podemos* is that, in just a few months, an inexperienced, underfunded, untested political party came to the forefront of Spanish politics and threatened to displace the dominant Spanish Socialist Party, thus rejuvenating the Left and situating the movement in a position to challenge the apparently unmovable domination of the duopoly of political power. The prediction of electoral analysts (including Miquel and Campos 2013) is that after the new elections in 2015, the only way for Conservatives and Socialists to repel the assault to their control of Spanish politics will be to form an alliance (the so-called "grand coalition"), either in parliament or in government. This is bound to further induce their loss of legitimacy, thus paving the way for the election of parties and political actors whose matrix could be found in the 2011 *Indignadas* movement. The challenge for these movement-induced political actors will be to carry with them into the institutional realm the values and practices that they learned in the movement and that prompted the hope they ultimately came to incarnate. Politics as usual or new, transformative politics is the dilemma confronted by the heirs of the networked social movements in Spain and elsewhere; a dilemma whose solution will determine the practice of democracy in the years to come.

## LEVERS OF POLITICAL CHANGE?

Networked social movements have the potential to affect changes in the political system, as shown in this volume and as I have emphasized in this chapter, reflecting on changes that took place in various countries in 2013–14. In all cases, the sources of change originate in the influence that these movements have on the minds of people, individually and collectively; both by articulating what they feel and think, and by opening up the possibility of resistance to the existing order, putting forward alternative projects of life and democracy. Of course, for social movements to affect politics, they have first to exist in this practice, and this is not the case until now in most countries of the world, even if there are social protests everywhere and in all cases nowadays they are present on Internet networks. But social movements are a different form of collective action, as I have tried to argue in this book and as I have characterized in their new social practices in the preceding chapter. However, once they do happen in a given society, their potential of inducing political change is not a necessary outcome. It depends on cultural and institutional specificity as much as on the actual practices of the movement and of the political actors. In the main instances of the powerful movements I have analyzed in this chapter, what I observe is the scant direct impact of the social movement on the political systems of countries as different as the United States or Turkey. In other cases, particularly in Greece, Chile, Brazil, and especially Spain, some openings took place in the political system, although not in the dominant political parties but at the level of the presidency or, in the case of Greece and Spain, in the institutional left of the political system. Under such conditions, there has been an alliance between the social movements and political leaders who recognize their legitimacy and channel willingly some of their aspirations, bringing the wind of dreams into the sails of their strategies for political reform. I have also identified, in the case of Spain, the birth of a new political actor, *Podemos*, mainly issued from the 15M movement, which attempts to be in coherence with the demands and proposals of the movement without pretending to be the movement, as the pragmatism of institutionalized politics imposes limits on the aspirations for utopian social change. Moreover, the electoral success of *Podemos* has inspired a large number of local coalitions that are trying to convert the outrage and hope of citizens into institutional transformations at the municipal level. It is not surprising that Spain has been the country where the social movement is finding a political expression in a relatively short time – about four years. Because Spain was, and is, the site of the most potent networked social movement in Europe, and also the first one to appear to the eyes of the world, after the Arab revolutions, to the point that it became the matrix and inspiration of other social movements, including Occupy Wall Street.

Yet, history is not written in advance, nor does it follow a linear trajectory toward positive social change. In fact, most historical experience shows the opposite. This is dramatically exemplified by the Arab revolutions of 2010–11. They did have extraordinary political effects, in fact, they turned upside down the entire Arab world. If anyone challenges the notion of networked social movements as agents of political change, the so-called Arab Spring is there to prove them wrong. Yet, I always objected to the Spring part of the labeling because, in the short term, Winter set down on a vast expanse of the Arab world as a result of the intervention of geopolitical interests and fundamentalist Islamic movements in the breaches opened by democratic, grassroots movements in the political systems of Egypt, Libya, and particularly Syria. A new military dictatorship, supported by the United States, is keeping a shaky hand on the still revolutionary Egyptian society where the movement is alive and well in its diversity, while Libya and Syria disintegrated in atrocious civil wars directly provoked by multiple foreign interventions that have destabilized the Middle East and the world at large. Only the original Arab revolution, Tunisia, in spite of the tensions between Islamism and secularism, appears to have found a way to coexist in the construction of a democracy of sorts. My point, however, is not to revisit here the Arab revolutions but to emphasize, on the one hand, the extraordinary political impact of unforeseen networked social movements on the Arab world and on the world at large; and on the other hand, saying that political change happened does not mean that it is the change we would like, let alone the change projected by the social movements themselves.

And so, we do not really know the ultimate political consequences of this first wave of networked social movements that represent the shape of social movements in our time because neither myself nor anyone else can predict anything in the process of social change, as all the usual pundits were taken by surprise by the explosion of social movements that were obviously in the making, as a number of analysts, including this author, had been writing for some time (Castells 2009; Shirky 2008). Since I know we cannot predict the future in rigorous terms, I cannot say if *Podemos* and its sequels will actually survive the onslaught of the entire Spanish political class because it will depend, among other things, on the process of constitutional crisis between Catalonia and Spain. Furthermore, I do not know if the seeds planted by Occupy in the minds of American people will surge in a moment of social crisis, although the massive mobilization against the impunity of police racist brutality in December 2014 shows that the spirit of resistance against injustice is alive and well. Or if new, insurgent candidacies to office will take place in the US on the ruins of the hope generated by the Obama legacy. Or if the re-elected Brazilian President Dilma Rousseff will take up the challenge of social movements that came close to deciding the 2014 election. What I think I can say confidently is that significant political change will result, in due time, from the actions of networked social movements, and that these movements will continue to spring up around the world, from Catalonia to Hong Kong. Because social crises and conflicts are arising in this period of historical transition we are in and because the current political institutions, almost everywhere, are ineffective and illegitimate in the minds of their citizens. Minds that are being opened up by the winds of free communication and inspire practices of empowerment enacted by fearless youth.

## NOTE

1  In September 2014, after a desperate attempt by Manuel Valls, the Socialist prime minister, to stop the collapse of his party in the polls by forming a new government, it was revealed that the newly appointed minister of international trade had not paid his taxes because, he explained, he was suffering from "administration phobia."

## REFERENCES

Calderon, F. and Castells, M. (forthcoming) Huellas del Futuro en America Latina. Santiago de Chile, Fondo de Cultura Economica.

Castells, M. (2003) *The Power of Identity*, 2nd edn. Blackwell, Oxford.

Castells, M. (2009) *Communication Power*. Oxford University Press, Oxford.

Flesher Flominaya, C. (2014) "Spain is Different." Podemos and 15-M. *Open Democracy*, May 29.

Frediani, C. (2014) How Tech-Savvy Podemos Became One of Spain's Most Popular Parties in One Hundred Days. TechPresident.com/news, August 11.

Grillo, B. and Casaleggio, P. (2011) *Siamo en Guerra: Per una nuova politica*. Perfect Paperback, Milan.

Miquel, J. and Campos, L.M. (2013) *Asaltad el Sistema*. Bubok Publishing, Madrid.

Pellizzetti P. (2014) No todo el que dice "redes, redes" entrara en el reino de los networks, *Vanguardia Dossier*, 50: 64–7.

Rizzo, S. and Stella, G. (2007) *La Casta*. Saggi Italiani, Rome.

Shirky, Clay (2008) *Here Comes Everybody. The Power of Organizing Without Organizations*. Penguin Books, New York.

# BEYOND OUTRAGE, HOPE:

## THE LIFE AND DEATH OF

## NETWORKED SOCIAL MOVEMENTS

It is not a crisis, it is that I do not love you any more.
> Banner in Occupied Plaza del Sol, Madrid,
> May 2011

The networked social movements, whose experiences you and I have shared in this book, will continue to fight and debate, evolve, and eventually fade away in their current states of being, as have all social movements in history. Even in the unlikely case that they transform themselves into a political actor, a party, or some new form of agency, they will cease their existence by this very fact. Because the only relevant question to assess the meaning of a social movement is the social and historical productivity of its practice, and the effect on its participants as persons and on the society it tried to transform. In this sense, it is too early to evaluate the ultimate outcome of these movements, although we can already say that regimes have changed, that institutions have been challenged and that the belief in the triumphant global financial capitalism has been shaken, perhaps in irreversible ways, in the minds of most people.

In the last analysis, the legacy of a social movement is made of the cultural change it has produced through its action. Because if we think differently about some critical dimensions of our personal and social lives, the institutions will have to yield at some point. Nothing is immutable, although changes in history do not follow a predetermined path because the supposed sense of history sometimes does not make sense. In this regard, what appears to be the possible legacy of the networked social movements still in the making? Democracy. A new form of democracy. An old aspiration, never fulfilled, of humankind.

In any social movement there are multiple expressions of needs and desires. These are moments of liberation when everybody empties her/his bag of frustrations and opens her/his magic box of dreams. Thus, we can find every possible human projection in the themes and actions of these movements: most notably, the stern critique of a merciless economic system that feeds the computerized Automaton of speculative financial markets with the human flesh of daily suffering. Yet, if there is an overarching theme, a pressing cry, a revolutionary dream, it is the call for new forms of political deliberation, representation, and decision-making. This is because effective, democratic governance is a prerequisite for the fulfillment of all demands and projects. Because if citizens do not have the ways and means of their self-government, the best-designed policies, the most sophisticated strategies, the more well-wishing programs may be ineffective or perverted in their implementation. The instrument determines the function. Only a democratic polity can ensure an economy that works as if people mattered, and a society at the service of human values and the pursuit of personal happiness. Again and again, networked social movements around the world have called for a new form of democracy, not necessarily identifying its procedures but exploring its principles in the practice of the movement. The movements, and the public opinion at large, coincide in denouncing the mockery of democratic ideals in most of the world (see Appendix). Since this is not just a matter of the subjectivity of political actors, who often are sincere and honest within their own mindframes, something must be wrong with "the system," this obscure entity that nobody has met personally but whose effects are pervasive in everybody's life. And so, from the depth of despair, everywhere, a dream and a project have surged: to reinvent democracy, to find ways for humans to manage collectively their lives according to principles that are largely shared in their minds and usually disregarded in their everyday experience. These networked social movements are new forms of democratic movements, movements that are reconstructing the public sphere in the space of autonomy built around the interaction between local places and Internet networks, movements that are experimenting with assembly-based decision-making and reconstructing trust as a foundation for human interaction. They acknowledge the principles that ushered in the freedom revolutions of the Enlightenment, while pinpointing the continuous betrayal of these principles, starting with the original denial of full citizenship to women, minorities, and colonized people. They emphasize the contradiction between a citizen-based democracy and a city for sale to the highest bidder. They assert their right to start all over again. To begin the beginning, after reaching the threshold of self-destruction by our current institutions. Or so they believe the actors of these movements, whose words I have just borrowed. The legacy of networked social movements will have been to raise the possibility of re-learning how to live together. In real democracy.

## Public opinion in selected countries toward Occupy and similar movements

*Source:* Figures elaborated by Lana Swartz on the basis of data collected from the sources cited for each graph.

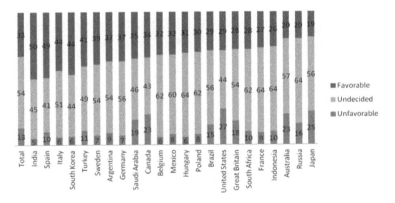

*Figure A1: Attitude toward "Occupy Wall Street" protests*

**Question:** How favorable or unfavorable are you toward the "Occupy Wall Street" protests, as far as you understand them? *Source:* Ipsos Global Advisor poll conducted on behalf of Reuters News. November 2011.

## Attitudes of citizens toward governments, political and financial institutions in the United States, the European Union, and the world at large

*Source:* Figures elaborated by Lana Swartz on the basis of data collected from the sources cited for each graph.

### European Union

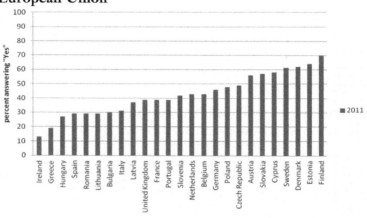

*Figure A2: Confidence in European financial institutions*

**Question**: In this country, do you have confidence in each of the following or not? Financial institutions and banks.
*Source*: Gallup. June 2011.

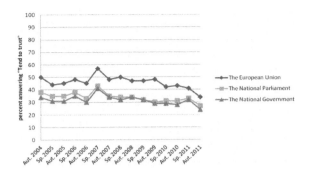

*Figure A3: Trust in European political institutions*

**Question**: I would like to ask you a question about how much trust you have in certain institutions. For each of the following institutions, please tell me if you tend to trust it or tend not to trust it: the European Union, the National Parliament and the National Government. *Source*: Eurobarometer.

## United States

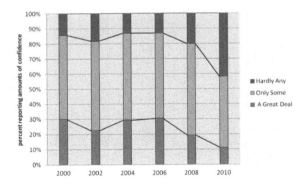

*Figure A4: Confidence in US banks and financial institutions*

**Question**: I am going to name some institutions in this country. As far as the people running these institutions are concerned, would you say you have a great deal of confidence, only some confidence, or hardly any confidence at all in them? Banks and financial institutions? *Source*: General Social Survey, National Opinion Research Center, University of Chicago.

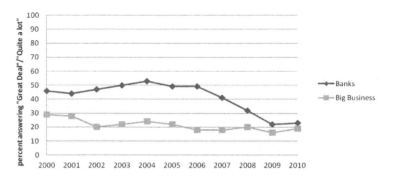

*Figure A5: Confidence in US financial institutions*

**Question**: Now I am going to read you a list of institutions in American society. Please tell me how much confidence you, yourself, have in each one – a great deal, quite a lot, some, or very little? Banks; big business. *Source*: Gallup.

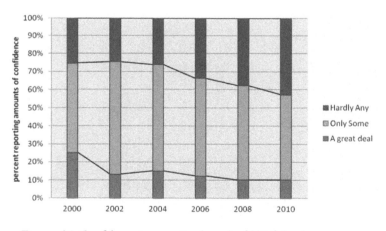

*Figure A6: Confidence in executive branch of US federal government*

**Question**: I am going to name some institutions in this country. As far as the people running these institutions are concerned, would you say you have a great deal of confidence, only some confidence, or hardly any confidence at all in them? The Executive Branch of the Federal Government. *Source*: General Social Survey, Conducted by National Opinion Research Center, University of Chicago.

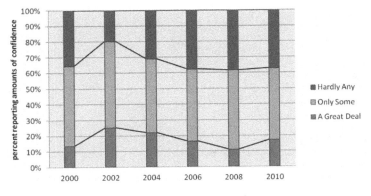

*Figure A7: Confidence in US Congress*

**Question:** I am going to name some institutions in this country. As far as the people running these institutions are concerned, would you say you have a great deal of confidence, only some confidence, or hardly any confidence at all in them? Congress. *Source:* General Social Survey, National Opinion Research Center, University of Chicago.

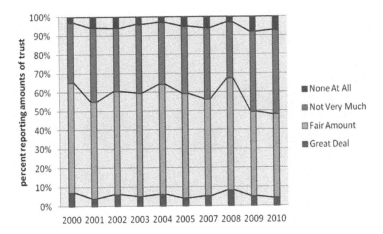

*Figure A8: Trust in US politicians*

**Question:** How much trust and confidence do you have in general in men and women in political life in this country who either hold or are running for public office – a great deal, a fair amount, not very much, or none at all? *Source:* Gallup.

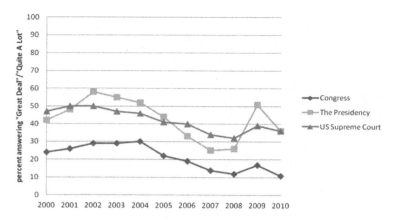

*Figure A9: Confidence in US political institutions*

**Question:** Now I am going to read you a list of institutions in American society. Please tell me how much confidence you, yourself, have in each one – a great deal, quite a lot, some, or very little? The United States Supreme Court, Congress, The Presidency.
*Source:* Gallup.

## World at large

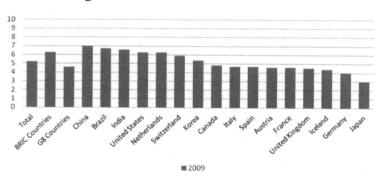

*Figure A10: Trust in government to manage the financial crisis*

**Question:** On a scale of 1 to 10 (where 1 means you don't trust at all and 10 means you trust completely), what is your level of trust in your government to manage the financial crisis? *Source:* ICM.

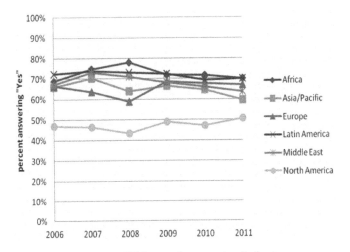

*Figure A11: Widespread corruption in business*

**Question**: Is corruption widespread within businesses located in this country, or not? *Source*: Gallup World View.

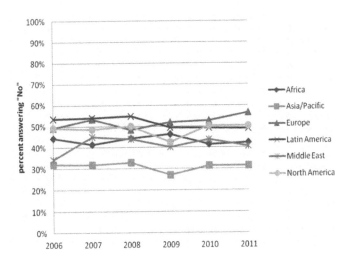

*Figure A12: Confidence in national government*

**Question**: In this country, do you have confidence in each of the following, or not? How about national government? *Source*: Gallup World Voice.

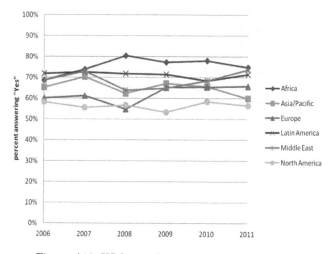

*Figure A13: Widespread corruption in government*

**Question**: Is corruption widespread throughout the government in this country, or not? *Source*: Gallup World Voice.

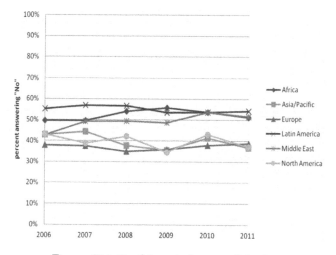

*Figure A14: Confidence in honesty of elections*

**Question**: In this country, do you have confidence in each of the following, or not? How about honesty of elections? *Source*: Gallup World View.